Case and Agreement in Abaza

SIL International and
The University of Texas at Arlington
Publications in Linguistics

Publication 138

Publications in Linguistics is a series published jointly by SIL International and the University of Texas at Arlington. The series is a venue for works covering a broad range of topics in linguistics, especially the analytical treatment of minority languages from all parts of the world. While most volumes are authored by members of the Institute, suitable works by others will also form part of the series.

Series Editors

Donald A. Burquest
University of Texas at Arlington

Mary Ruth Wise
SIL International

Volume Editors

Mary Ruth Wise
Rhonda Hartell

Production Staff

Bonnie Brown, Managing Editor
Virginia Larson, Proofreader
Margaret González, Compositor
Hazel Shorey, Graphic Artist

Case and Agreement in Abaza

Brian O'Herin

SIL International
and
The University of Texas at Arlington

©2002 by SIL International
Library of Congress Catalog No: 2002109893
ISBN: 1-55671-135-2
ISSN: 1040-0850

Printed in the United States of America

All Rights Reserved

09 08 07 06 05 04 03 02   10 9 8 7 6 5 4 3 2 1

No part of this publication may be reproduced, stored in a retrieval system, or transmitted in any form or by any means—electroni, mechanical, photocopy, recording, or otherwise—without the express permission of SIL International, with exception of brief excerpts in journal articles or reviews.

Copies of this and other publications of SIL International may be obtained from

International Academic Bookstore
SIL International
7500 W. Camp Wisdom Rd.
Dallas, TX 75236-5699
Voice: 972-708-7404
Fax: 972-708-7363

Email: academic_books@sil.org
Internet: http://www.ethnologue.com

Contents

List of Tables	ix
Acknowledgments	xi
Abbreviations	xiii
1 Introduction and Background	1
1.1 Grammatical sketch of Abaza	6
1.1.1 Phonology	7
1.1.2 Morphology and syntax	9
1.2 Theoretical framework	33
1.2.1 Levels of representation	33
1.2.2 X-bar theory	34
1.2.3 A and A-bar positions	37
1.2.4 Government and the ECP	38
1.2.5 Case theory	39
1.2.6 Theta theory	39
1.2.7 Binding theory	40
2 Basic Case Assignment	43
2.1 Preliminary discussion	43
2.1.1 Agreement and its relation to Case	44
2.1.2 Case assignment and feature checking	45
2.1.3 Word formation	45
2.2 Ergative Case assignment	49
2.2.1 Case assignment to the nominal possessor	49
2.2.2 Case assignment to the object of a postposition	53

        2.2.3 Case assignment to the subject of a transitive verb . 55
        2.2.4 Case assignment to the indirect object of a
              ditransitive verb 58
    2.3 Absolutive agreement 63
        2.3.1 Agreement with the subject of an intransitive verb . 63
        2.3.2 Agreement with the direct object of a transitive or a
              ditransitive verb 66
    2.4 The position of agreement projections 69
        2.4.1 AGRP-TP-AGRP 70
        2.4.2 The relative positions of ABSP and ERGP 70
    2.5 Nesting paths 79
        2.5.1 Allowing movement 79
        2.5.2 Motivating nesting movement 81
    2.6 Summary 90

3 Stative Predicates 91
    3.1 Lexical categories as heads of stative clauses 92
        3.1.1 Stative verbs 93
        3.1.2 Stative postpositions 94
        3.1.3 Stative nominals 97
        3.1.4 Stative adjectives 100
    3.2 Statives clauses are CPs 102
        3.2.1 Mood 103
        3.2.2 Tense 104
        3.2.3 Distribution of stative CPs 106
        3.2.4 Extended projections 109
    3.3 Subject position and case assignment 110
        3.3.1 Subject position 111
        3.3.2 Integrated phrase structure 111
        3.3.3 A potential alternative analysis 118
    3.4 The verb $ak^{'w}$ 121

4 Causatives 125
    4.1 The causative of dynamic verbs 126
        4.1.1 The causative of intransitive dynamic verbs 126
        4.1.2 The causative of transitive dynamic verbs 132
        4.1.3 The causative of ditransitive dynamic verbs 140
    4.2 Reflexives 146
        4.2.1 General account 146
        4.2.2 Reflexives and the causative construction 150
    4.3 The causative of statives 153
        4.3.1 The causative of intransitive stative verbs 154

Contents

    4.3.2 The causative of transitive stative verbs 157
    4.3.3 Possessed nouns, transitive postpositions, and the causative. 158
  4.4 Subject positions. 160
  4.5 Double causatives 161
  4.6 Conclusion 165

5 Derived Inversion 167
  5.1 The potential of ditransitive verbs 169
  5.2 The potential of transitive and intransitive verbs 179
  5.3 Reflexives and derived inverted verbs 185
  5.4 Interaction of the potential and causative. 186

6 Lexically Inverted Verbs 193
  6.1 Inherent Case 194
  6.2 Inverted verbs and inherent Case 194
  6.3 Expletives 199
  6.4 Reflexives 202
  6.5 The potential of inverted verbs 204
  6.6 Lexically inverted verbs and the causative 207

7 Postposition Incorporation 213
  7.1 Oblique arguments in the verb complex 213
    7.1.1 Benefactives and adversatives 214
    7.1.2 Comitatives 215
    7.1.3 Locatives 216
    7.1.4 Instrumentals 217
  7.2 Motivation for a postposition incorporation analysis. . . . 217
    7.2.1 The UTAH 218
    7.2.2 Independent postpositions in Abaza 219
    7.2.3 The use of applicatives versus independent PPs . . . 223
  7.3 The incorporation of $\text{AGR}^\circ\text{-P}^\circ$ 224
    7.3.1 Empirical differences 224
    7.3.2 Baker's applicative analysis 230
    7.3.3 Case assignment in Abaza 231
  7.4 Adjunction positions 235
    7.4.1 Order of morphemes 235
    7.4.2 Li's Generalization 237
    7.4.3 Coreference possibilities. 237
    7.4.4 Word order 239

	7.4.5	The position of locative PPs	241
	7.5	Legal movement	244
	7.5.1	Proper government within VP	244
	7.5.2	Proper government outside VP	246
8	Wh-Agreement	249
	8.1	Wh-agreement data	250
	8.1.1	Wh-agreement patterns with other agreement	250
	8.1.2	[wh] as a φ-feature	264
	8.2	The manner adverbial *yačʷəya*	265
	8.3	*Pro*-drop	269
	8.4	Wh-agreement under coreference	270
	8.5	Conclusion	275
Appendix	277
References	279

List of Tables

1 Consonants	7
2 Order of dynamic verbal prefixes	19
3 Order of dynamic verbal suffixes	27

Acknowledgments

The 1995 version of this study was presented to the University of California at Santa Cruz as a Ph.D. dissertation. It is hard to imagine a better committee than I had. I am pleased to have had Judith Aissen as chair. At every point, her comments and suggestions made the work better, both in terms of writing and analysis. Jim McCloskey also gave very helpful feedback on many of the chapters at various stages of development. Many thanks to both of them for the time and energy put into reading and commenting on various drafts. Jorge Hankamer pointed me in the right direction in understanding several constructions, since even though Abaza is not Turkish, there are many similarities. I appreciate Johanna Nichols' willingness to be involved in the process in spite of the extra travel distance for her. Her knowledge of the languages, cultures, and peoples of the Caucasus was a real help in shaping this book. Each of my committee members was a model of combining excellent linguistics and field work.

Thanks to the faculty of the Linguistics Board at the University of California at Santa Cruz, including Judith Aissen, Sandy Chung, Donka Farkas, Jorge Hankamer, Junko Itô, Bill Ladusaw, Jim McCloskey, Armin Mester, Jaye Padgett, and Geoff Pullum. Each of them added to my understanding of linguistics. It was an inspiration to see how well they balance high quality research with excellent teaching and a real concern for their students. The academic climate was further enhanced by my fellow students of linguistics.

My deepest thanks to my Abaza friends for their hospitality, help, and patience as I worked to learn and understand their language. Special thanks go to Ferit Sardogan, Zafer Uluç and his family, Hadzhismel

Adzhibekov, Bilyalyu Hasaroqua, Rauf Klychev, and Sergei Pazov. Without their help the dissertation would never have been completed.

Numerous SIL colleagues contributed to this project in a variety of ways, including technical support, training, fruitful discussions, and encouragement. Special thanks are due to Andy and Cheri Black for, among other things, their friendship and computer expertise, especially with AMPLE, which made relevant examples so much easier to find. They encouraged me to come to UCSC in the first place.

Graduate studies and families do not always mix well. Thanks to my wife, Julie, and our sons, Kevin and Steven, for their patience when I needed to study and write instead of participate in a myriad of other activities. Kevin and Steven provided much needed relief with "wrestle breaks" when I needed them. Our time as a family in Santa Cruz was much richer for our friends and fellowship at University Baptist Church.

My parents, also friends, have loved and encouraged me since before I can remember. Their positive influence has affected me, academically and otherwise, in ways neither they nor I fully recognize.

Finally, I would like to thank our many friends and supporters for their prayers, encouragement, and financial support throughout this study program. I am also grateful to the Linguistics Board at UCSC for financial support in the form of teaching assistantships, to the UCSC Graduate Division for support of my research in Russia through the Research and Travel Fund, and to SIL International for a study grant from the Corporation Academic Scholarship Fund.

This book is dedicated to God, who created language, including the Abaza language. Without His strength, I never would have finished.

Abbreviations

Abbreviations for references to example sources.[1]

ADCPR	K'lych, 1988
AL	Genko, 1955
AOD	Tobyl', 1992
ARD	Tugov, 1967
AT	Allen, 1965
GAL	Tabulova, 1976
IAT	Tygv, 1987
LA	Serdyuchenko, 1955
NART	Nartiraa, 1975
PAL	Pazov, 1990
RAD	Zhirov and Ekba, 1956
RAP	Dzhandar, 1991
SGSAL	Serdyuchenko, 1956
SSAVC	Allen, 1956
STBMF	Chkadua, 1970
VS	Chzykl'a, 1991

Other abbreviations

1s	first-person singular
2sf	second-person singular feminine
2sm	second-person singular masculine
3sf	third-person singular feminine

---

[1] Examples without references are from my own field notes, gathered 1986–1990, summer 1992, and summer 1994.

3si	third-person singular irrational/inanimate
3sm	third-person singular masculine
3sr	third-person singular rational/animate
1p	first-person plural
2p	second-person plural
3p	third-person plural
A	adjective
ABS	absolutive prefix
ABSP	absolutive agreement phrase
ADV	adverb
ADV	adversative or malefactive
AGR	agreement
AGRP	agreement projection/phrase
AGT	agent
Alv	alveolar
AOR	aorist
AP	adjectival phrase
APPL	applicative
ASP	aspectual
AUX	auxiliary
AV	adverbializer
AWH	absolutive series wh-agreement
BEN	benefactive
C/COMP	complementizer
CAP	closer agreement principle
CAUS	causative
CFC	complete functional complex
CFPP	case frame preservation principle
COM	comitative
COND	conditional
CONT	continuative
CP	complement phrase
CS	causative subject
CV	causative verb
D/DET	determiner
DEF	definite
DEG	degree
DEGP	degree phrase
DEP	dependent
DESID	desiderative
DIR	directional

Abbreviations

DO	(base) direct object
DP	determiner phrase
DYN	dynamic
ECP	Empty Category Principle
EPP	Extended Projection Principle
ERG	ergative prefix
ERGP	ergative agreement phrase
EWH	ergative series wh-agreement
FAC	factive
FREQ	frequentative
FUT	future
FUT1	future1
FUT2	future2
GB	Government and Binding
GC	Governing Category
GTC	Government Transparency Corollary
HAB	habitual
INDEF	indefinite
INF	infinitive
INFL	inflection
INST	instrumental
INT	intensifier
IO	(base) indirect object
IP	inflectional projection
LAB	labial
LF	logical form
LOC	locational
MAS	masdar
N	noun/adjective root
NEG	negative
NEG IMP	negative imperative
NFF	non-finite future
NUM	number
NWC	Northwest Caucasian language family
OBL	oblique prefix
OP	operator
OP	object agreement prefix (in Baker's examples only)
P	incorporated postposition
P	postposition root, pre/postposition
Pal	palatal/palato
PASS	passive

PCC	Path Containment Condition
PERF	perfective
PF	phonetic form
Phar	pharyngeal
PL	plural
PO	postpositional object
POT	potential prefix
POT	potential
PP	postpositional phrase
pro	null pronoun
PRO	an item which is +pronominal, +anaphor
PRS	present
PS	possessor
PSP	past participle
PST	past
PSTI	past incompletive
PTC	(present) participle
PV	preverb
RECIP	reciprocal
REFL	reflexive
REL	relative clause
REP	repetitive
RPL	rational plural
RWH	reason wh-agreement
S	(base) subject
SG	singular
SP	subject agreement prefix
STP	stative present
SUBJ	subjunctive
T	tense
TAG	tag question
TP	tense phrase
TSC	Transitive Subject Condition
UTAH	Uniformity of Theta Assignment Hypothesis
V	verb, verb root
VP	verb phrase
WHQ	wh-question
WHQI	irrational wh-question
WHQR	rational wh-question

Abbreviations

XP	phrase
YNQ	yes-no question
YP	adjunct phrase

1
Introduction and Background

The goal of this study is to give an account of the rich agreement system of Abaza, a language of the Northwest Caucasian family spoken primarily in the Caucasus Mountains of Russia, including a large corpus of data from a language previously discussed only minimally in the literature.

The first published description of Abaza appeared in German (Bouda 1940). Three notable works concerning Abaza have appeared in English: Colarusso (1975/1988) is a phonological analysis of the various Northwest Caucasian languages, including a chapter on the dialects of Abaza; Allen (1956) is a description of the verbal morphology with some limited discussion of the related syntax; Allen (1965) is an analysis of a brief text, giving a complete parsing of every word in the text and including a commentary.

Most published work on Abaza is in Russian and is not readily available outside of the former Soviet Union. Genko (1955), Serdyuchenko (1955), and Tabulova (1976) are fairly comprehensive descriptions of the phonology and morphology of Abaza. Two dictionaries have been published: Russian to Abaza edited by Zhirov and Ekba (1956) and Abaza to Russian edited by Tugov (1967). Chkadua (1970) is an analysis of the tense system of Abaza and Abkhaz, again focusing on morphology. Pazov (1990) is a discussion of idiomatic expressions in Abaza. I know of no other accounts in any language of the syntactic structure of Abaza.

As a non-Indo-European SOV language with an ergative-absolutive pattern of agreement, Abaza represents a type of language underrepresented in the literature along several parameters. There has been a long discussion in the literature on the question of whether the phenomenon of ergativity reflects properties of syntactic organization or is an essentially morphological phenomenon independent of the syntax (e.g., Anderson 1976, Dixon 1979, Marantz 1984, Campana 1992, Woolford 1993, and Bittner and Hale 1996a, 1996b). Abaza's agreement system is morphologically ergative, i.e., agreement with an intransitive subject is registered in the same way as agreement with a direct object, and differently from agreement with a transitive subject. I treat this distinction as a syntactic difference as well as a morphological difference, in that direct objects and intransitive subjects occupy a syntactic position not shared by transitive subjects.

A central concern of this study is the relationship between syntax and morphology. Abaza has a highly complex morphology. The verb word, especially, indicates a variety of information often associated with specific syntactic structure. I assume that there is a direct relationship between the order of morphological constituents and the corresponding syntactic structure. This follows from Baker's (1985) Mirror Principle. Specifically, I assume that morphemes in the verb word introduce features which must be checked in the syntax in the same order as the morphemes occur. The order of morphemes within the verb word is thus directly related to syntactic structure. To the extent that this volume is successful in accounting for the Abaza data, it provides support for the Mirror Principle.

The question of how agreement should be analyzed is another core concern. This issue is not unique to languages exhibiting an ergative-absolutive agreement or case pattern. In my analysis of Abaza, I have chosen to analyze agreement as mediated through syntactic agreement phrases, AGRP. In this analysis, each occurrence of an agreement morpheme is related to a syntactic agreement phrase, AGRP. This provides a single syntactic configuration in which morphological agreement is realized.

One possible approach could have been to demonstrate that an analysis involving agreement phrases is superior to an analysis lacking them. I have not focused on this, although I believe that the use of agreement phrases has made the overall analysis much more elegant and coherent. One advantage of agreement phrases is that they provide for the possibility of a position which mediates agreement that is not necessarily adjacent to the category normally associated with that agreement. This fits the empirical facts of Abaza very nicely at several key points, e.g., with causatives and lexically inverted verbs.

Accounting for the ergative-absolutive agreement pattern is another core issue in my analysis of Abaza. There is a growing body of literature within recent formal frameworks concerning how to account for this pattern (e.g., Levin 1983, Levin and Massam 1984, Marantz 1984, Bok-Bennema 1991,

Bittner 1992, Campana 1992, Johns 1992, Murasugi 1992, Boboljik 1993a, 1993b, and Bittner and Hale 1996a, 1996b). Virtually all of these accounts focus on the ergative-absolutive pattern within transitive and intransitive clauses only. I seek to give a comprehensive account of all constructions involving agreement in Abaza, going beyond simple intransitive and transitive clauses. This provides a richer body of empirical material bearing on the nature of ergative agreement systems.

One of the core questions in the recent discussion of ergativity has been whether the locus of absolutive case and agreement is syntactically higher or lower than the locus of ergative case and agreement. A wide variety of arguments, both empirical and theory-internal, have been presented on both sides of the issue. In looking at cases more complex than simple transitive and intransitive clauses, my analysis comes down firmly on the side having the locus of absolutive agreement higher than that of ergative agreement. Although the alternative may account for simple transitive and intransitive verbs, increasingly complex constructions require increasingly ad hoc stipulations to provide an account of the data. In my analysis, this is not so. The basic set of principles I adopt does not require major revisions as we look at increasingly complex constructions, but these principles predict the actual behavior in most cases.

I have chosen to use a formal framework (Principles and Parameters) in my analysis of the agreement patterns in Abaza, since I believe that this approach provides considerable insight into the principles underlying Abaza word and sentence structure.[2] One thing to be gained from this investigation is that constructions can be compared cross-linguistically with respect to their formal properties. Such comparison can show similar properties across languages, in spite of surface differences. For example, with respect to the incorporated postpositions discussed in chapter 7, similarities can be seen between Abaza and a group of languages as diverse as the Bantu languages of Africa, Rama (Chibchan) of Nicaragua, Nadëb (Maku) of Brazil, and Winnebago (Siouan) of North America.

A second advantage of this approach is that it generates a set of clear predictions about what is and is not possible with respect to formal properties. For example, there are more logically possible morphological and syntactic configurations in Abaza than actually occur. A formal theory can explain why many of these do not occur (barring accidental gaps). For

---

[2]The first version of this study was completed in early 1995. At that point, the Minimalist Program was still in its early stages of development (Chomsky 1991, 1992). The data here is presented in such a way that the reader may recast it in terms of the Minimalist Program or some other syntactic theory. It is my view, however, that the Principles and Parameters approach remains superior to the Minimalist Program for analyzing Abaza, particularly with respect to (a) ergativity and (b) structures involving more than two agreement projections.

instance, the relative order of potential and causative prefixes is fixed in Abaza. The formal theory I use accounts directly for why it is fixed in that order, and why the opposite order is impossible.

Finally, given a precise analysis of the formal properties of different constructions in a language, it is possible to make clear predictions about the formal interactions of those constructions. If the independently motivated principles for different constructions are accurate, they should be valid when those constructions interact with other constructions. This provides a means of testing a theory's accuracy. If a small set of general principles correctly accounts for a large variety of constructions, including the complex interaction of more simple constructions, then the theory is successful. If, on the other hand, new principles are required to "fix things up" as more complex constructions are encountered, it suggests that the general principles may be in need of revision.

I believe that the general set of principles I establish for Abaza correctly accounts for a wide range of constructions in the language, as well as the interaction of those constructions with each other. For example, the interaction of the potential with both lexically inverted verbs and the causative is directly accounted for in my analysis, without the need for additional machinery. My analysis will be successful to the extent that a small set of general principles accounts for the full range of data. I hope that the success of my overall analysis convinces those not familiar with formal theories that there is much to be gained from such theories in terms of understanding language.

A brief grammatical description of the language is given in §1.1. Constructions which are discussed in more detail in subsequent chapters are described only briefly, but included here in order to put them in the context of the language system as a whole. Section 1.2 is an overview of Principles and Parameters theory.[3] It is not intended to be a comprehensive account of the theory, but to provide sufficient background so that those unfamiliar with the theory can follow the discussion in the remainder of the book.

Chapter 2 is the core chapter. In it, I present the basic agreement patterns found in intransitive, transitive, and ditransitive verbs, in possessed nouns, and in postpositions; and I propose a single unified framework which accounts for these patterns. Two fundamental principles are established here: that absolutive agreement occurs in a higher syntactic phrase marker than ergative agreement and that movement to the specifier positions in which agreement morphology is licensed follows a nested pattern of movement. This contrasts with the crossing pattern required by some

---

[3]Black (2000:5–17) also summarizes the basic assumptions of Principles and Parameters, the successor of Government and Binding.

accounts of ergativity within the Minimalist Program (Chomsky 1992, Boboljik 1993a, 1993b).

Also crucial to my analysis is the claim that agreement is mediated through the specifier-head relationship within functional agreement projections. The use of agreement phrases raises a number of questions, which have not been conclusively resolved in the literature. One such question is how agreement phrases are licensed. In Abaza, it cannot be the case that each agreement projection is licensed in a position immediately dominating a certain type of projection, e.g., lexical or INFL/T, since the number of agreement morphemes which may occur in a single word in Abaza may exceed the number of such potential licensing projections. Another key principle, then, is that a certain type of agreement phrase (ERGP) may be freely generated within a verbal extended projection. This relates to another question concerning the nature of agreement phrases. Chomsky (1992) suggests that there is a single type of agreement phrase (AGRP), and differences in the overt manifestation of agreement are determined by the structural configuration of the agreement phrase, e.g., AGRP dominating VP results in accusative case while AGRP dominating TP results in nominative case. My analysis requires the two types of agreement phrases, ERGP and ABSP, to be distinct.

Subsequent chapters show that the framework established in chapter 2 correctly accounts for a variety of other constructions in Abaza with a minimum of modification. All of the major constructions and patterns involving agreement in Abaza are covered in these chapters. Chapter 3 deals with stative predicates, which include predicates headed by any lexical category in the language. Chapter 4 deals with the causative prefix, which I analyze as syntactically heading a VP. Chapter 5 deals with the phenomenon of derived inversion, in which the addition of one of several affixes triggers a rearrangement of the agreement pattern. Chapter 6 discusses a class of two-argument verbs, lexically inverted verbs, which have a pattern of agreement distinct from (in fact, opposite to) the normal transitive pattern. Chapter 7 accounts for a set of verbal prefixes which indicate various oblique relationships. I treat these as postpositions which incorporate into the verb. In chapter 8, I discuss a type of agreement beyond simple person and number agreement which is used with wh-questions and relative clauses. This wh-agreement pattern is part of the agreement paradigm, and consequently I treat [wh] as a φ-feature.

1.1 Grammatical sketch of Abaza

Abaza is spoken by roughly 40,000 speakers in Russia, primarily along the Kuban, Greater Zelenchuk, and Lesser Zelenchuk rivers on the north slopes of the Caucasus in the Karachayevo-Cherkessk Republic.[4] Additionally, there are between 10,000 and 30,000 speakers in Turkey,[5] who settled there after fleeing the war between the Ottoman Empire and the (Tsarist) Russian Empire during the 1870s.[6]

Abaza is a member of the Northwest Caucasian (NWC) language family. The closest related language is Abkhaz, with which it forms a subgroup of the NWC family. Three other languages constitute the remainder of the NWC family: Ubykh, Kabardian, and Adyghe.

The NWC languages are sometimes referred to, collectively or individually, as Circassian. The relation among these languages is relatively well established. (See, for example, Colarusso 1989.) The status of the NWC family with respect to other language families is the subject of much debate. The potentially related language families include South Caucasian or Kartvelian (including Georgian, Mingrelian, Laz, and Svan), Northeast Caucasian (including many of the languages of Daghestan), and Indo-European. For an attempt to support proto-NWC's connection to proto-Indo-European, see Colarusso (1992).

The primary dialect of Abaza is Tapanta, on which the official literary language in the Soviet Union was based, and this continues to be the standard dialect for media (television, radio, and newspaper) and education.[7] Those living in Turkey speak a descendant of this dialect, which is relatively unchanged from that spoken in Russia. The major differences between the Russian and Turkish varieties of the Tapanta dialect are lexical, due to borrowings into the language from Russian and Turkish. Stylistically, the Turkish dialect appears to use the deictic pronoun *awəy* 'that' as the third-person singular pronoun to a much greater degree, perhaps because of the influence of Turkish, which has a single third-person pronoun, while the Russian dialect differentiates three third-person singular

---

[4]The 1989 census places the number at 32,983 (Ionova 1993). Previous censuses gave 19,591 (1959), 25,448 (1970), and 29,000 (1979).

[5]Aydemir (1973, 1974, 1975), whose numbers I use, counts Abaza and Abkhaz together for a total number of speakers of about 31,000. From my experience meeting speakers, and from the villages listed by Aydemir, I believe that the majority of these 31,000 are Abkhaz. Thus, 10,000 is probably a closer estimate for the number of Abaza speakers in Turkey than 30,000.

[6]For discussion of the history and culture of the Abaza, see Zamakhshirievna (1989).

[7]The orthography based on the Cyrillic alphabet and currently used in Russia was developed in 1938 by Soviet scholars.

1.1 Grammatical sketch of Abaza

pronouns (he, she, it). I use data from both dialects, noting other differences as appropriate.

Section 1.1.1 provides an overview of the phonological system of Abaza. Section 1.1.2 presents the basic structure of phrases of the three main categories of Abaza, postposition, noun, and verb. This includes both morphological alternations and syntactic alternations, particularly with respect to word order.

1.1.1 Phonology

Abaza has roughly sixty consonants.[8] This rich consonant system is balanced by a minimal vowel inventory, which consists of just two vowels, /a/ and /ə/ (or /ɨ/), distinguished solely by the feature [±high]. The consonant inventory can be seen in table 1.[9]

Table 1. Consonants

	Stops			Affricates			Fricatives		Sonorants	
Bilabial	b	p	p'						m	w
Labio-dental							v	f		
Alveolar	d	t	t'	dz	c	c'	z	s	n	l, lʲ, r
Palato-Alv.				ǰ	č	č'	ʒ	ʃ		
Pal. Pal.-Alv.				ǰʲ	čʲ	č'ʲ	ʒʲ	ʃʲ		y
Lab. Pal.-Alv.				ǰʷ	čʷ	č'ʷ	ʒʷ	ʃʷ		
Velar	g	k	k'				ɣ	x		
Pal. Velar	gʲ	kʲ	k'ʲ				ɣʲ	xʲ, ɬ		
Lab. Velar	gʷ	kʷ	k'ʷ				ɣʷ	xʷ		
Uvular		q	q'							
Pal. Uvular			q'ʲ							
Lab. Uvular		qʷ	q'ʷ							
Pharyngeal							ʕ	h		
Lab. Phar.							ʕʷ	hʷ		
Glottal			ʔ							

The symbols I use differ from the IPA in a few respects. I use [y] instead of [j] for the palatal semivowel. I use [h] (and [hʷ]) instead of [ħ] for the

---

[8] The number of consonant phonemes is imprecise due to variations in both analysis and dialect.

[9] For a fuller discussion of the Abaza consonant inventory, including in the various dialects, see Colarusso (1975/1988).

pharyngeal fricatives. I use [ǰ] and [č] for the palato-alveolar affricates instead of [dʒ] and [tʃ].

The velar fricatives are in relatively free variation with corresponding uvular fricatives.[10] In some, perhaps most, dialects, /ɫ/ and /xʲ/ have merged into a single phoneme.

Except for regressive voicing assimilation under certain conditions, and word-final devoicing for some speakers, there are few rules affecting the quality of the consonants. The voiceless stops and affricates are aspirated, some of them rather strongly. Voiced stops and affricates which are devoiced word-finally are not aspirated, so even in this environment there is little chance for losing contrasts.

The two vowels are the high vowel /ə/ (or /ɨ/) and the low vowel /a/. Most of the phonological alternations in Abaza affect the vowels. One of the most salient alternations is the assimilation of roundness and frontness from neighboring consonants (a neighboring labialized consonant may turn [a] into [o] and [ə] into [u] in the right context; a neighboring palatalized consonant may turn [a] into [e] and [ə] into [i] in the right context). Throughout this study, both assimilated and underlying vowels will be used in transcription, depending on the source of the example. Most verbal and a few nominal suffixes involving semivowels, specifically the tense morphemes -y, -w, and -wa and the conjunction -y, undergo additional modification in certain morphological environments such that they merge with neighboring vowels, and the combination becomes [+high]. Specifically:

(1) a. [ə] + [y] → [i],
    b. [a] + [y] → [i],
    c. [ə] + [w] (+ [a]) → [u],
    d. [a] + [w] (+ [a]) → [u].

A second salient alternation concerns the presence and absence of the high vowel. The presence of this vowel is highly, but not completely, predictable. There are few cases in which the presence or absence of this vowel results in a difference in meaning.[11] Finally, geminate vowels are not allowed. If two vowels are juxtaposed, and at least one is low, the result is a single low vowel. If neither is low (a very rare occurrence), the result is a single high vowel.

---

[10]Colarusso (1975/1988) claims that the underlying position is actually uvular, and that velar fricatives have entered the language through Circassian (Kabardian).

[11]It is for this reason that Kuipers (1965) argues that Abaza has a one vowel system: /a/ versus ∅.

Stress is contrastive, but will not be marked here. For a discussion of stress in Abaza, see Dybo, Nikolaev, and Starostin (1978) and O'Herin (1992b, 1994).[12]

1.1.2 Morphology and syntax

Abaza is highly agglutinative, involving a great deal of morphological alternation, particularly in the verb complex and, to a lesser degree, in the noun complex. Syntactically, Abaza is strongly head-final. The following sections discuss the basic morphological alternations and the basic syntactic structure of postpositional phrases (1.1.2.1), nominal phrases (1.1.2.2), and verbal phrases (1.1.2.3). Paradigms for the agreement of a postposition with its object, a noun with its possessor, and a verb with its subject, object, and indirect object are not presented here, but can be found in chapter 2.

1.1.2.1 Postpositional phrases. As the name suggests, postpositions follow their complements. Agreement with the object of the postposition is registered with a prefix on the postposition. Postpositions are mostly locative and temporal, but there are comitative and benefactive postpositions, as well. Many relations expressed by prepositions or postpositions in other languages are expressed by prefixes in the verb complex. (See chapter 7 for a treatment of these verbal prefixes as incorporated postpositions.)

Example (2) shows a temporal postposition with a third-person singular irrational or inanimate complement, i.e., object. Example (3) shows a locative postposition with a first-person singular complement.

(2) awəy   a-mʃtax^j
    that   3si-after
    after that

(3) sara   s-pnə
    I   1s-at
    at my house, by me

1.1.2.2 Nominal phrases. Abaza nouns morphologically mark a variety of grammatical distinctions, including number, definiteness, and agreement with a possessor. Adjectives are generally compounded with the noun. Conjunction is marked morphologically on each conjunct.

---

[12]Spruit (1986) offers a detailed account of stress in Abkhaz, which is similar to Abaza.

Plurality is marked with the suffix -kʷa, as in (4) and (5). In addition, a second plural suffix, -čʷa, may be used for rational (human) nouns, either alone or between the root and the suffix -kʷa, as in (6). For some words referring to the young of animals, and ending in [əs] or [is] (/əys/), this ending is replaced by [ara] to form the plural, as in (7). Except for cases like (7), there is no overt marking to indicate nonplurality.

(4) a-sabəy-kʷa
    DEF-child-PL
    the children

(5) ha-kʷa
    pear-PL
    pears

(6) y-aʃ-čʷa-kʷa
    3sm-brother-RPL-PL
    his brothers

(7) a. kʷč'ʲ-əs
       chick-SG
       chick

    b. kʷc'-ara
       chick-PL
       chicks

The kind of information carried by determiners in other languages is signaled morphologically on the noun in Abaza. The definite marker is the prefix a-. It appears to be used in a wider range of contexts than the definite article in English. The indefinite marker is the suffix -k'.

(8) a. a-ləmharəʕʷ
       DEF-butterfly
       the butterfly

    b. ləmharəʕʷ-k'
       butterfly-INDEF
       a butterfly

1.1 Grammatical sketch of Abaza

Deictics and demonstratives, such as *awə* 'this' and *arə* 'that', are independent words and occur to the left of the head noun, as in (9).[13] Quantifiers, such as *zəmʕʷa* 'all, every' and *mačʼ* 'few', occur to the right of the head noun, as in (10). In this way they behave as adjectives. These determiners can also all be used pronominally.

(9) arə   a-qacʼa
    that   DEF-man
    that man

(10) a. gʷəp   zəmʕʷa[14]
       group   all
       the whole group

    b. a-qacʼa-kʷa   zəmʕʷa-ta
       DEF-man-PL   all-AV
       all the men

The plural and indefinite suffixes may co-occur, with the interpretation 'some'. The indefinite suffix occurs outside the plural suffix.

(11) wəs-kʷa-kʼ
     thing-PL-INDEF
     some things

The suffix *-kʼ* is also used to indicate the number 'one', so that (8b) can also mean 'one butterfly'. Numerals between two and ten are indicated by prefixes, plus the obligatory suffix *-kʼ*. This suffix differs from the indefinite suffix in its distributional properties in that it may occur with the definite prefix and within stative predicates.

(12) ʕʷ-qʼama-kʼ
     two-dagger-NUM
     two daggers

---

[13] The definite prefix is identical to the third-person singular irrational (nonhuman or inanimate) agreement marker. Thus, the form in (9) could also mean 'that (irrational) one's man'. It is likely that the definite marker either developed from the agreement marker, or that a definite reading is one use of this marker.

[14] In the dialect I am most familiar with, which is unwritten, *zəmʕʷa* tends to form a phonological unit with the head noun. The literary dialect in the former Soviet Union (T'ap'anta) writes *zəmʕʷa* as a separate word, though adjectives may be written together with their respective nouns (as compounds). In either case, the quantifiers occupy a position to the immediate right of the noun.

(13) x-q'ama-k'   three daggers
    pʃ-q'ama-k'   four daggers
    xʷ-q'ama-k'   five daggers
    c-q'ama-k'   six daggers[15]
    bəʒʲ-q'ama-k'   seven daggers
    ʕa-q'ama-k'   eight daggers
    ʒʷ-q'ama-k'   nine daggers
    ʒʷa-q'ama-k'   ten daggers

Possessors occur to the left of the head noun, and agreement with the possessor is registered on the head noun with a prefix in the ergative agreement series. Examples of possessed NPs can be seen in (14) through (16).

(14) ahmet   y-tdzə
     Ahmet   3sm-house
     Ahmet's house

(15) ac'əys   a-ʕʷara
     DEF-bird   3si-nest
     the bird's nest

(16) a-phas   lqac'a
     DEF-woman   3sf-man
     the woman's husband

The definite article may not co-occur with either the numerals or the possessive prefixes, but the possessive prefixes may co-occur with the numerals. In that case, the possessive prefix occurs outside, i.e., to the left of, the numeral.

(17) sosrəqʷ'a   yə-ʕʷ-ʃamqa-k'
     Sosruko   3sm-two-knee-INDEF
     Sosruko's two knees   NART, 51[16]

Modifiers (adjectives) are suffixed to the noun root, forming a compound. Plural and indefinite morphology occurs to the right of adjectives. The adjective is compounded with its respective head in (18) through (20), demonstrating its position inside both the indefinite marker and the

---

[15]The prefix for 'six' is a rapid diagnostic for differentiating between Abaza and Abkhaz. It is c in Abaza, and f in Abkhaz.

[16]See abbreviations list for source of cited examples.

1.1 Grammatical sketch of Abaza

plural marker. Multiple adjectives may also be compounded to the right of the noun head, as in (21) and (22).

(18) čə-dəw-k'
 horse-big-INDEF
 a big horse

(19) a-mʃʷ-dəw-kʷa
 DEF-bear-big-PL
 the big bears

(20) qac'a-bzəy-kʷa
 man-good-PL
 friendly men

(21) qʷmarga-pʃdza-dəw
 toy-pretty-big
 pretty big toy

(22) wasa-kʷayč'ʷa-psəla-dəw
 sheep-black-plump-big
 big plump black sheep

A second way of forming nominal modification is as an adverbial adjunct, marked with the adverbializer *ta*, as in (23). This construction has a more limited distribution. Note that in both types of adjectival modification, the modifier is to the right of the noun head, which is unexpected considering the strong preference for head-final structures in the language.

(23) čə-k'   dəw-ta
 horse-INDEF big-AV
 a big horse

Relative clauses precede their heads, as in (24). When both possessor and relative clause are present, the possessor precedes the relative clause, as in (25).

(24) x-wasa-k'   z-ʃə-z   a-la
 three-sheep-INDEF EWH-kill-PST DEF-dog
 the dog that killed three sheep

(25) *ahmet   yə-m-ca-wa   yə-wandər*
     Ahmet   AWH-NEG-go-PTC   3sm-car
     Ahmet's car that doesn't work

In addition to these affixes, conjunction is marked by the suffix *-y* on each conjunct. This is also true if there are more than two conjuncts.

(26) *s-anə-y   s-aba-y*
     1s-mother-and 1s-father-and
     my mother and father

(27) *s-anə-y   s-aba-y   s-aʃa-y*
     1s-mother-and 1s-father-and 1s-brother-and
     my mother and father and brother

The conjunction *-y* can be supplemented with the intensive suffix *-gʲə*, which likewise occurs on each conjunct.

(28) *s-anə-gʲə-y   s-aba-gʲə-y*
     1s-mother-INT-and   1s-father-INT-and
     my mother and father

(29) *s-anə-gʲə-y   s-aba-gʲə-y   s-aʃa-gʲə-y*
     1s-mother-INT-and   1s-father-INT-and   1s-brother-INT-and
     my mother and father and brother

It is possible for the intensive suffix *-gʲə* to occur on only the final conjunct, but it has a slightly different interpretation, in which the final conjunct is somehow separate from the other(s).

(30) *s-anə-y   s-aba-y   s-aʃa-gʲə-y*
     1s-mother-and 1s-father-and 1s-brother-INT-and
     my mother and father, and my brother (separately)

These conjunctions are the only nominal affixes shown here which can also occur with pronouns.

(31) *sara-y   wara-y*
     1s-and   2sm-and
     you and I

1.1.2.3 Verbal phrases. The most basic distinction in the Abaza verbal system is between dynamic and stative verbs. These have independent systems of affixation. Note that predicates of nonverbal categories take morphology from the stative system. See chapter 3 for a discussion of stative predicates.

Dynamic verbs. The dynamic verb in Abaza may host a wide variety of affixes. Prefixes include various agreement markers, preverbs, directionals, causative, potential, and markers of various oblique relationships. Suffixes include tense, aspect, and mood markers. Negation occurs as either a prefix or a suffix.

Prefixes. One of the most salient sets of prefixes in the Abaza verbal system is the set of agreement markers. The verb in Abaza registers agreement with all of its arguments, including subject, object, and indirect object. Agreement morphemes are all prefixes, with the series that registers agreement with intransitive subjects and transitive direct objects (absolutive) occurring to the left of the other basic agreement series (ergative), which is used to register agreement with transitive subjects, indirect objects, causative subjects, (see chapter 4), and various oblique relationships including benefactive, instrumental, comitative, and various locatives (see chapter 7). (See chapter 2 for a discussion and analysis of the basic agreement system.)

Reflexive and reciprocal constructions are signaled morphologically by prefixes. Reflexivity is indicated by the use of the prefix č-, which occurs in the same position as the absolutive series of prefixes. The reflexive prefix replaces the absolutive prefix which would otherwise agree with the object. The subject continues to be registered in the ergative series. (See sections 4.2 and 6.4 for further discussion of reflexives.)

(32) č-s-kʷaba-d
 REFL-1s-bathe-DYN
 I bathed myself.

Reciprocity is indicated by one of several reciprocal prefixes, the most common being *aba-*. (The choice of reciprocal prefix is lexically determined.) The subject is registered in the absolutive series, and there is nothing other than the reciprocal prefix to indicate the presence of a direct object. In this sense, the reciprocal prefix detransitivizes a transitive verb, while a reflexive does not. For presumably pragmatic reasons, the reciprocal occurs only with plural subjects.

(33) h-**aba**-ba-d
 1p-RECIP-see-DYN
 We saw each other.

(34) ʃʷ-**aba**-ba-d
 2p-RECIP-see-DYN
 You (PL) saw each other.

(35) y-**aba**-ba-d
 3p-RECIP-see-DYN
 They saw each other.

Some verbs have complex roots. For these verbs with two distinct parts, various elements, including the ergative agreement marker, may occur between the two parts, but both are obligatory. This can be seen, for example, with the complex root *pq* 'break'. Following the tradition of Caucasianists, I refer to the part of the verb to the left of the ergative marker as the preverb, and the part to the right as the verb (root). In glossing examples, I simplify by glossing preverbs as PV, and assigning the overall meaning of the preverb-root combination to the root. In actuality, it is the combination of preverb plus root which gives the overall meaning. In examples in which the preverb and root are contiguous, I generally do not separate them into preverb and root, but give a single gloss for the combination.

(36) y-p-s-qə-d
 3si-PV-1s-break-DYN
 I broke it.

The preverbs have no independent (compositional) meaning. Some roots, or SUFFIXOIDS (K'lych 1988), however, may occur with different preverbs, which results in different complex verbs. Certain roots may also occur without a preverb, but with a distinct meaning from the counterpart having a preverb. (For more discussion of preverbs, see K'lych 1988 and Klychev 1994.)

Other prefixes occurring in the verbal complex include the directional markers, ʃa- and na-. These prefixes indicate action towards and away from the speaker, respectively, although the reference point of the directionality is not absolutely fixed. They occur between the ergative and absolutive agreement series. These prefixes are common, especially

1.1 Grammatical sketch of Abaza

ʕa-, and highly productive. They also serve various discourse functions. (See O'Herin 1985 for a discussion of the discourse functions.)

(37) a. **ʕa**gra (< ʕa-ga-ra DIR-carry-MAS) to bring
     b. **na**gra (< na-ga-ra DIR-carry-MAS) to take

There is a set of spatial prefixes with more specific locational meanings than the directionals. Examples, taken from Genko (1955:171–172), are given in (38). None of these are ever associated with agreement or an overt argument.

(38) k'a-   movement downwards
     ǰʷəkʷ-, ǰʷəl-   movement outwards
     čk'ara- (čk'arə-)   in, from the corner
     ʃt'a- (ʃt'ə-)   down flat
     pqa- (pqə-)   forward, in front of
     čʕʷa- (čʕʷə-)   at, from the hearth
     ta- (tə-)   into, inside
     bja- (bjə-)   amidst, from among
     čaʒʷ-   on horseback, by horse
     čpən-   on the shore
     pč'a-   before, in front of [17]
     wahʷta-   behind (location)
     ʕʷna-   at home, inside
     k'əla- (k'əl-)   through
     ʃk'la-   behind (direction)

Example (39) shows the prefix k'a- in a fully inflected form.

(39) a-čə   awaʔa   y-**k'a**-ha-d
     DEF-horse there   3si-**down**-fall-DYN
     The horse fell there.   NART, 89

Preverbs, directionals, and these spatial prefixes share the property that there is never agreement associated with any of them. They occur in the same general morphological space between the absolutive and ergative agreement series. Although there are minor differences in position, there seems to be a relatively fixed order among them. The primary difference between the preverbs, on the one hand, and directionals and spatial

---

[17] Some Abaza speakers have glossed this as 'against', so that it contrasts with pqa-. See pč'a-gəl-ra 'resist (lit., against-stand-MAS)'.

prefixes on the other, is that the preverbs are obligatory, while the others are optional. The directionals differ from the spatial prefixes in that they are much freer in their distribution and in that they may serve certain discourse functions. In a few cases, directionals or spatial prefixes occur as obligatory preverbs.[18]

Certain oblique functions can also be expressed in the verb complex, including the benefactive, the comitative, the instrumental, and various locatives. These are indicated through the use of prefixes and, as already mentioned, there is agreement with the oblique argument. (See chapter 7 for a treatment of these as incorporated postpositions.)

(40) y-s-z-a-č^{j}pa-d
    3si-1s-BEN-3si-do-DYN
    It did it for me.   SSAVC, 163

The causative prefix, r-, increases the number of arguments registered through agreement by one. The causative subject is registered in the ergative series to the immediate left of the causative morpheme. (See chapter 4 for a discussion of the causative construction.)

(41) d-q^{w}əc-i-t'
    3sr-think-PRS-DYN
    S/he thinks.   GAL, 178

(42) d-a-r-q^{w}əc-i-t'
    3sr-3si-CAUS-think-PRS-DYN
    It made him/her think.   GAL, 178

The potential prefix, z-, indicates permission or ability for an action to be performed. (For a discussion of the potential construction, see chapter 5.)

(43) yə-s-h^{w}a-y-t'
    3si-1s-say-PRS-DYN
    I say it.

(44) y-s-zə-h^w-i-t'
    3si-1s-POT-say-PRS-DYN
    I can say it.   GAL, 116

---

[18] I assume that these are in transition between the two relevant types.

1.1 Grammatical sketch of Abaza

Schematically, the dynamic verbal prefixes can be seen in table 2. The absolutive and ergative agreement series (ABS, ERG) are interspersed with the other categories. The ergatives and the obliques (OBL) may include multiple prefixes of the same type. The column indicated by LOC includes both locative obliques and the spatial prefixes. The obliques and locative obliques involve agreement with the oblique argument in addition to the oblique prefix itself. Sample morphemes are given under each type.

Table 2. Order of dynamic verbal prefixes

ABS	OBL	DIR	PV	LOC	ERG	POT	ERG	CAUS	ROOT
s-, b-, w-, d-,...	z-, čʷ-, la-, c-	ʕa-, na-	p-, ...	ta-, k'a-; kʷ-, dzqa-,...	s-, b-, w-, l-,...	z-	s-, b-, w-, l-, ...	r-	V

Null absolutive agreement. In one limited set of cases, absolutive agreement is obligatorily missing where one would otherwise expect it to be present in the verb complex. Additionally, in these cases the nominal and the verb complex tend to form a tighter phonological (prosodic) unit than when the absolutive marker is present, so that [a'dzaʒʷd] forms a single stress unit in (45).[19]

(45) a-la   a-dz   a-ʒʷ-d
    DEF-dog DEF-water 3si-drink-DYN
    The dog drank the water.

According to Allen (1956:134), Tabulova (1976:113), and Sergei Pazov (pers. comm.), both of the conditions in (46) must be met for absolutive agreement to be absent.

(46) a. the nominal with which the missing absolutive marker would register agreement is either 3si or 3p (the two absolutive forms which have the phonological form *y*),[20] and
    b. the nominal with which the missing absolutive marker would register agreement must occur immediately before the verb complex.

---

[19]See Allen (1956) for a fuller discussion of the phonological properties of this construction.
  [20]The + wh form, which is also phonetically *ya*, does not participate in this alternation. It is further distinguished from the other two *y* forms phonologically in its stress properties. See O'Herin (1992b, 1994) for further discussion of stress in Abaza.

This contrast can be seen in (47)–(50). In (47), the conditions are met for null absolutive agreement, and the absolutive agreement marker is null. In (48), the conditions are met for null absolutive agreement, but there is an overt absolutive prefix. Such forms are highly disfavored, but marginally acceptable, especially in very slow speech. In (49), the conditions are not met for null absolutive agreement because the adverb ʃaʃta 'early' intervenes between the direct object and the verb, so the absolutive prefix is obligatory. Contrast (50), in which the conditions for null absolutive agreement are not met, but in which the absolutive prefix is missing. This leads to full ungrammaticality.

(47) sara   a-mʃʷ   s-ba-y-t'
     I   DEF-bear   1s-see-PRS-DYN
     I see the bear.

(48) ??sara   a-mʃʷ   yə-s-ba-y-t'
     I   DEF-bear   3si-1s-see-PRS-DYN
     I see the bear.

(49) sara   a-mʃʷ   ʃaʃta   yə-s-ba-y-t'
     I   DEF-bear   early   3si-1s-see-PRS-DYN
     I see the bear early.

(50) *sara   a-mʃʷ   ʃaʃta   s-ba-y-t'
     I   DEF-bear   early   1s-see-PRS-DYN
     (I see the bear early.)

It is irrelevant to the generalization in (46) which syntactic position is registered by the absolutive prefix. The above examples demonstrate direct objects of transitive verbs. Other positions which are registered by absolutive agreement include the subject of an intransitive verb, (51) and (52), the direct object of a ditransitive verb, (53), the subject of an inverted verb, (54), and the subject of a stative predication, (55). (See chapter 3 for further discussion of stative predicates, and chapter 5 for inverted verbs.) Each of these positions allows null absolutive agreement when the corresponding nominal occurs to the immediate left of the head bearing this (null) absolutive agreement, as shown in the following examples.

(51) a-qac'a-kʷa   nxa-y-d
     DEF-man-PL   work-PRS-DYN
     The men are working.   SSAVC, 152

1.1 Grammatical sketch of Abaza

(52) a-ʒʷ   gʷəmxa   a-hamač   a-zə-ʕanxa-t'
     DEF-cow   bad   DEF-shed   3si-BEN-remain-DYN
     The shed is the bad cow's lot.   GAL, 112

In (52), the subject of the intransitive verb ʕanxa 'remain' is ahamač 'shed' which occurs to the immediate left of the verb. The DP aʒʷ gʷəmxa 'the bad cow' is a benefactive object.

(53) sara   wara   a-čʲʷa   na-wə-s-tə-y-d
     I   you   DEF-apple   DIR-2sm-1s-give-PRS-DYN
     I give you the apple.

(54) a-la   ʕa-sə-cha-t'
     DEF-dog   DIR-1s-bite-DYN
     The dog bit me.

(55) sara   tədzə-k'   s-əma-b
     I   house-INDEF   1s-have-STP
     I have a house.

The conditions for null absolutive agreement in (46) are relaxed somewhat in two circumstances. The overt form, y, may occur in slow speech even when the nominal with which it registers agreement occurs to the immediate left. This is not unexpected if the rule is dependent (partially or wholly) on phonological environment, since an extra pause may be involved in slow speech that is not present in normal rates. If the pause counts as something intervening between the two elements for the purpose of (46), this conforms to the rule.

The second situation in which restrictions on (46) are relaxed is in the case of stative predicates. (See chapter 3 for further discussion.) Null absolutive agreement is often possible even when the nominal with which it registers agreement is either null itself or not immediately adjacent to the head bearing absolutive agreement. The most common such occurrences are with certain meteorological statements, as in (56) and (57). It is also possible, but not required, if the stative predicate begins in a consonant, especially an obstruent, as in (58) and (59).

(56) ʕʷazə-b
     fog-STP
     It is foggy.

(57) px^{j}aʕb
    hot-STP
    It is hot.

(58) q'raḽ^j-b
    country-STP
    It is the country, homeland. NART, 50

(59) sana-b   lə-x^{j}əz
    sana-STP   3sf-name
    Her name is Sana.[21] NART, 50

The generalization in (46) is purely dependent on the surface string of constituents. The rule must have access to the morphological structure (and shape) of the verb complex on the right (to see that the absolutive agreement prefix is 3si/3p) and the syntactic structure of the nominal to its left (to see that the nominal is that which is registered by the absolutive agreement prefix in question). It must be a relatively late rule, which also has access to phonological information (to guarantee that the two parts form a prosodic constituent). I propose, then, that this rule deletes the 3si/3p absolutive agreement prefix in (or on the way to) the PF component under the right conditions. Note that this requires that this level of representation have access to syntactic and morphological structural information.

Suffixes. The categories of tense, aspect, and mood are expressed in the verbal suffix system.[22] Dynamic verbs distinguish six basic tenses, plus various complex tenses. For indicative verbs, the basic tense forms are as in (60).[23]

(60) a. Past completive   s-ca-∅-d
                            1s-go-AOR-DYN
                            I went.

     b. Past incompletive   s-ca-w-n
                            1s-go-PSTI-PST
                            I was going.

---

[21] The subject, *lax^{j}əz*, occupies the anti-topic position to the immediate right of the verb.
[22] See Chkadua (1970) for a fuller discussion of tense and mood in Abaza.
[23] I will henceforth not indicate null aorist (or other null) affixes. I also will refer to FUT1 as just FUT, as this is the considerably more common future tense.

1.1 Grammatical sketch of Abaza

c. Past dependent   *s-ca-Ø-n*
                              1s-go-AOR-DEP
                              I was going (and...)

d. Present   *s-ca-y-d*
                              1s-go-PRS-DYN
                              I go, am going.

e. Future definite   *s-ca-b*
                              1s-go-FUT2
                              I will (definitely) go.

f. Future indefinite   *s-ca-waʃ-d*
                              1s-go-FUT1-DYN
                              I will go.

These same tense distinctions hold in other moods, but some forms differ slightly in their phonological form, for example the present tense is generally -wa in nonindicative moods.

(61) a. Past completive   *s-ca-Ø-ma*
                              1s-go-AOR-YNQ
                              Did I go?

b. Past incompletive   *s-ca-wə-z-ma*
                              1s-go-PSTI-ASP-YNQ
                              Was I going?

c. Past dependent   —[24]

d. Present   *s-ca-wa-ma*
                              1s-go-PRS-YNQ
                              Do I go?, Am I going?

e. Future definite   *s-ca-rə-ma*
                              1s-go-FUT2-YNQ
                              Will I (definitely) go?

---

[24]There is no past dependent yes-no interrogative question form.

f. Future indefinite   s-ca-waʃ-ma
                         1s-go-FUT1-YNQ
                         Will I go?

There are various aspectual suffixes which occur either between the root and the tense marker, or between the tense and mood markers, depending on the individual suffix. These include -x 'repetitive', -rkʷ'a 'continuative', -la 'frequentative', etc.

(62) a. d-qʷmar-**xə**-y-t'
         3sr-play-**REP**-PRS-DYN
         S/he plays again.

   b. y-a-z-qʷəcə-**rkʷ'a**-y-t'
       3p-3si-BEN-think-**CONT**-PRS-DYN
       They still think about it.

   c. d-qʷmar-**la**-y-t'
       3sr-play-**FREQ**-PRS-DYN
       S/he often plays.

   d. d-**ata**-ca-**xə**-y-t'
       3sr-**ONCE**-go-**MORE**-PRS-DYN
       S/he goes one more time.[25]

The possible moods in Abaza include at least indicative, yes-no interrogative, content-interrogative (rational and irrational), imperative, conditional, nonfinite, relative, gerund, subjunctive, and desiderative. These various moods are demonstrated in (63) all in the aorist tense, which has a null tense marker (not marked), where applicable for the tensed forms.

(63) a. indicative   d-ca-d
                             3sr-go-DYN
                             S/he went.

   b. yes/no interrogative   d-ca-ma
                             3sr-go-YNQ
                             Did s/he go?

---

[25]The morphemes *ata-* and *-xə* form a discontinuous constituent meaning *one more time*.

1.1 Grammatical sketch of Abaza

c. content interrogative (rational)
yə-ca-da
AWH-go-WHQR
Who went?

d. content interrogative (irrational)
yə-caʕya
AWH-go-WHQI
What went?

e. imperative
ʃʷ-ca
2p-go
Go! (PL)

f. conditional
dʕcaʕrkʷən
3sr-go-COND
If s/he goes, ...

g. nonfinite
dʕcaʕnəs
3sr-go-INF
for him/her to go

h. relative
yəʕca
AWH-go
(the one) who went

i. gerund
dʕca
3sr-go
going, s/he...

j. subjunctive
d-caʕrən
3sr-go-SUBJ
S/he would go.

k. desiderative
d-caʕnda
3sr-go-DESID
Would that s/he go!

The two types of content questions and the relative form all require exactly one argument to be registered with wh-agreement. (See chapter 8 for a fuller discussion.) The relative and gerund forms are identical except that the gerund has no [+wh] arguments. These two forms lack overt mood suffixes, but do exhibit normal tense distinctions.

The imperative lacks both tense or mood suffixes. The subject must be second person. Of all the moods and tenses, only the imperative causes any change in the pattern of agreement markers. If the imperative is positive, the subject is singular, and the verb is transitive, the ergative marker is obligatorily absent. Otherwise, agreement is as in other moods. This obliterates the masculine versus feminine distinction for the imperative of transitive verbs.

(64) w-ca
    2sm-go
    Go! (m)

(65) b-ca
    2sf-go
    Go! (f)

(66) ʃʷ-ca
    2p-go
    Go! (PL)

(67) y-∅-ga
    3si-2s-carry
    Get (carry) it! (SG)

(68) y-ʃʷ-ga
    3si-2p-carry
    Get (carry) it! (PL)

None of the mood suffixes may occur when there is a separate overt complementizer, such as *asqan* 'while, when', as example (69) demonstrates. The verb complex *anpčə*, which is in the clause having the overt head *asqan*, has no mood marker on it.

(69) a-haqʷ   an-pčə   asqan sosrəqʷ'a awaʔa   d-ʕatəʃʷt-d
    DEF-stone when-break   when   Sosruko   there   3sr-fell-DYN
    When the stone broke, Sosruko fell there.   NART, 54

Schematically, the order of dynamic verbal suffixes can be charted as in table 3.

1.1 Grammatical sketch of Abaza

Table 3. Order of dynamic verbal suffixes

ROOT	(ASPECT)	TENSE	(ASPECT)	MOOD
V	xə, rk'ʷa, la, ...	w, wa, waʃ, y, ra, ...	z, ...	d, b, n, ma, ya, da, ...

Masdars. The masdar, a type of nominalization, is used as the citation form of verbs.[26] The masdar-forming morpheme, -ra, is a suffix. This suffix may also be used with roots of nonverbal categories to give an abstract noun, as in (71).

(70) *ca-ra*
  go-MAS
  to go, going

(71) *dəw-ra*
  big-MAS
  bigness

There are actually two distinct masdar constructions, verbal and nominal.[27] Both are formed by the addition of the masdar suffix to a verb. They differ in that the nominal masdar may take only nominal modification (adjectives to the right of the masdar), while the verbal masdar may take only verbal modification (adverbials to the left of the masdar). Compare the nominal masdar in (72) with the verbal masdar in (73).

(72) *apxʲa-ra-bzəy*
  study-MAS-good
  good studying

(73) *larbaʃʷəga-la   də-s-ba-ra*
  glasses-INST   3sr-1s-see-MAS
  ... me to see him with glasses

---

[26] "Masdar" is the traditional Caucasianist term for the derived forms described in this section.

[27] The verbal masdar is not common. In a text of roughly 6,600 words, there is one clear case of a word which is possibly a verbal masdar. (The other option is a future2 participle, which has the same phonological form.) There are over a hundred nominal masdars in the same text. Most of my examples of verbal masdars are elicited, and these are likewise rare.

They differ also in their agreement patterns. The nominal masdar may have only a single ergative agreement prefix, which registers agreement with the possessor. The nominal masdar is the only form in the language involving a verb root that does not allow absolutive agreement. Compare the nominal masdar in (74) with the verbal masdar in (75).

(74) s-ba-ra
    1s-see-MAS
    my seeing, seeing me

(75) sə-y-ba-ra
    1s-3sm-see-MAS
    ... him seeing me

For nominal masdars, this ergative agreement series occurs external to all other prefixes, regardless of its normal relative order in the verbal prefix system. The verbal masdar exhibits an agreement pattern identical to that in a normal (nonmasdar) verb. Compare the nominal (76) and the verbal (77) with respect to the reflexive prefix.

(76) *s-č-kʷaba-ra*
    1s-REFL-wash-MAS
    my self-washing

(77) *č-s-kʷaba-ra*
    REFL-1s-wash-MAS
    washing myself, to wash myself

Finally, the nominal masdar may have nominal morphology, such as the plural suffix and definite and indefinite articles.

(78) *a-ca-ra*
    DEF-go-MAS
    the going

(79) *ca-ra-k'*
    go-MAS-INDEF
    a going

1.1 Grammatical sketch of Abaza

(80) ca-ra-kʷa
go-MAS-PL
goings

Negation. Negation, which is also morphologically marked in the verb complex, occurs in four major patterns, depending on the tense and mood of the verb. The four patterns are given in (81). Examples of these four patterns are shown in (82). There appear to be two suffix positions for the negative morpheme, immediately following the verb root, as in (82a), and final, as in (82c).[28]

(81) a. the negative suffix, -m, only,
  b. the negative prefix, m-, only,
  c. the negative suffix, -m, plus the intensive prefix g^j-, and
  d. the negative prefix, m-, plus the intensive prefix g^j-.

(82) a. conditional   d-ca-m-ztən
                               3sr-go-NEG-COND
                               if s/he hadn't gone

  b. imperative   wə-m-ca-n
                               2sm-NEG-go-PSTI[29]
                               Don't go!

  c. present indicative   s-g^j-ca-wa-m
                               1s-INT-go-PRS-NEG
                               I'm not going.

  d. aorist yes-no question   d-g^j-m-ca-ma
                               3sr-INT-NEG-go-YNQ
                               Didn't s/he go?

Nothing more will be said in this study about negation and the intensive prefix, as the distribution and analysis is quite complex and not directly relevant to the general issues discussed. (See O'Herin 1992a for further discussion.)

---

[28] When the negative suffix occurs in final position, there is no overt mood suffix.
[29] The negative imperative idiosyncratically requires the mood suffix -n in Tapanta. In the Anatolian dialects, this has been replaced by a second instance of -m.

Constituent order. Abaza clauses are verb-final. Thus, for intransitive verbs, the order is subject-verb. Subjects precede other arguments, so transitive clauses are subject-object-verb. In ditransitive clauses, the basic order places the indirect object before the direct object, giving the order subject-indirect object-direct object-verb.

(83) ada ačtə-y-d
 frog croak-PRS-DYN
 The frog is croaking.

(84) a-čʲkʼʷən a-hʷəhʷ-kʷa y-ʕaza-y-d
 DEF-boy DEF-dove-PL 3sm-raise-PRS-DYN
 The boy raises doves.

(85) awəy sara axčʲa ʕa-sə-y-t-d
 s/he I money DIR-1s-3sm-give-DYN
 He gave me money.

There are at least two privileged nonargument positions, including a focus position to the immediate left of the verb, as in (86), and an antitopic position to the immediate right of the verb, as in (87).[30] The antitopic position is apparently reserved for an XP which is already salient in a discourse. In the text containing (87), Sosruko is the main character, and he is mentioned by name in the immediately preceding sentence.

(86) s-kʲtab dəzda y-na-z-axʷ
 1s-book who 3si-DIR-EWH-take
 Who took my book?

(87) totraʃ-əyʃtə-y, pʃay-y, wagʷawaɉʲə-y d-gʲ-rə-m-gʷapxa-d
 Totrash-even-and Pshey-and Wagwoj-and 3sr-INT-3p-NEG-like-DYN

 sosrəqʷa
 Sosruko
 But Totrash, Pshey, and Wagwoj weren't pleased with Sosruko.
 NART, 57

Adverbs can occur relatively freely with respect to the arguments. They generally occur to the left of the verb complex, but there may also be one adverb to the right of the verb complex, possibly in the antitopic position.

---
[30]Compare similar structures in Turkish (Hankamer, pers. comm.) and other languages (Vallduví 1990). I treat this as right-adjunction to CP.

1.1 Grammatical sketch of Abaza

Abaza is a pro-drop language, in that pronouns are allowed to be null (*pro*) when their features are indexed on a governing element. Verbal agreement cannot be interpreted as pronominal incorporation, since verbal agreement with arguments is obligatory, regardless of whether there is an explicit nominal or not. In addition, Abaza has independent overt pronouns, and agreement occurs even when these are present.

It is not unexpected that pronominal argument DPs may be null in Abaza, given the rich agreement system. Basic information is not lost when there is a null argument, since the relevant features of the null argument are recoverable from agreement on the lexical head that licenses the null pronoun. This is consistent with the condition proposed in Rizzi (1986:520):

(88) Let X be the licensing head of an occurrence of *pro*: then *pro* has the grammatical specification of the features on X co-indexed with it.

Stative verbal morphology. Stative verbs generally express predicates which are states rather than actions or events. The classification of verbs as stative or dynamic is lexical, however, and does not conform exactly to the semantic distinction. A few verbs can occur with either stative or dynamic morphology with different interpretations based on this morphology.

Stative verbs differ from dynamic verbs with respect to prefixes in that certain prefixes available for dynamic verbs are not available for stative verbs. These include directionals and other spatio-temporal prefixes. The stative system differs from the dynamic system with respect to suffixes in that stative verbs lack a number of distinctions available in the dynamic system. For example, stative morphology distinguishes only two tenses, past and present, in contrast to the eight seen in the dynamic system. Certain moods are also unavailable in the stative system, for example the imperative.

Most stative tense and mood suffixes are phonologically identical to those of dynamic tense and mood suffixes. Compare the dynamic yes-no question paradigm in (61a) and (61d) with its stative counterpart in (89).

(89) a. Past   y-ʃʷ-əma-∅-ma
                   3si-2p-have-AOR-YNQ
                   Did you (PL) have it?

     b. Present   y-ʃʷ-əma-w-ma
                   3si-2p-have-PRS-YNQ
                   Do you (PL) have it?

The most notable difference between dynamic and stative tense and mood morphology occurs with the indicative mood suffixes. The present stative indicative suffix is -*b* and the past stative indicative suffix is -*n*, as in (90). Tense and mood are combined in these suffixes. This contrasts with the dynamic indicative suffix -*d*, which requires a distinct tense suffix. (Compare examples (60a) and (60d) with (90a) and (90b), respectively.)

(90) a. Past   *y-s-əma-n*
                 3si-1s-have-PST
                 I had it.

     b. Present   *y-s-əma-b*
                 3si-1s-have-STP
                 I have it.

1.1.2.4 Cross-categorial morphology. Adverbs do not require or allow agreement within the verbal complex (or elsewhere). There are two suffixes, which are probably better analyzed as clitics, that turn a phrase of any category into an adverb. These are *la* and *ta*. They are attached to the right of the last word in the phrase. The clitic *la*, exemplified in (91), is generally treated as an instrumental suffix in the literature. (My analysis in chapter 6 will treat *la* as a type of postposition.) The clitic *ta*, exemplified in (92), has been treated in diverse ways in the literature, including as an adverbializer (Genko 1955), as a factitive case marker indicating what the host phrase becomes (Serdyuchenko 1956), and as a verbal suffix (Sergei Pazov, pers. comm.). In actual fact, the range of usage for both these clitics is much wider. (See example 23.) An account of them is beyond the scope of this study. The crucial point for present purposes is that no agreement is required or allowed with phrases having these clitics/suffixes.

(91) *ha-ʃt'axʲ-la*   *dəzda*   *y-aʕʷs*
      1p-after-AV   who   AWH-pass
      Who passed by behind us?

(92) *sabəy-ta*   *də-l-ʕaza-n*
      baby-AV   3sr-3sf-raise-PST
      She brought him up as a baby/since he was a baby.   NART, 50

1.2 Theoretical framework

I analyze Abaza agreement within the theory of Principles and Parameters whose main principles and framework were primarily developed in Chomsky (1981, 1986a, 1986b, 1991) beginning with Government and Binding (GB) theory. This section is intended to give background so that the reader unfamiliar with this theory is able to follow my analysis and discussion. It is not intended to be a complete presentation or explication of the theory. For a more complete introduction, see Sells (1985, chapter 2), Baker (1988, chapter 2), Lasnik and Uriagereka (1988), and Haegeman (1991).

1.2.1 Levels of representation

The structure of a sentence is factored into four representations, each referred to as a level of representation. These are d-structure, s-structure, LF, and PF. Each of these levels of representation expresses constituency relationships, usually represented as a tree or labeled bracketing. Rules map one level of representation onto another level of representation.

The lexicon provides the basic elements which enter into the constituency relationships of the levels of representation. These are the lexical elements (words). The lexicon also specifies the idiosyncratic properties of each lexical element, such as what category of complement, if any, is required, and what thematic (or participant) relationships hold. A lexical item which requires a particular type of complement is said to SUBCATEGORIZE for that argument. For example, a transitive verb subcategorizes for its direct object. The PROJECTION PRINCIPLE requires that the lexical properties of each element be represented in parallel ways at each level of representation.

D-structure, or underlying structure, is the level of representation at which all of the thematic relationships, or participant roles, are expressed. D-structure is mapped onto s-structure either by the general rule, Move-α, which permits the movement of any constituent to any position in the structure, or by deletion. There are thus no specific rules of movement. Movement to illegitimate positions is ruled out by various constraints on movement, some universal and some language-specific. Some cross-linguistic variation is accounted for by parameterizing these constraints on movement.

LF (logical form) is the level of representation at which various scopal relationships are interpreted, including those of quantifiers and operators. S-structure representations are mapped onto LF representations by applications of the rule Move-α, or possibly by deletions.

PF (phonetic form) is the level of representation which connects with the actual acoustic output. S-structure representations are mapped onto PF representations by various stylistic and phonological rules.

The relationship among these levels is represented in (93).

(93)
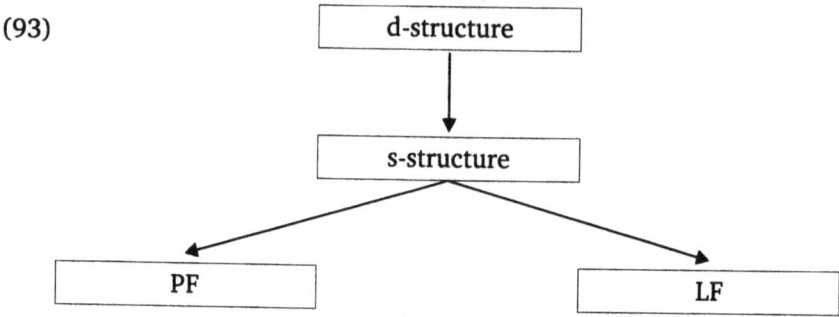

1.2.2 X-bar theory

In Principles and Parameters, possible constituency relationships are constrained by the phrase structure schemata of X-bar theory. In X-bar theory, a HEAD determines the category of the phrase (at every level from the head to the maximal phrase). The phrase involves several levels, referred to as bar-levels. The lowest of these is the head or X° or zero-bar level. The intermediate level is the single-bar level or X'. The highest level is the phrasal level, also called the double-bar level or XP. The XP and X' levels may branch. Elements which branch from the same node are said to be sisters. The sister of the head is referred to as the COMPLEMENT of the head. These two constituents branch from the X' node. Common complements include verbal and adpositional objects. The sister of the X' node is the SPECIFIER of the phrase. Among elements analyzed as specifiers are subjects (specifiers of VP) and possessors (specifiers of NP). Phrases may also move into empty specifier positions, subject to constraints on movement and feature-compatibility.

The relationship between a head and its specifier, the specifier-head relationship, is important in many respects. Crucially, certain features are shared in this relationship, such as agreement features within an agreement phrase. Complements and specifiers are necessarily maximal phrases. These relationships can be seen in the tree in (94).

1.2 Theoretical framework

(94)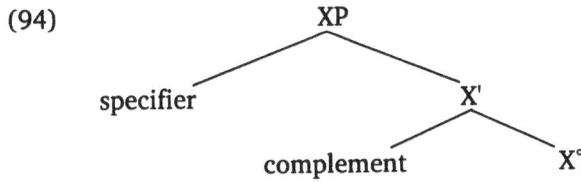

Some cross-linguistic variation in basic word order can be accounted for by having the specifier either to the left or to the right of X', and the complement either to the left or to the right of X°. With specifiers fixed to the left of X', basic SOV word order is accounted for by having complements to the left of X°, while basic SVO has complements to the right of X°. This provides an account of basic SVO, SOV, OVS, and VOS orders, but does not account for the subject-medial orders VSO or OSV. These are accounted for in the theory through movement. (See Black (2000) for a detailed discussion of VSO order.)

There is one additional structural relation, which allows a fuller phrasal structure. ADJUNCTION attaches an element, Y, to another element, X, without changing the bar-level of X. An element may only adjoin to another element of the same bar-level, so heads may adjoin only to heads and phrases (XPs) may adjoin only to phrases. Thus, in (95), YP and Y° have been adjoined to XP and X°, respectively. Following May (1985), the upper and lower XP or X° in these structures are taken to jointly constitute a single complex node. The individual XP and X° elements in (95) are known as SEGMENTS of that category. This assumption has the consequence (important for certain purposes) that the full complex node XP in (95a) does not dominate YP, and similarly for X° and Y° in (95b).

(95) a. 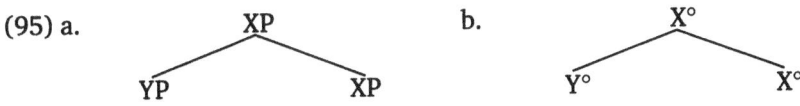 b.

The intuition underlying these assumptions is that adjunction involves the positioning of a phrase at the edge of some other phrase—neither fully within it nor fully external to it.

Abstracting away from the order of elements, then, all phrasal structure conforms to the X-bar schemata in (94) plus the possibility of adjunction as in (95).

A number of important relationships are defined in terms of structural (tree-geometric) configuration. One of the most important of these is C-COMMAND, as in (96). A head, X°, c-commands its complement and everything within its complement (and a complement XP c-commands the head which is its sister). The specifier in a phrase XP c-commands X°, the complement of X°, and everything within that complement.

(96) α c-commands β iff α does not dominate β and every γ that dominates α dominates β.[31]

A relationship similar to c-command is M-COMMAND, whose definition is like that in (96) except that γ must be a maximal projection (XP). A head m-commands both its complement and its specifier and everything within them. The complement of a head, X, and the specifier of X m-command each other.

Like most theories, Principles and Parameters recognizes two classes of word-level elements, open-class elements and closed-class elements (lexical and functional, respectively, in the usual terminology). The lexical categories are N (noun), V (verb), A (adjective), and P (pre/postposition). Functional categories which I utilize include C or COMP (complementizer), AGR (agreement), T (tense), and D or DET (determiner). Heads of functional categories can, but need not, be null. When the head of a functional XP is null, evidence for the presence of the functional XP can often be seen in the syntactic behavior of overt elements in relation to them, for example if an overt element moves into the specifier of XP.

COMP, which may be headed by complementizers such as *that* in English, is the highest verbal functional category. In Abaza, features of mood (indicative, yes-no question, wh-question, etc.) reside in C°. I propose that the complement of C° in Abaza is an agreement phrase, and that this agreement phrase is the locus of absolutive agreement, which I label ABSP. The complement of ABS° is TP.[32] In Abaza, a second agreement phrase occurs as complement to T° in transitive clauses. I will argue that this is the locus of ergative agreement, which I label ERGP. The verbal projection is complement to the lower AGR° (ERG°) in transitive clauses and to T° in intransitive clauses. The structure of an SOV transitive clause is thus as in (97).[33] (See chapter 2 for further discussion.)

---

[31] Crucially for adjunction structures, α is dominated by β only if α is dominated by every segment of β.

[32] In earlier versions of the theory, agreement and tense were combined in a single category I or INFL (inflection). In analyses of English, the subject was required to occur in the specifier of IP, either being generated there directly or having moved from a position within VP.

[33] I follow Koopman and Sportiche (1988, 1991) in adjoining the subject to VP, rather than placing it in the specifier of VP. See §4.4 for justification of this position.

1.2 Theoretical framework

(97)
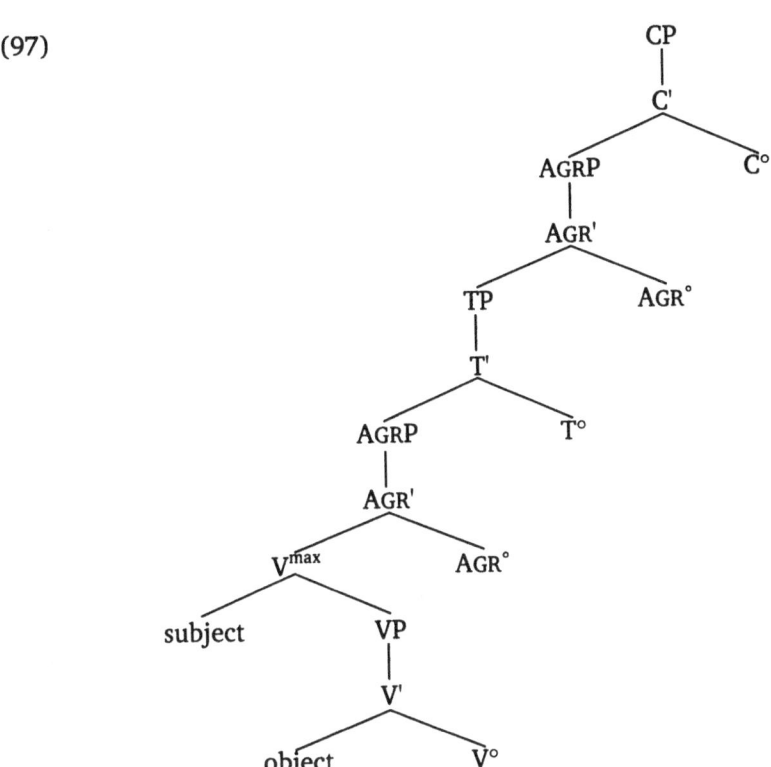

Abney (1987) observed the parallel between nominal phrases and verbal phrases and argued for a nominal functional category dominating NP. He termed this DP (for the determiner which heads this phrase). I utilize this structure, as well. (Again, see chapter 2 for the relevant structure.)

1.2.3 A and A-bar positions

Chomsky (1981) distinguished two types of positions: A-positions, to which a theta-role can be assigned, and A-bar positions, to which a theta-role cannot be assigned. A-positions include argument positions within VP and the subject position, as well as the positions of possessors and adpositional objects. This distinction is crucial for relativized minimality (Rizzi 1990), in which only positions of the same type interfere with one another for purposes of licensing their traces (see §1.2.5). This distinction is also used to rule out certain types of movement. Specifically, A-movement (movement to an A-position) from an A-bar position is excluded as IMPROPER MOVEMENT.

Historically, the subject was assumed to originate in the specifier of IP, where it was assigned the verb's external theta-role. The specifier of IP was thus treated as an A-position. With the introduction of the VP-internal subject hypothesis (Kitagawa 1986, Kuroda 1988, Koopman and Sportiche 1988), the question arises as to the nature of the subject position external to VP, i.e., the specifier of IP. The nature of the specifiers of other functional projections also arises, particularly the specifiers of agreement projections. Campana (1992) considers the specifier of AGRP to be an A-position.[34] Bittner and Hale (1996a, 1996b) consider the specifier of IP to be an A-bar position. I assume that the specifier positions of agreement projections are A-bar positions.

1.2.4 Government and the ECP

One of the core relations in Principles and Parameters is that of GOVERNMENT. Government requires three properties: the governor must c-command the governee,[35] the governor must be "close" enough to the governee (measured in terms of barriers), and the actual governor must be the closest possible governor (defined in terms of relativized minimality). This relation is utilized in a number of the modules of Principles and Parameters, as seen below.

(98) α governs β iff
α c-commands β,
every barrier[36] for β dominates α, and
minimality is respected.

Roughly, minimality is respected if there is no potential governor of the same "type" as the actual governor intervening between the actual governor and the governee (see Rizzi 1990). The possible types include heads, A-positions, and A-bar positions.

When a phrase or head moves in accordance with the rule Move-α, it leaves a (null) TRACE in the position it moved from. One of the most active constraints on possible movement is a condition on traces. This constraint is the Empty Category Principle (ECP), as in (99).

---

[34]Campana utilizes Mahajan's (1990) terminology in which argument positions in VP and the specifiers of agreement projections are L-positions, and in contrast with L-bar positions.

[35]Some definitions of government which have been proposed utilize m-command instead of c-command.

[36]See §7.5 for a definition of barrier.

1.2 Theoretical framework

(99) Empty Category Principle:
   Traces must be properly governed.

PROPER GOVERNMENT is a more restrictive type of government, which will be discussed more fully in §7.5.1.

1.2.5 Case theory

Case theory involves the licensing of overt noun phrases and null pronouns (*pro*). Every overt noun phrase must be licensed through a relation termed CASE ASSIGNMENT. Only certain heads, i.e., Case-assigning heads, may license noun phrases for purposes of Case theory. The noun phrase to be licensed must stand in a particular structural relationship with the licensing head. Government is the relationship traditionally required for the assignment of Case. In some recent proposals involving syntactic agreement projections, AGRP, Case is assigned only in the specifier-head relationship within agreement phrases.[37] This requires the movement of all DPs to the specifier of an AGRP in order to occur in the correct relation with a Case-assigning head.[38] In my analysis of Abaza, I assume that all Case assignment occurs in the specifier-head relationship within one of two types of agreement phrase, absolutive agreement phrases (ABSP) and ergative agreement phrases (ERGP). The core constraint of the Case module is the Case Filter.

(100) Case Filter:
   Every overt DP must be assigned Case.

Note that Case for purposes of licensing differs from morphological case. The licensing of noun phrases is assumed to involve the assignment of abstract Case even in languages lacking morphological case. In this sense, Case licensing is really a kind of positional licensing.

1.2.6 Theta theory

Theta theory accounts for the association of participant roles (theta-roles, or θ-roles) with syntactic arguments. Each lexical head has a set of θ-roles associated with it. For example, a transitive verb like *carry*

---

[37]The specifier-head relationship also involves the government relation under the definition of government utilizing m-command instead of c-command.
[38]I assume that inherent or lexical Case is also assigned in the specifier-head relationship within agreement projections. (See chapter 5.) In some versions of the theory, inherent Case is assigned to a nominal phrase directly by the (lexical) head which governs it.

has an agent role, which is assigned to the subject, and a theme role, which is assigned to the object. A lexical head assigns its θ-role to syntactic arguments in certain positions with respect to the lexical head at d-structure. A distinction is often made between internal and external θ-roles. An external θ-role is a single privileged θ-role, which is assigned to the highest argument (normally the subject for verbs). How internal and external θ-roles are differentiated depends on where the subject is assumed to occur. For Abaza, I assume that subjects are adjoined to VP, forming V^{max}. The external θ-role is assigned to this position. Internal θ-roles are all assigned to arguments within the maximal projection of the head which assigns the θ-roles.

One of the core principles of theta theory is the Theta Criterion, which guarantees a one-to-one relation between syntactic arguments and θ-roles.

(101) Theta Criterion:
Each argument is assigned exactly one θ-role, and
each θ-role is assigned to exactly one argument.

The Theta Criterion applies at all syntactic levels. An argument phrase which moves to another position keeps the θ-role it is assigned in its d-structure position. This relationship is maintained through the argument-trace chain which is formed by this movement. It is not possible for an argument to be assigned one θ-role at one level, such as d-structure, and a different θ-role at another level, such as s-structure or LF.

1.2.7 Binding theory

Binding theory determines the distribution of nominals and the binding and coreference relations they may enter into, based on the two features [±pronominal] and [±anaphor]. Phrases with the features [+pronominal, −anaphor] include pronouns, both null (*pro*) and overt. Phrases with the features [+anaphor, −pronominal] are anaphors, including reflexives and reciprocals. Phrases with minus values for both features are r-expressions (for referring), and include overt non-pronominal, non-anaphor noun phrases. A single item, PRO, has positive values for both features, and its presence is subject to the conditions on both pronouns and anaphors.

The core constraints of the binding theory are found in the three principles of the Binding Conditions.

1.2 Theoretical framework

(102) Binding Conditions:
    a. An anaphor must be bound in its governing category.
    b. A pronoun must be free in its governing category.
    c. An r-expression must be free.

BINDING refers to the relationship between two co-indexed elements when one c-commands the other, as in (103). An element which is free is not bound.

(103) Binding:
    α binds β iff α c-commands β, and α and β are co-indexed.

The GOVERNING CATEGORY (GC) of an element, α, is the smallest maximal phrase (XP) which (1) contains α and a governor for α and (2) is a COMPLETE FUNCTIONAL COMPLEX (CFC). A governing category is a CFC if "all grammatical functions compatible with its head are realized in it" (Chomsky 1986b:169). This requires the presence of a subject for a verbal CFC.

This concludes our preliminary discussion of the Principles and Parameters theory. There are additional principles which are not directly relevant to this study, such as control theory, which determines how PRO is interpreted, bounding theory, which is another type of restriction on movement, and predication theory. More detailed discussion of these principles will be raised as warranted.

2
Basic Case Assignment

This chapter describes the most basic principles by which Case is assigned in Abaza. The overall analysis is that there are two types of agreement projections, AGRP, which mediate ergative and absolutive agreement. An ergative agreement projection is licensed by a lexical head, while an absolutive agreement projection is licensed by TP. In a transitive clause, the direct object originates lower than the subject, yet it ends up in a position higher than the subject. This creates a nesting pattern of movement, which reflects the basic architecture of Abaza syntactic structure. I propose the Nesting Condition for Abaza, similar to Pesetsky's (1982) Path Containment Condition, in order to account for this movement pattern.

2.1 Preliminary discussion

This section presents some assumptions and background necessary for the ensuing discussion. Section 2.1.1 spells out the assumptions I make concerning the relationship between overt agreement in Abaza and the assignment of abstract Case. Section 2.1.2 discusses the means of Case assignment and its interaction with feature checking. Section 2.1.3 discusses the way words are formed and the relationship of this to different interpretations of head movement.

2.1.1 Agreement and its relation to Case

Grammatical relations are marked overtly in the morphology of many languages. The two basic ways of accomplishing this are (1) through agreement and (2) through morphological case. Nichols (1986) refers to these patterns as head-marking and dependent-marking, respectively. Many languages use a combination of these two patterns, for example Russian, which has an extensive morphological case system as well as agreement of a verb with its subject.

Abaza utilizes the head-marking pattern in the extreme. Virtually every noun phrase is registered through agreement on the head which licenses it. This means that nouns register agreement with their possessors, postpositions register agreement with their objects, and verbs register agreement with their subjects, direct objects, and indirect objects.

One component of the theory of Principles and Parameters is the Case module. The core principle of the Case module is the Case Filter, as in (104). The idea behind the Case Filter is that a noun phrase must be licensed, and abstract Case is the means of this licensing.[39]

(104) Case Filter:
    Every overt DP must be assigned abstract Case.[40]

In my analysis of the agreement patterns of Abaza, I make the fundamental assumption in (105).[41] That is, morphological agreement in Abaza is an overt realization, and thus a diagnostic, of Case assignment.

(105) Agreement of X with YP reflects Case assignment by X to YP.[42]

The assumption that the morphological structure of a language interacts with and reflects syntactic structure has as a precursor the Mirror Principle, proposed by Baker (1985:4).

---

[39]Note the difference between abstract Case (often capitalized) and morphological case. Abstract Case is assumed to occur in all languages and may be morphologically absent. Its presence and influence can be seen in languages lacking overt case morphology in ways not relevant to us here. Morphological case is a property of just those languages which mark DPs depending on their semantic role or syntactic position.

[40]This includes the null pronoun *pro*. The other empty (null) categories, PRO and traces, do not require Case, although wh-traces receive Case by virtue of the chain in which they occur.

[41]This is also a foundational assumption of the Minimalist Program (Chomsky 1992).

[42]As will be seen below, a verb word, for example, may actually involve multiple heads. The presence of agreement, then, in a verb word does not necessarily indicate Case assignment by the verb head itself, but by some head expressed in this complex of heads.

2.1 Preliminary discussion

(106) The Mirror Principle:
Morphological derivations must directly reflect syntactic derivations (and vice versa).

In practical terms, I assume that the order of affixes reflects syntactic structure, such that affixes which are closer to the relevant head or root correspond to syntactic material which is closer to the syntactic head. In most cases, this is equivalent to the claim that affixes which are closer to a head correspond to syntactic structure which is lower in the tree.

2.1.2 Case assignment and feature checking

I assume that Case is assigned through the specifier-head relationship within an agreement projection. This configuration arises when a noun phrase needing Case moves into the specifier position of an AGRP. Under this assumption, it is only the head of AGRP, in either of its two types, ABSP or ERGP, which may assign Case.[43]

I further assume that the features which are registered through agreement are checked in this configuration. That is, a noun phrase in the specifier position of an agreement projection must bear the same set of relevant features (φ-features) as the agreement head. If these features do not match, the structure is ill-formed. The features of the agreement heads are overtly realized in the various agreement prefixes.

2.1.3 Word formation

There are two possible views of how words are formed in Abaza. One is that each word is formed in the lexicon (through word-formation rules and/or a morphological template), and the relevant features are encoded in the lexical entry, perhaps as a structured bundle of features. The word, having these features already encoded, is inserted into the syntactic tree, and the relevant features are checked as the word (head) moves into each relevant position.[44] If all the features successfully check, the structure survives and is well-formed (providing other modules pass the structure as well). If some feature of the lexical entry does not successfully check in the appropriate position, the structure is ill-formed.

---

[43]Another possibility which has been proposed is that it is the combination of an agreement head plus some other licensing head which moves into it that assigns Case. See, for example, Chomsky (1992).

[44]Under this view, the movement of the lexical head can be viewed as substitution into a phonetically null (head) position, rather than adjunction.

The second possible view is that the root is a head which is inserted from the lexicon directly into the syntactic tree. The affixes are themselves heads which are also inserted directly into the syntactic structure. As the root head moves through the syntactic structure (by head-movement), it (or the complex of heads which develops as the structure is built up) adjoins to each of the affixes in turn. For example, a verb is inserted from the lexicon into the syntactic tree under V°. This verbal head then raises through a series of functional projections to C°, by successive steps of head movement. As it raises, it adjoins to each functional head. Movement under the adjunction interpretation can be motivated by the need for these various affixes to have a certain type of host. This can be seen in (107).[45]

(107)

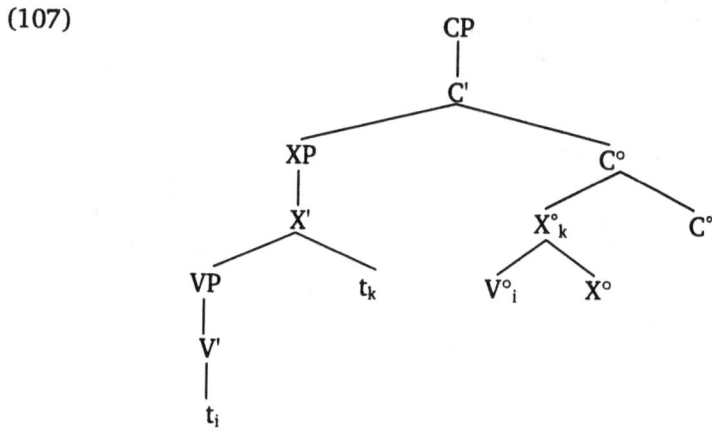

In this structure, t_i is the trace of V°. Whatever is licensed by this head is checked first, and any morphological realization of this checking will appear closest to the verb root. From that position, V° raises to adjoin to X° (at t_k in the tree). The V°-X° complex checks the relevant features of whatever X° licenses. Any morphological realization of this checking appears next closest to the verb root, outside of morphology associated with earlier checking. The V°-X° then raises to adjoin to C°, leaving a trace, t_k. The [[V°-X°]-C°] complex then checks for relevant features on whatever C° licenses, and morphological realizations of this feature or set of features must appear at one of the edges of the complex word (left or right),

---

[45]It is crucial that the relevant heads antecedent govern their traces. The multiple adjunction structure requires the segmental notion of adjunction (see May 1985).

2.1 Preliminary discussion

outside all other affixes. X° actually consists of several heads, but the principles are exactly as described here, repeated for each head.[46]

Either of these modes of word construction is consistent with the analysis I propose for Abaza. An advantage of the adjunction interpretation over the substitution interpretation is that it derives the Mirror Principle. Morphological structure mirrors syntactic structure because syntactic operations build morphological structure.

For the substitution interpretation, it is less clear what motivates the Mirror Principle, or at least it is less clear that the Mirror Principle is directly tied to some morphological or syntactic process. The Mirror Principle, of course, can be maintained as an independent principle, perhaps stipulated. One possible way to account for this relation between syntax and morphology is for the morphology to associate with each word a structured feature bundle which the syntax has access to. Features corresponding to morphology closer to the root are structured in the feature bundle so that they are checked in the syntax prior to features corresponding to morphology further from the root. Although Abaza utilizes both prefixes and suffixes, the relative position of the features in the structured feature bundle can be determined by the relative position of the corresponding syntactic structure. (See Inkelas 1993 for a similar proposal.) The features are thus checked from the inside out.

The structured feature bundle for a transitive verb like that in (108) is given in (109), with each feature bracketed inside the features which are checked later.

(108) ʃʷə-l-ba-waʃ-d
2p-3sf-see-FUT-DYN
She will see you (PL).

---

[46]Following Allen (1956), I refer to the verb word, including the root and all its associated morphology, as a "verb complex". A verb complex has the following properties: (1) it occupies the sentence-final position in the unmarked order, (2) it morphologically indicates tense, aspect and/or mood, or the nonfinite categories associated with the same functional heads, and (3) it involves a predication. Parallel to this, I refer to the word having these properties in stative predications as a "stative complex". It differs only in the category of the lowest head of the complex.

(109)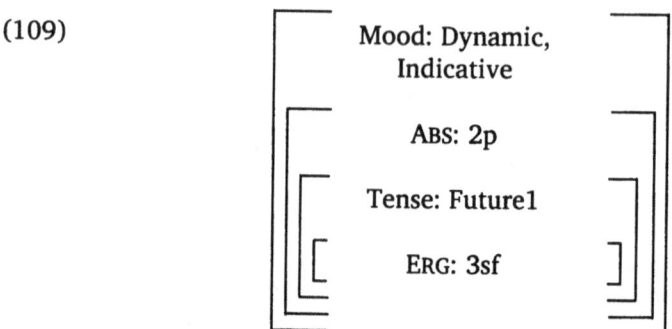

When the innermost feature is checked, the corresponding layer of bracketing disappears, and the next innermost feature needs to be checked. The deletion of a checked feature has the result that it is always the innermost feature which is checked, thus providing a principled way to keep track of which features have been checked and which still require checking. For example, when the ergative features in (109) have been checked, the feature bundle will be:

(110)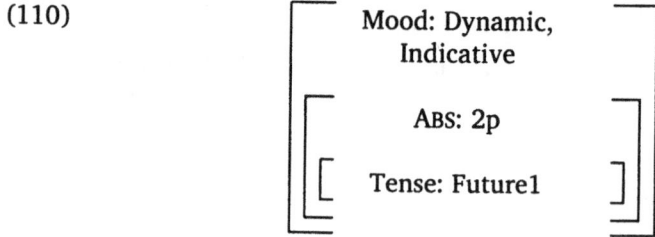

An additional advantage of the adjunction analysis is that it accounts for the fact that the order of some affixes is (relatively) free. (See especially §7.3.1 on multiple incorporated postpositions.) If complete words are built in the lexicon according to some morphological template, there must be more than a single template to account for the possible variations. Of course, this is less problematic for a more dynamic morphological theory not using simple templates.

An advantage of the substitution proposal is that it is easier to account for morphological affixes which are not motivated by the presence of any syntactic head, since they can be treated as not introducing a feature which must be checked in the syntax. For example, some verbal affixes, such as directionals and certain spatial affixes, are arguably not heads of any syntactic constituent. Nevertheless, they occur in the verbal prefix

2.2 Ergative Case assignment

array in specific morphological positions. It is not clear how to account for their presence there under a pure adjunction analysis.[47] Additionally, substitution provides a simpler account of morphologically discontinuous constituents. Specifically, preverb plus root combinations should have a single lexical entry, but the two constituents are separated by other morphological material. If this other morphological material consists of heads adjoining to the complex of heads, it should not be able to occur between the constituents of the lexical root.[48]

Because I view the potential difficulties of the non-head morphological affixes as more serious than either the question of motivating the Mirror Principle or having multiple morphological templates, I will assume the substitution interpretation. Syntactic trees will reflect this. Nothing crucial in my analysis hinges on this choice, however.

2.2 Ergative Case assignment

One agreement series is used to register agreement with nominal possessors, objects of postpositions, transitive (and ditransitive) subjects, and indirect objects. This agreement is analyzed here as mediated through an agreement projection, ERGP, which dominates each of the relevant lexical heads.

2.2.1 Case assignment to the nominal possessor

Abaza nouns register agreement with their possessors. This agreement is indicated by a prefix, agreeing with the possessor in person, number, and, in the second and third person singular, gender or rationality (human versus nonhuman). The paradigm of *tdzə* 'house' is shown in (111), with the abbreviations used throughout this volume shown to the right.

---

[47] One possibility would be to treat them as adverbial heads, ADV°, which are adjoined at certain specified positions and then incorporate into the complex verbal head as it passes that adjoined underlying position. This raises certain ECP difficulties, however, as well as questions about legitimate adjunction.

[48] It may be possible to provide an adjunction analysis for these discontinuous constituents similar to that of Speas (1990) for Navajo in which some adjunction is treated as morphological infixation. For Abaza, the most plausible such account is to treat the preverbs as extrametrical. This would presumably require at least two levels in the phonological derivation, one in which the preverb was extrametrical and one in which it was not. I find this plausible on phonological grounds. For example, ergative prefixes assimilate in voicing to following obstruents where absolutive prefixes do not. This analysis is not without problems, however, and I do not pursue it further.

(111) a. s-tdzə   my house   1s
      b. b-tdzə   your (f) house 2sf
      c. w-tdzə   your (m) house 2sm
      d. l-tdzə   her house   3sf
      e. y-tdzə   his house   3sm
      f. a-tdzə   its house   3si
      g. h-tdzə   our house   1p
      h. ʃʷ-tdzə   your (PL) house 2p
      i. r-tdzə   their house   3p

The possessor precedes the noun it possesses in accord with the head-final nature of the language. It is also possible for the possessor to be null, with agreement on the head noun indicating the person and number of the possessor. In these cases, I treat the possessor position as occupied by a null pronoun, *pro*, bearing the relevant features of person, number, gender, and rationality. Examples of possessed nouns can be seen in (112)–(115). There are no obligatorily possessed nouns. All possessors are optional.

(112) a-phas   l-qas'a
      DEF-woman   3sf-man
      the woman's husband

(113) a-s'əys   a-ʕʷara
      DEF-bird   3si-nest
      the bird's nest

(114) (wara)   w-nap'ə
      you (m)   2sm-hand
      your (m) hand

(115) ahmet   y-tdzə
      Ahmet   3sm-house
      Ahmet's house

I adopt the DP-hypothesis proposed by Abney (1987). This proposal posits a functional projection, DP (for determiner phrase), above the lexical projection, NP. Together they form an extended nominal projection (see Grimshaw 1991). The DP structure provides a position for the agreement projection I will propose. A simple structure consisting solely of NP does not provide enough structure to account for all the syntactic material

2.2 Ergative Case assignment

in these constructions. Following standard practice, e.g., Abney (1987) and Longobardi (1994), I posit the possessor in a specifier position within the nominal extended projection, and not in a complement position.[49] Specifically, I assume that the possessor DP originates in the specifier of NP position.

I propose that the agreement of a noun with its possessor is mediated by an agreement projection. One question, then, is where in the DP structure this agreement projection occurs. The two possible positions are (1) above the DP and (2) between the NP and the DP. I opt for the position between NP and DP. The resulting underlying structure of a possessed nominal in Abaza is shown in (116). A nominal without a possessor lacks a DP in the specifier of NP and the entire agreement projection between NP and DP.

(116)
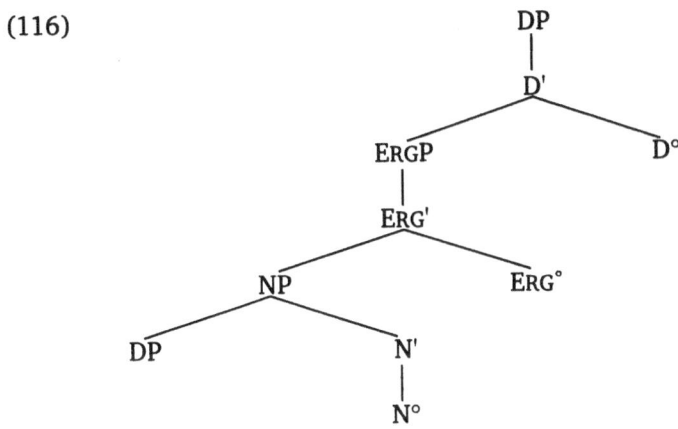

There are two reasons for choosing this structure over one having the agreement projection above the DP, both of them having to do with making the nominal structure similar to other well-motivated structures.[50] The first is that the structure of nominal phrases is parallel to the structure

---

[49]One reason for assuming this distinction is that the possessor is not selected in the same way that the object of a preposition or postposition or the direct object of a transitive verb is. Note that in many languages, e.g., German and Russian, prepositions select the particular case of their objects. It is not the case that languages allow nouns to select the case of their subjects (possessors). There are other selectional restrictions that split along this same dimension. A further factor motivating this distinction is that the possessor of a noun can be treated parallel to a verbal subject in terms of structure, while an adpositional object can be treated parallel to a verbal object.

[50]Longobardi (1994) argues for independent reasons that a possessor occupies the specifier of the highest projection in the nominal extended projection below DP. My account is entirely consistent with his analysis.

of verbal phrases, as shown below. One of the factors motivating Abney's original proposal was the structural similarity between the verbal and nominal constructions. In this regard, DP corresponds to CP as the highest functional projection. The second reason for choosing the structure in (116) is that it allows the generalization that there is a single uniform structural position for this agreement projection across the entire Abaza system, immediately above a lexical maximal projection, VP, PP, and NP. The distributional property of the head of this agreement projection is that it takes a lexical XP, without regard to category. (This generalization is modified somewhat in §2.2.4.)

An obvious place to look for evidence as to the relative positions of DP and ERGP is in the relative order of the determiner and agreement morphology. If the agreement marker is inside, i.e., closer to, the noun root than the determiner, that would argue for the DP being higher. If the agreement marker were outside the determiner, that would argue for the ERGP being higher. Unfortunately, there is no such evidence either way, since the definite determiner and the agreement markers are in complementary distribution; they cannot co-occur.[51]

Given the underlying structure in (116), the post-movement structure is as in (117).

(117)

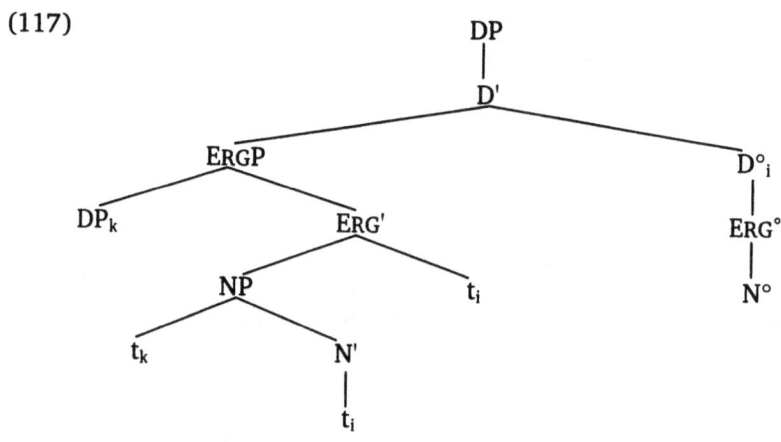

---

[51]Various language-specific constraints are possible which filter out forms having both determiner and agreement marker. For example, if words are formed in the lexicon (which requires an autonomous morphology), they can be assigned the same morphological "slot", with the possibility of only one occurring. This is not surprising, since the definite determiner seems to have developed historically from the third person singular irrational agreement marker (they are both *a*).

2.2 Ergative Case assignment

In this construction, the head N° substitutes for ERG°. This movement leaves a trace, t_i, which is subject to (and satisfies) the restrictions on traces. The possessor DP moves to the specifier of ERGP in order to get Case, and this movement also leaves a trace, t_k. In this configuration, the relevant features can be checked through the specifier-head relationship. The ERG°-N° complex then substitutes for D°, leaving a second trace, t_j. The movement of the agreement head (complex) into the determiner head is invisible in this structure, since overt determiners may not co-occur with agreement morphology. I assume that the movement occurs, however, because of parallels with other structures. The head N° overtly incorporates into D° in nonpossessive DPs, as evidenced by the fact that the determiners occur affixed to the root (see §1.1.2.1). In verbs having this same agreement projection, the verbal head, V°, moves overtly all the way to C°. Having N° move all the way to D° in structures with possessors maintains the parallel between DP and CP.

2.2.2 Case assignment to the object of a postposition

Most postpositions must register agreement with their objects.[52] This can be seen in the paradigm in (118) for the postposition *pnə* 'by, at'. The agreement series which registers agreement with the object of a postposition is phonologically identical to the series which registers agreement with the possessor of a noun.

(118) a. *s-pnə*   by me (at my house)   1s
      b. *b-pnə*   by you (f) (at your house)   2sf
      c. *w-pnə*   by you (m) (at your house)   2sm
      d. *l-pnə*   by her (at her house)   3sf
      e. *y-pnə*   by him (at his house)   3sm
      f. *a-pnə*   by it   3si
      g. *h-pnə*   by us (at our house)   1p
      h. *ʃʷ-pnə* by you (PL) (at your house)   2p
      i. *r-pnə*   by them (at their house)   3p

Postpositions follow their objects, as seen in (119) and (120), again in accord with the head-final nature of the language. The object of a postposition can be overt or null.[53] In the latter case, it is treated as a null

---

[52]There is also a small class of suffixes, which I analyze as postpositions, which do not allow agreement with any object, and which are cliticized to their object (accounting for their appearance as suffixes). It is possible that the objects of these postpositions satisfy the Case Filter through incorporation rather than through an agreement projection. See Baker (1988) and Rizzi and Roberts (1989) for analyses along these lines.

pronoun, *pro*, with the relevant features. It is also possible to have a clausal complement (usually in the gerundive form, but masdars and purposives are also possible) to at least one postposition, *qaz* 'for', which is used to indicate reason, as shown in (121). A CP object is registered by third-person singular irrational (default) agreement. I assume that the objects of postpositions occupy the postposition's complement position, although this assumption is not crucial to the analysis presented here.

(119) *awǝy   a-mʃtax*ʲ
      that   3si-after
      after that

(120) { *sara, pro* }   *s-pnǝ*
      { I, *pro* }   1s-at
      at my house, by me

(121) *yǝ-čʷǝ-y-t'*   *y-ʕapsa-wa*   *a-qaz*
      3p-sleep-PRS-DYN   3p-tired-PTC   3si-for
      One sleeps because one is tired.

As in the nominal structure, I propose that agreement between a postposition and its object is mediated by an agreement projection. This agreement projection occurs directly above the lexical phrase, PP. The underlying structure is as in (122).

(122)
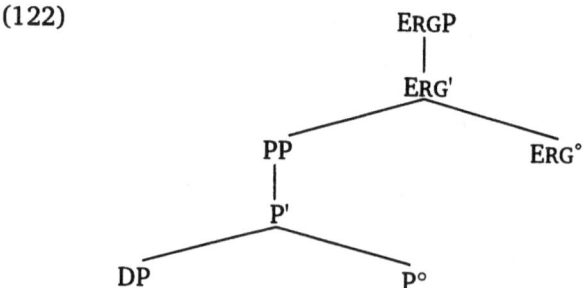

In this structure, the head P° substitutes for the head of the agreement projection. Like the possessor in the nominal construction, the DP complement moves into the specifier of the agreement projection, where the relevant features of the DP can be checked through the specifier-head relationship. This produces the structure in (123).

---

[53]Not all postpositions allow null third-person objects.

2.2 Ergative Case assignment

(123)
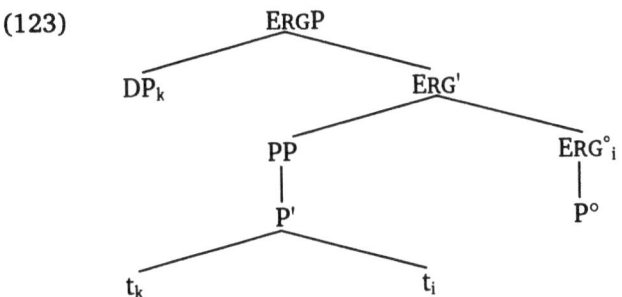

2.2.3 Case assignment to the subject of a transitive verb

The verb in Abaza overtly registers agreement with the subject of a transitive or a ditransitive verb. The corresponding agreement series is phonologically identical to that which registers agreement with the possessor of a noun and the object of a postposition. These prefixes can be seen in bold between the third-person singular rational object (absolutive) prefix *dә-* (the absolutive agreement series is discussed in §2.3) and the verb *ʃә* 'kill' in the paradigm in (124). The final *d* indicates indicative mood for dynamic verbs.

(124) a. dә-**s**-ʃә-d   I killed him/her.
     b. dә-**b**-ʃә-d   You (f) killed him/her.
     c. dә-**w**-ʃә-d   You (m) killed him/her.
     d. dә-**l**-ʃә-d   She killed him/her.
     e. dә-**y**-ʃә-d   He killed him/her.
     f. d-**a**-ʃә-d   It killed him/her.
     g. dә-**h**-ʃә-d   We killed him/her.
     h. dә-**ʃʷ**-ʃә-d   You (PL) killed him/her.
     i. dә-**r**-ʃә-d   They killed him/her.

This agreement can, and I argue should, be treated in the same way as the agreement already discussed. That is, an agreement projection above VP mediates this agreement. Because the series used to register agreement with transitive subjects contrasts with the series used to register agreement with both the subjects of intransitive verbs and the direct objects of transitive verbs, I refer to it as the ergative series. In addition, I refer to the agreement projection which mediates this agreement as ERGP.

I assume the version of the VP-Internal Subject Hypothesis proposed by Koopman and Sportiche (1988, 1991). In this analysis, the subject is adjoined to VP, creating a node which they label V^{max}. They argue that although structurally in an adjunction configuration, the subject is in an A-position, and the V^{max} node is a basic part of the verb phrase. For now, I adopt this structure without argument. It will be shown below, however, that this configuration best accounts for the Abaza data because it is the only version of the VP-Internal Subject Hypothesis which provides a position for the indirect object in ditransitive verbs.[54] A VP-internal structure is preferable to one in which the subject occupies the specifier of some functional projection dominating VP (such as Bowers 1993) because the VP-internal structure provides a position for the subject of the complement to the causative verb. (See chapter 4.) The (partial) underlying structure for a transitive verb phrase is shown in (125). Again, the basic Abaza order of SOV is accounted for directly by having heads occur uniformly on the right.

(125)

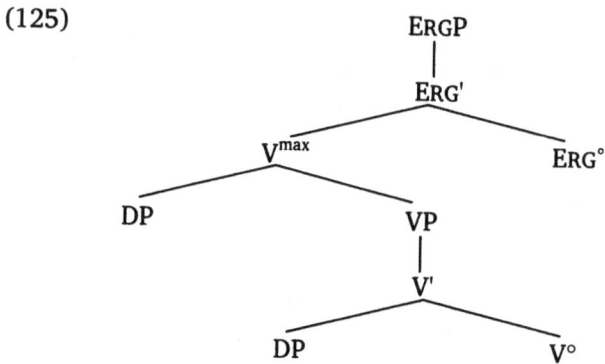

As in the two constructions we have already seen, ergative agreement is mediated through the ergative agreement projection when the lexical head raises to substitute for ERG°, and the relevant DP raises into the specifier of ERGP. The resulting substructure is as in (126).

---

[54]Assuming binary branching, the VP-internal subject proposed by Kitagawa (1986) and Kuroda (1988) occupies the specifier of VP, which leaves no open position for the indirect object.

2.2 Ergative Case assignment

(126)
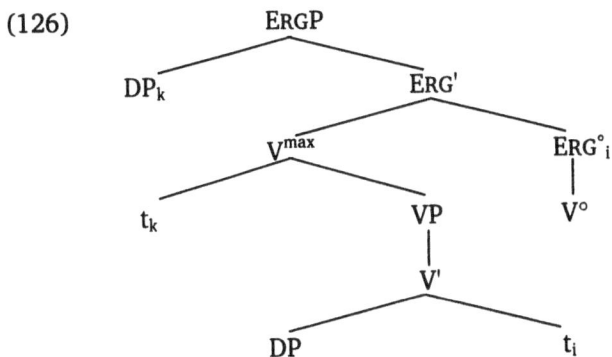

For reasons to be seen in chapter 6, I assume that a transitive verb assigns a feature to its subject which requires the subject to occur in an ergative agreement specifier.[55] This, along with the Nesting Condition discussed in §2.5.2, accounts for the movement of a transitive subject to the specifier of an ergative agreement projection. Treating ergative Case as a lexical Case is consistent with the analyses of Mahajan (1989), Harbert and Toribio (1991), and Woolford (1993). I refer to this as the Transitive Subject Condition.

(127) Transitive Subject Condition:
The subject of a transitive verb is assigned the feature [+ERG].

To summarize, there is a single agreement series which registers agreement with nominal possessors, complements of postpositions, and subjects of transitive (and ditransitive) verbs. This series can be given a unified analysis in which there is an agreement projection, ERGP, immediately dominating the corresponding lexical phrases, NP, PP, or VP (V^{max}). In each case, the lexical head raises to substitute for ERG°, and the relevant DP moves into the specifier position of the agreement projection, where it receives Case and where the features of the DP are checked against the agreement features marked on the lexical head.

Here, we can make a first approximation of the licensing conditions of ERGP. The ergative agreement projection is licensed by the presence of a lexical XP. In the examples seen thus far, the lexical phrase is always sister to ERG°. In terms of selection, this could be expressed in the generalization that ERG° selects lexical XP. In terms of extended projections (see

---

[55]This is equivalent to assigning an inherent Case.

Grimshaw 1991), which is how I will express these relationships, the distribution of ERGP can be accounted for as seen in (128).[56]

(128) Lexical XP extends to ERGP.

2.2.4 Case assignment to the indirect object of a ditransitive verb

With a ditransitive verb, agreement with the indirect object is registered by an ergative series in addition to the series which registers agreement with the subject. Agreement with the subject is registered in the ergative series to the immediate left of the verb root, and agreement with the indirect object is registered in a series to the left of that. The direct object is registered in the absolutive series, like the direct object of transitive verbs. A paradigm of agreement with the indirect object of the verb *t* 'give' can be seen in bold in (129). In each case, the subject is third-person singular feminine, indicated by the ergative marker *l-*. The direct object is indicated by *y-*, followed by the directional prefix ʕa-. The suffix -waʃ indicates future tense, and indicative mood is indicated by the final -*t'*.

(129) a. *y-ʕa-sə-l-t-waʃ-t'*   She will give it to me.
     b. *y-ʕa-bə-l-t-waʃ-t'*   She will give it to you (f).
     c. *y-ʕa-wə-l-t-waʃ-t'*   She will give it to you (m).
     d. *y-ʕa-lə-l-t-waʃ-t'*   She will give it to her.
     e. *y-ʕa-yə-l-t-waʃ-t'*   She will give it to him.
     f. *y-ʕ-a-l-t-waʃ-t'*   She will give it to it.
     g. *y-ʕa-hə-l-t-waʃ-t'*   She will give it to us.
     h. *y-ʕa-ʃʷə-l-t-waʃ-t'*   She will give it to you (PL).
     i. *y-ʕa-rə-l-t-waʃ-t'*   She will give it to them.

The basic word order of ditransitive constructions, which places the indirect object between the clause-initial subject and the direct object, is S-IO-DO-V,[57] as seen in (130)–(133).

---

[56]An extended projection is a lexical XP plus its associated functional projections. A functional head does not select its complement in the same way that a lexical head does.

[57]This basic order is given also by Colarusso (1976). Allen (1956) implies that the basic order is S-DO-IO-V, as in (i). This order is often possible, perhaps either as some sort of dative shift or else as a focusing of the indirect object (see chapter 8), but I argue that it is not the basic underlying order.

(i)   a-qac'a   a-la   a-phʷəspa   y-lə-yt-d
      DEF-man   DEF-dog   DEF-girl   3si-3sf-3sm-give-DYN
      The man gave the dog to the girl.   SSAVC, 157

2.2 Ergative Case assignment

(130) sara   wač̣ʷa   sphas   aɫən   lə-s-t-waʃ-d
     I   tomorrow   1s-woman   ring   3sf-1s-give-FUT-DYN
     I will give my wife a ring tomorrow.

(131) s-ʃwza   zak'ə   yə-s-tə-y-d
     1s-friend   something   3sm-1s-give-PRS-DYN
     I give something to my friend.

(132) awəy   hara   a-č̣ʷa-kʷa   ʃa-ha-y-tə-y-d
     s/he   we   DEF-apple-PL   DIR-1p-3sm-give-PRS-DYN
     He gives us the apples.

(133) sara   wara   p'aɫa   w-s-t-x-wa...
     I   you(m)   agreement   2sm-1s-give-ASP-PRS
     I, making a date with you,... (lit., I, giving you an agreement,...)
                                                                               NART, 89

The underlying structure of the VP can be accounted for under the Koopman and Sportiche analysis of the VP-Internal Subject Hypothesis by positing the indirect object in the specifier of V position.

(134)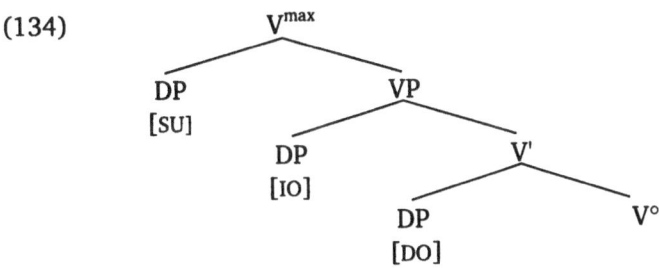

This structure differs from proposals made for ditransitives by Larson (1988) and Bowers (1993). Larson proposed two separate VPs, with the subject in the specifier of the higher VP, the direct object in the specifier of the lower VP, and the indirect object in the complement of the lower VP. This move is taken in order to provide enough positions within VP, but it is not necessary given the structure in (134). Since Larson's proposal utilizes two lexical heads for a single lexical item, the availability of an alternative proposal lacking this nonstandard move is preferable. Furthermore, Larson's proposal predicts the objects in the reverse order.

Bowers (1993) provides data arguing against Larson's proposed structure and proposes a structure of his own in which a functional category,

PrP (predication), dominates VP. The subject (external argument) occupies the specifier of PrP, the direct object occupies the specifier of VP, and the indirect object is the complement (sister) of V°. Other oblique arguments of the verb are adjoined to V'. Bowers' analysis differs from mine in two respects: the presence of an additional functional projection and the relative position of the direct and indirect objects. I argue in chapter 4 that the subject must occupy a position within the lexical projection of VP rather than the specifier of a functional projection. The relative position of direct and indirect objects proposed by Bowers is problematic in that it predicts the wrong order of syntactic constituents for Abaza. Furthermore, it is shown below that the direct object must be in the lowest structural position in order to end up in the specifier of the highest agreement projection because of the nesting pattern of movement to the specifiers of agreement projections in Abaza. The structure in (134), therefore, accounts for the Abaza data better than either of the structures proposed by Larson or Bowers.

In order to account for the agreement pattern within Abaza ditransitive verb complexes, I propose that there are two ergative agreement projections stacked above VP. The underlying substructure I propose is as in (135).

(135)

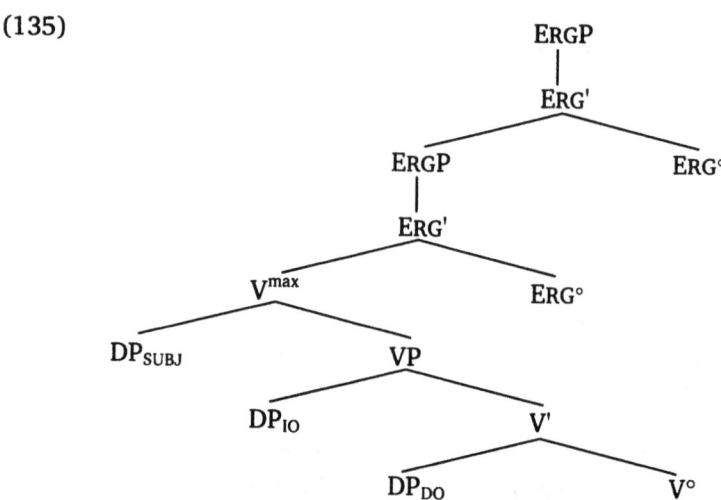

From this underlying structure, the subject moves into the specifier of the lower ergative agreement projection, and the indirect object moves into the specifier of the higher ergative agreement projection, resulting in a nesting pattern as shown in (136). (Head movement is not shown.)

2.2 Ergative Case assignment

(136)
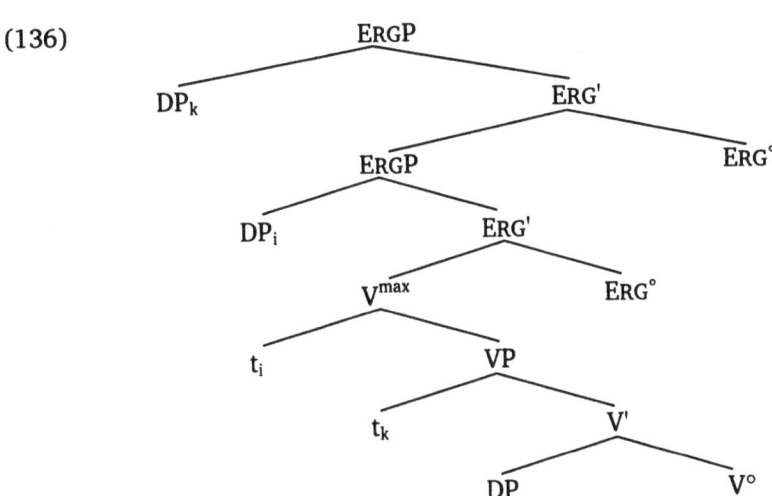

The question arises, what licenses these two ergative agreement projections, since they are not present with every occurrence of a lexical head? I propose that they may be generated freely within a verbal extended projection, in accordance with the language-specific principle (137). As will be seen more clearly in chapter 5, ergative agreement projections are not limited to positions directly above the lexical verb (or other ergative agreement projections), but may be interspersed among other functional projections in the extended projection.

(137) Lexical VP licenses ERGP* freely within its extended projection.

Such a principle potentially creates structures with a proliferation of ergative agreement projections. I rule out these excess structures with the two restrictions in (138) and (139).

(138) Unused Agreement Filter:
    Structures having an agreement projection whose specifier is unoccupied are ill-formed.

(139) Closer Agreement Principle:
    Given two trees structurally identical except for the position of ERGP, both of which satisfy other conditions equally, the structure involving the lower ERGP is used.

The Unused Agreement Filter in (138) guarantees that only as many ergative agreement projections will occur as are used, by eliminating structures which have ergative agreement phrases that do not mediate any actual agreement.[58] Besides preventing unused excess structure, this filter can be motivated by the need for an agreement head to check the features of its specifier within the normal specifier-head relationship. If there is no specifier, however, the relevant features of the head cannot be checked.

Whereas the Unused Agreement Filter in (138) restricts the number of ergative agreement projections, the Closer Agreement Principle in (139) restricts their position in the structure by requiring them to be as low as possible. In the normal case, this puts them immediately above the lexical VP. Furthermore, (139) prohibits an ergative agreement phrase from occurring, for example, above TP or AbsP, which are discussed in the next section. This principle also accounts for the relative order of phrases within the potential construction, discussed in chapter 5. One possible motivation for such a filter is so that movement can be as short as possible.[59]

Within the verbal extended projection, then, ERGP may be freely instantiated, subject to the restrictions (138) and (139). This is not so within nominal or postpositional extended projections. In these cases, only one ergative agreement projection may occur, and only in the position immediately dominating NP or PP. The licensing conditions for ergative agreement phrases in (128) must thus be modified to include only these categories, as in (140).

(140) Lexical NP, PP extend to ERGP.

The overall licensing conditions for ERGP, then, are those given in (137) and (140), plus the restrictions in (138) and (139). These restrictions

---

[58]It is not simply the case that ditransitive VP licenses two ergative projections stacked above it. Two ergative agreement projections above the causative verb are required for the causative of transitive verbs, and three are required for the causative of ditransitive verbs (see chapter 4). This would require an extension of the number of possible stacked ERGPs to three. Furthermore, it must be stipulated that the causative verb, which is not ditransitive, must be able to license multiple ergative projections. This is even more problematic in that the transitivity of the causative VP does not itself determine the number of ergative agreement phrases in the causative case, but the transitivity of the complement of the causative VP. This, and the fact that all but the lowest ERGP are non-adjacent to the VP, leads to non-local relationships which determine the presence of certain phrases. Additionally, there are cases in which a non-agreement functional projection intervenes between an ergative agreement phrase and the lexical VP (see chapter 5 for further discussion).

[59]Compare the principle of Shortest Move in Chomsky (1992).

apply to both licensing conditions. The Unfilled Agreement Filter, for example, prevents ERGP from being licensed with NP if there is no possessor to fill the ergative specifier. The Closer Agreement Principle applies vacuously to (140), since the latter only licenses ERGP in the lowest possible position.

2.3 Absolutive agreement

We turn now to an account of the second agreement series, which is used to register agreement with the subject of an intransitive verb and the direct object of a transitive or a ditransitive verb. Section 2.3.1 addresses the former, while §2.3.2 deals with the latter. The primary motivation for utilizing an absolutive agreement projection is to provide a uniform structural position from which absolutive Case is assigned, regardless of the particular construction involved.

2.3.1 Agreement with the subject of an intransitive verb

Agreement with the subject of an intransitive verb is registered by an agreement series phonologically and positionally distinct from the ergative series. Positionally, it always occurs left-most in the verb complex. Phonologically, it is distinguished from the ergative series in each of the third-person forms. Because this series is used to register agreement with the subjects of intransitive verbs and the objects of transitive verbs, in contrast with the subjects of transitive verbs, I refer to this as the absolutive series.[60] The absolutive series can be seen to the left of the intransitive verb root $q^w mar$ 'play' in (141). Glosses for each of the prefixes used throughout this book are given in the right column.

(141) a. sʕqʷmarʕd   I played.   1s
      b. bʕqʷmarʕd   You (f) played.   2sf
      c. wʕqʷmarʕd   You (m) played.   2sm
      d. dʕqʷmarʕd   S/he played.   3sr
      e. yʕqʷmarʕd   It played.   3si
      f. hʕqʷmarʕd   We played.   1p
      g. ʃʷʕqʷmarʕd   You (PL) played. 2p
      h. yʕqʷmarʕd   They played.   3p

---

[60]Russian grammars refer to the absolutive series as the D-series, corresponding to the third-person singular rational absolutive prefix d-. They refer to the ergative series as the L-series, corresponding to the third-person singular feminine ergative prefix l-. These two forms each occur only in the series which bear their name.

Examples (142)–(146) show intransitive verbs with overt subjects in the canonical position to the left of the verb.

(142) *a-phas   d-ʕay-d*
  DEF-woman 3sr-come-DYN
  The woman came.

(143) *y-čə   aʒʷə-t'*
  3sm-horse age-DYN
  His horse grew old.   IAT, 65

(144) *ʃʷara   ʃʷ-ʕʷə-y-d*
  you (PL) 2p-run-PRS-DYN
  You run.

(145) *awəy   də-nxa-y-d*
  s/he 3sr-work-PRS-DYN
  S/he works.

(146) *a-mara   ʕa-qalə-y-d*
  DEF-sun dir-go.up-PRS-DYN
  The sun rises.

I propose that absolutive agreement is mediated through an agreement projection, ABSP. The underlying structure for (142) is represented in (147). Note that the absolutive agreement projection is located directly below CP and above TP. (This proposal is justified in §2.4.)

2.3 Absolutive agreement

(147)
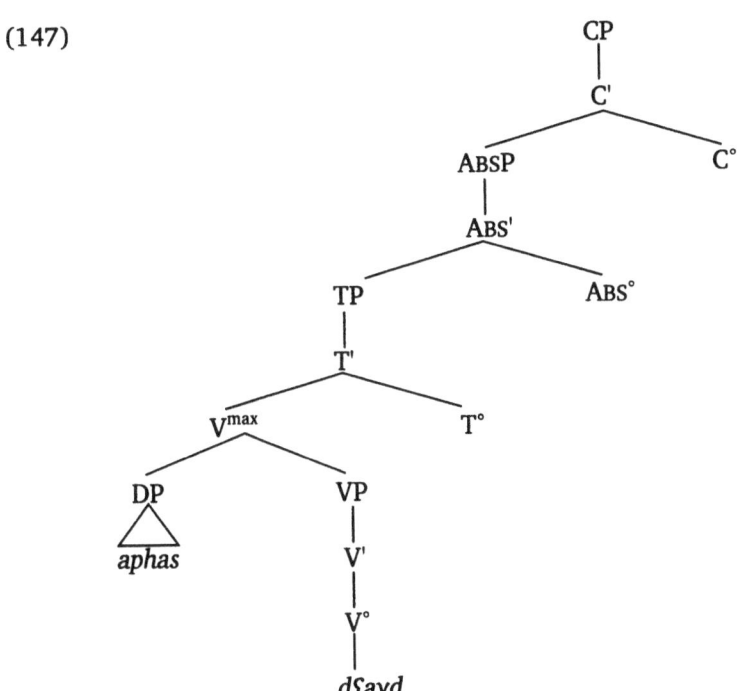

The verb form *dʕayd* is built in the lexicon and inserted in the tree with (at least) the features [tense: aorist] and [mood: dynamic indicative], as well as [absolutive: third-person singular rational]. The verb head substitutes for T°, where the tense feature is checked, and a trace, t_i, is left at V°. From this position, the V°-T° complex substitutes for ABS°, leaving a second trace, t_i, at T°. In order to be licensed, the subject DP moves into the specifier position of ABSP, where the features of the DP are checked against the features of the absolutive agreement head. The moved DP leaves a trace, t_k, in its original position. The [ABS°-[V°-T°]] complex next substitutes for C°, where the mood features are checked.[61] Again, a trace, t_i, is left at ABS°. The resulting structure is seen in (148).

---

[61] I assume that the mood markers in Abaza are complementizers. This is consistent with the claim made by Cheng (1991) that "typing particles," such as the Abaza mood suffixes, are generated in C°.

(148)

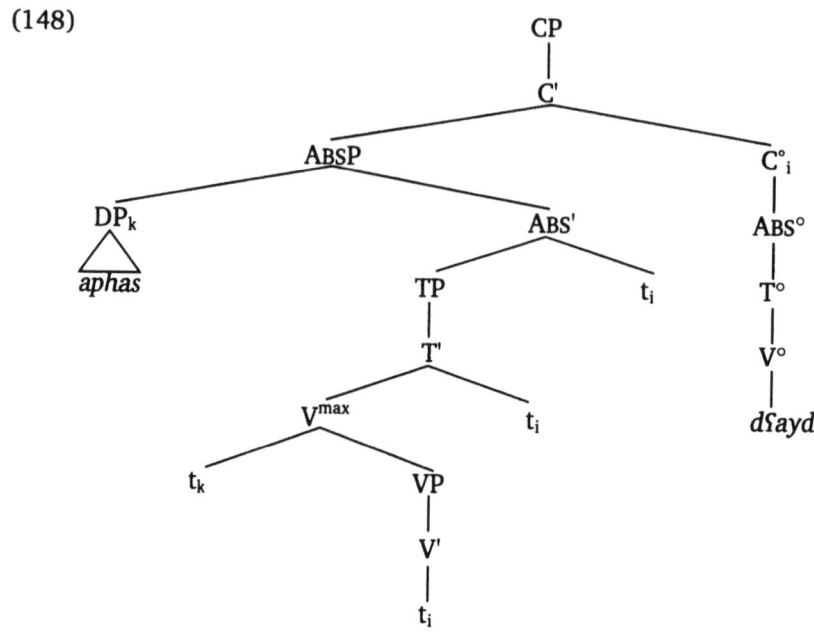

2.3.2 Agreement with the direct object of a transitive or a ditransitive verb

Agreement with the direct object of a transitive verb utilizes the same set of agreement markers as the series used for the subjects of intransitive verbs. This can be seen in the paradigm in (149) of the transitive verb *ba* 'see', with the third-person singular feminine subject registered in the ergative series with the marker *l-* and the dynamic indicative mood with the suffix *-t'*. The absolutive marker is initial in each case.

(149) a. *sə-l-ba-t'*   She saw me.
      b. *bə-l-ba-t'*   She saw you (f).
      c. *wə-l-ba-t'*   She saw you (m).
      d. *də-l-ba-t'*   She saw him/her.
      e. *yə-l-ba-t'*   She saw it.
      f. *hə-l-ba-t'*   She saw us.
      g. *ʃʷə-l-ba-t'*   She saw you (PL).
      h. *yə-l-ba-t'*   She saw them.

With overt arguments, the order is SOV.

2.3 Absolutive agreement

(150) a-phas-kʷa   a-halə   r-sə-y-d
      DEF-woman-PL   DEF-carpet 3p-weave-PRS-DYN
      The women are weaving the carpet.

(151) zaǰʷə   a-phas   də-y-ʃa-y-d
      someone DEF-woman   3sr-3sm-hear-PRS-DYN
      Someone hears the woman.

(152) a-ʒʷ-kʷa   dz-ʃarda   r-ʒʷə-y-d
      DEF-cow-PL   water-much   3p-drink-PRS-DYN
      The cows drink a lot of water.

With the ergative agreement projection directly above V^{max}, and the absolutive agreement projection between TP and CP, as claimed above, the underlying structure of the transitive sentence is given in (153).

(153)

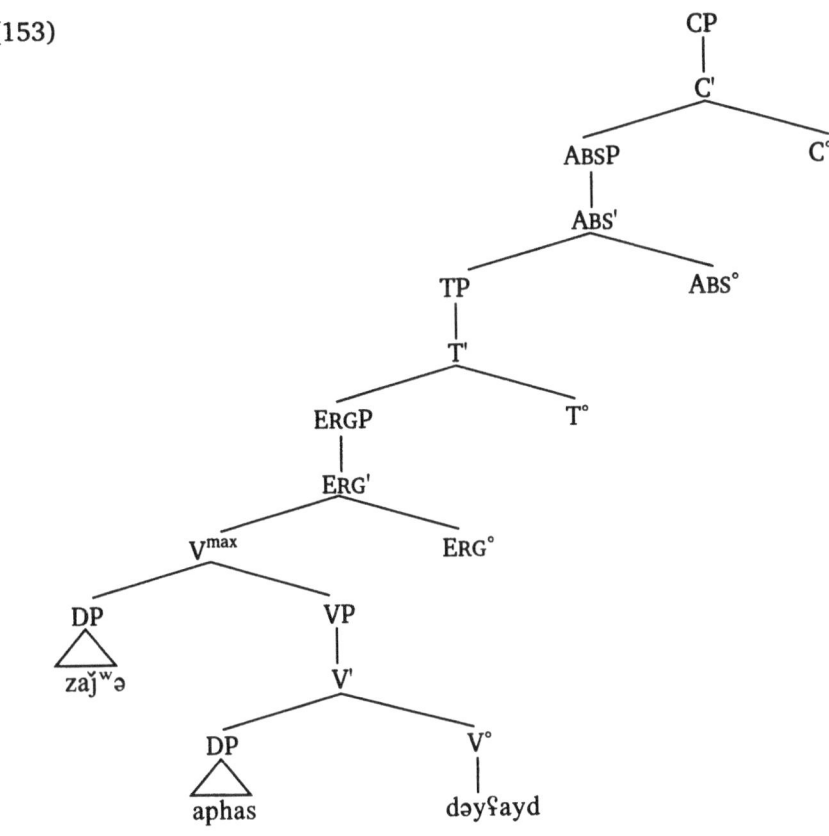

68   *Basic Case Assignment*

The structure of this transitive sentence after movement can be seen in (154). The verb complex is formed in the lexicon and inserted under V° as *dəyʕayd*. From this position the verb head substitutes for ERG°, leaving a trace, t_i. The subject DP raises from its position adjoined to VP into the specifier of ERGP, in order to get Case, and thus be licensed under the Case Filter. The moved DP leaves a trace, t_j, in its original position. These two movements produce a configuration in which Case can be assigned (ERG° is a Case-assigning head), and in which the features of agreement can be checked via the specifier-head relationship. The V°-ERG° complex moves to T°, leaving a second trace, t_i. The tense features are checked here, and the [[ERG°-V°]-T°] complex substitutes for ABS°. Again, a trace, t_i, is left in the vacated position. The relevant features are checked against the DP in the specifier of ABSP, which has moved there from the object position within VP in order to get Case, leaving the trace t_k. Finally, the whole [ABS°-[[ERG°-V°]-T°]] complex moves to C°, leaving the highest trace, t_i.[62]

(154)

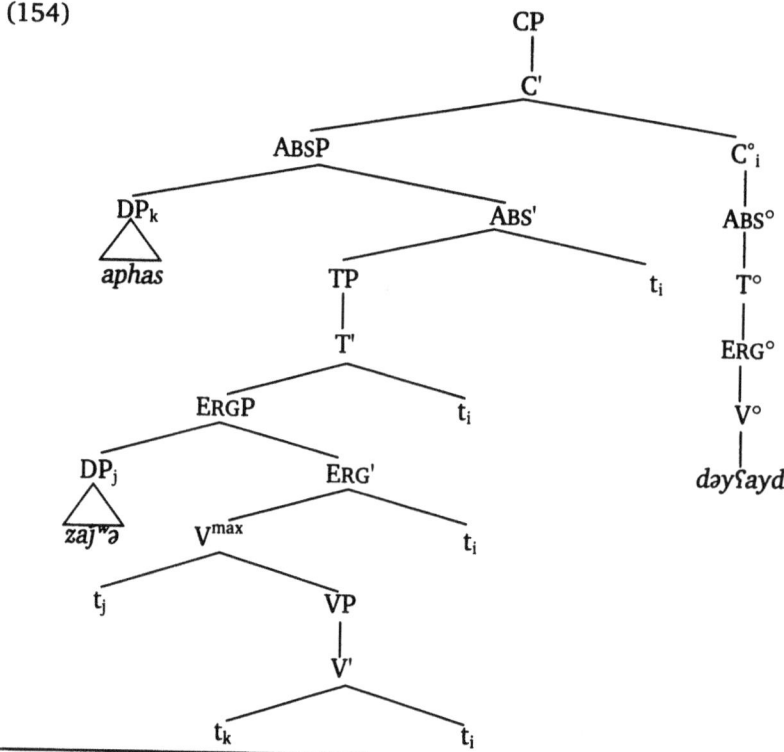

---

[62]For reasons of space, I will henceforth include in trees only the highest head in structures involving a series of substituted heads. This is merely shorthand for the structures in (148) and (154), however.

One potential difficulty with the post-movement structure for transitive clauses is that the word order (OSV) does not correspond to actual Abaza word order (SOV). An account of this is relatively straightforward under the assumption that the movement of the object into the specifier position of the absolutive agreement projection (for checking) takes place at LF and not in the syntax. It is generally assumed that such checking can be accomplished either in the syntax or at LF (Huang 1982, Campana 1992, Chomsky 1992). This means that the Case Filter must apply at LF instead of in the visible syntax (i.e., at s-structure). If this movement takes place at LF, then the object remains in its underlying position as the sister of V' throughout the syntax (ignoring other possible movement, such as focus and antitopicalization). This position as complement to the verb is to the right of the subject, and places the object in the correct surface order.

One question this proposal raises is whether movement into the specifier of the ergative agreement projections takes place in the syntax or at LF. Like movement to the absolutive specifier, this also occurs at LF, for similar reasons. The underlying order of subject and indirect object places the subject to the left of the indirect object. Once these two DPs have moved to their respective ergative specifiers, this order is reversed, with the indirect object to the left of the subject. Since the subject occurs to the left of the indirect object in the actual surface order, movement to the ergative specifiers must take place at LF.[63]

This analysis predicts that LF-sensitive mechanisms should all work "backwards" in Abaza, with objects taking scope over subjects. Unfortunately, I do not have the necessary data to confirm or disprove this prediction. I, therefore, leave this as an issue for further research.

2.4 The position of agreement projections

We turn now to a discussion of the positions of the agreement projections within the verbal extended projection. Section 2.4.1 discusses the analysis in which the two agreement projections are separated by TP. This is consistent with analyses following Pollock's (1989) proposal that there are more functional projections between CP and VP than just IP. Section 2.4.2 addresses the question of which of the two agreement projections occupies the higher position. Further evidence is presented (beyond the generalization that ERGP is licensed by lexical heads) that the absolutive agreement projection is higher than the ergative agreement projection.

---

[63]The movement of DPs to the specifiers of agreement projections is not forced until LF. This does not prevent such movement if forced by other factors. See, for example, focus movement, which is discussed in chapter 8.

2.4.1 AGRP-TP-AGRP

Since Pollock (1989), there have been a number of proposals concerning various types of functional projections within the verbal extended projection. Much of this discussion involves functional projections which mediate agreement, usually termed AGR (e.g., Iatridou 1990, Chomsky 1992).[64] Other functional projections which have been discussed include negation or NEGP (Laka 1990, Ouhalla 1990, Ernst 1992, Déprez and Pierce 1993), polarity or ΣP (Laka 1990, Schafer 1994), transitivity or TrP (Murasugi 1992), predication or PrP (Bowers 1993), aspect or AspP (Ouhalla 1990), modal or MP (Rivero 1994) and, within the nominal extended projection, quantifier or QP (Shlonsky 1991). A full discussion of all the arguments in favor of and against these proposals is beyond the scope of our present study.

Crucial to our discussion, Pollock (1989) demonstrated the need for a separate specifier position between VP and IP, and treated this as an agreement phrase, AGRP. Previously, agreement had been considered a component of INFL, along with tense. Pollock renamed IP TP for tense, thus separating the components of INFL into two separate projections. Ouhalla (1988) has shown the possibility for an agreement projection between TP and CP.

Chomsky (1992) adopts the use of two agreement phrases, one for the subject and one for the object. He places them in the two positions argued for, AGR_SP (for the subject) between TP and CP and AGR_OP (for the object) between TP and VP. For nominative-accusative languages the nominative projection is the higher of the two. AGR_SP is associated with TP, in the sense that the presence of (certain values of) TP licenses it, or that TP extends to AGR_SP. The lower agreement projection, AGR_OP, is associated with VP in the same way. This provides a uniform position for the two types of agreement projection in that each dominates the phrase of which it is an extension. I also adopt the structure in which the higher agreement phrase occurs between CP and TP and the lower agreement phrase(s) occur between TP and VP, although nothing crucial rests on their relative position with respect to TP.

2.4.2 The relative positions of AbsP and ErgP

Recent work on ergative-absolutive languages has divided into two camps. One group places the locus of ergative agreement higher than the locus of absolutive agreement (Levin and Massam 1984, Massam 1985,

---

[64]In analyses involving two agreement projections, they are sometimes differentiated with the subscripts S and O (for subject and object, respectively): AGR_S, AGR_O.

2.4 The position of agreement projections

Chomsky 1992, Bobaljik 1993a, b). The other group places the locus of absolutive agreement higher than the locus of ergative agreement (Bok-Bennema 1991, Bittner 1992, Campana 1992, Murasugi 1992, Bittner and Hale, 1996a, b). My analysis is clearly in line with the latter group.

Section 2.4.2.1 presents Bobaljik's (1993a, b) analysis as representative of more recent proposals in which the ergative agreement projection is higher than the absolutive agreement projection. Section 2.4.2.2 presents various reasons for preferring an analysis in which the absolutive agreement projection is higher in the structure than the ergative agreement projection.

2.4.2.1 ERGP higher than ABSP.
Following Chomsky (1992), and working within the Minimalist Program, Bobaljik (1993a, b) argues that in ergative-absolutive languages, the agreement projection mediating ergative agreement is the higher of the two agreement projections. The original motivation for the move by Chomsky (1992),[65] and followed by Bobaljik (1993a), was to account for ergative-absolutive languages within the Minimalist Program, where no nesting dependencies are allowed, for theory-internal reasons discussed below. Bobaljik (1993b) extended the argumentation to show that transitive subjects in both nominative-accusative and ergative-absolutive languages behave alike in contrast to the objects of transitive verbs. This can be seen, for example, with respect to reflexivization. The underlying subject must asymmetrically c-command the underlying direct object in order for the binding conditions to be observed. Chomsky (1992) has suggested that the binding conditions operate at LF. Bobaljik argues that since subject and object move to the specifiers of their respective agreement projections also at LF, the binding condition configuration requires that the subject agreement

---

[65]Chomsky's (1992) discussion of ergative languages is limited to the following:

> Suppose that VP contains only one NP. Then one of the two AGR elements will be "active" (the other being inert or perhaps missing). Which one? Two options are possible: AGR_s or AGR_o. If the choice is AGR_s, then the single NP will have the properties of the subject of a transitive clause; if the choice is AGR_o, it will have the properties of the object of a transitive clause (Nominative-Accusative and Absolutive-Ergative languages, respectively). These are the only two possibilities, mixtures apart. The distinction between the two language types reduces to a trivial question of morphology, as we expect. (Chomsky 1992:13)

It is Bobaljik who fleshes out this analysis for ergative-absolutive languages.

projection (ergative) be higher than the object agreement projection (absolutive).[66]

The Abaza data present additional difficulties for the Minimalist Program, in which Boboljik works. The principles which work together to force the crossing pattern of movement to agreement specifiers are Shortest Move and Domain Extension. The principle of Shortest Move requires that movement be to the closest available specifier position, which prohibits a moving DP from crossing over a filled specifier position, whether open or filled. Domain Extension is a principle which allows two specifier positions to be considered equidistant for purposes of Shortest Move. When a head, $X°$, incorporates into the next higher head, $Y°$, the specifier of XP and the specifier of YP are considered equidistant for the complement of $X°$.[67] These two principles force a crossing pattern of movement with respect to the subject and object of a transitive verb into their respective agreement specifiers. This can be observed in the structure in (155) (with irrelevant material omitted, and utilizing Chomsky's labeling).

(155)

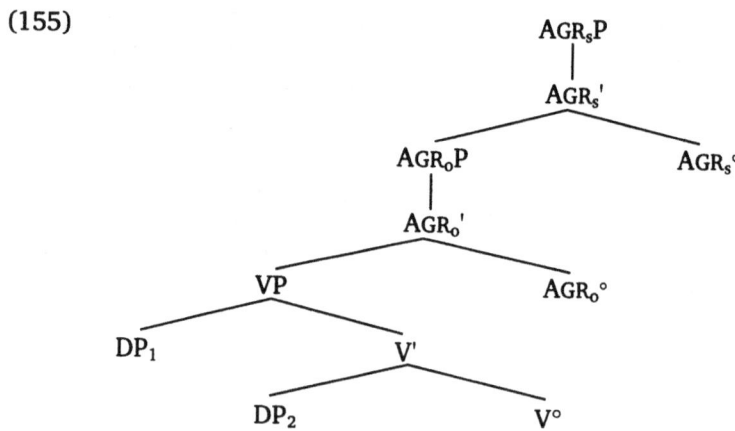

From this structure, only the subject, DP_1, would be able to move into the lower agreement specifier, since the object, DP_2, would have to cross

---

[66]Note that this argument disappears outside of the Minimalist Program, where the binding conditions may operate at some level other than LF.

[67]"Equidistance" is not transitive. That is, in the structure [[[ZP]YP]XP], when the head of XP incorporates into the head of YP, the specifiers of XP and YP are equidistant for movement from within XP. When the head of YP then incorporates into the head of ZP, the specifiers of YP and ZP are equidistant for movement from within YP. Although the specifiers of XP and YP are equidistant in one context and the specifiers of YP and ZP are equidistant in another, there is no possibility for the specifiers of XP and ZP to be equidistant for movement from within XP.

2.4 The position of agreement projections

the specifier of VP to reach that position, inducing a violation of the Shortest Move condition. However, when V° incorporates into $AGR_o°$, Domain Extension makes the specifiers of VP and AGR_oP equidistant from any lower position, thus allowing the object to move into the specifier of AGR_oP. The subject must then cross over the specifier of AGR_oP, but the incorporation of $AGR_o°$ into $AGR_s°$ results in Domain Extension making the specifiers of AGR_oP and AGR_sP equidistant for the subject.

This derivational pattern results in crossed dependencies, as seen in (156).

(156) ... DP_{SUBJ} ... DP_{OBJ} ... [$_{VP}$ ... t ... t ...]

Crossing dependencies are thus legal. This pattern is in fact the only possible outcome from the structure in (155). Nesting of dependencies, as in (157), is ruled out in principle.

(157) ... DP_{SUBJ} ... DP_{OBJ} ... [$_{VP}$ ... t ... t ...]

To see why this is so, consider how (157) would have to be derived. If the subject were to first make the Shortest Move into the lower agreement specifier, Domain Extension resulting from the movement of V° to $AGR_o°$ would have no detectable effect, since only the specifiers of VP and AGR_oP are rendered equidistant by this move. For the object, the two specifiers in this extended domain are both occupied, blocking movement to either position. The object must now move to the specifier of the higher agreement projection to be licensed, but this is impossible. Movement of $AGR_o°$ into $AGR_s°$ does not allow the object to move to the specifier of AGR_s, since this makes only the specifiers of AGR_o and AGR_s equidistant, but movement to either would violate Shortest Move since the specifier of V is closer. The result of the interaction of these two principles is that a crossing movement pattern is forced in general in such situations.

These assumptions fail to take into account movement patterns when there are more than two arguments which must move into the specifiers of agreement projections, as in the ditransitive examples in Abaza. The Minimalist Program makes the basic assumption that overt agreement is mediated by agreement phrases, thus requiring three such projections in Abaza. The problem is that there is no way for three DPs to move out of

VP, since the third one (in whichever order is used) will necessarily violate Shortest Move.[68] This can be seen in the tree in (158).

(158)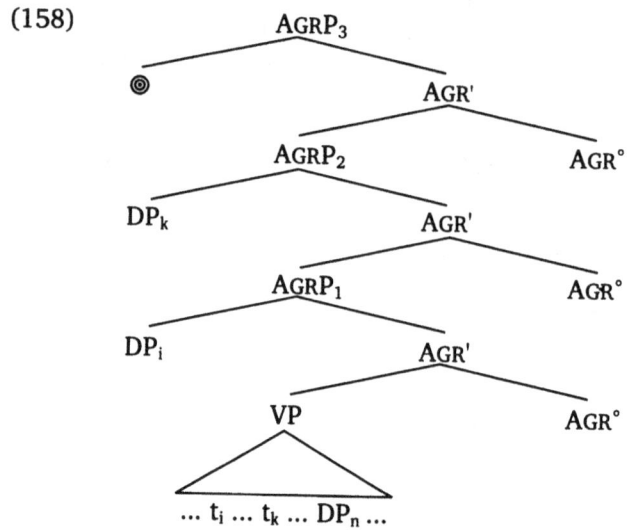

Simplifying so that no specifier position within VP is taken into account (which would further limit movement), the first argument to move, DP_i, moves to the specifier of the lowest agreement phrase, $AGRP_1$. The head of this phrase substitutes for the head of the next highest agreement phrase, $AGRP_2$. This allows Domain Extension to apply, so that the specifier positions of $AGRP_1$ and $AGRP_2$ are equidistant for the second argument, DP_k, to move out of VP. DP_k may thus move to the specifier of $AGRP_2$, satisfying Shortest Move. For the third argument, DP_n, however, Domain Extension makes the specifiers of $AGRP_1$ and $AGRP_2$ equidistant, but these are both occupied. Domain Extension makes the specifiers of $AGRP_2$ and $AGRP_3$ equidistant, but DP_n cannot move to the open specifier of $AGRP_3$ because the specifier of $AGRP_1$ is closer, and a violation of Shortest Move would result.

In order to allow movement to three agreement phrases within the Minimalist Program, then, either Domain Extension must be modified to allow a third DP to escape VP, or the Principle of Shortest Move must be weakened. Either of these revisions undermines the argument that a crossing movement pattern is forced, however.

---

[68]This is true also in a split VP structure for ditransitives following Larson (1988), unless the subject agreement phrase is above the higher VP shell, and both the direct object and indirect object agreement phrases occur between the two VP shells.

2.4 The position of agreement projections

Having demonstrated that basic motivations for placing ergative agreement structurally higher than absolutive agreement are untenable, we turn to evidence that absolutive agreement must be higher than ergative agreement.

2.4.2.2 AbsP higher than ErgP. In this section, three factors supporting the claim that ErgP is lower than AbsP in Abaza are presented: (1) the association of absolutive Case with tense or inflectional material and the association of ergative Case with VP (and other lexical XPs), (2) the Mirror Principle (Baker 1985) and the order of affixes, and (3) the Extended Projection Principle (EPP) in conjunction with expletive facts.

One basic argument in favor of having AbsP high is its close connection to Infl-like properties. Abstracting away from the position of the arguments to which the various Cases are assigned, a comparison of nominative-accusative Case assignment and ergative-absolutive Case assignment shows some useful similarities between the two systems, with respect to which categories assign which Cases. Intransitive verbs in both systems are associated with a single Case, while transitive verbs are associated with two (different) Cases, one of which is the same Case that occurs with intransitive verbs. Under the assumption that (one of) the difference(s) between transitive and intransitive verbs is that the former have the ability to assign (a particular) Case,[69] while the latter do not, it is entirely reasonable to conclude that the Case which does not occur with intransitives is assigned by the (transitive) verb, either directly or indirectly through AGRP. The Case associated with intransitives can then be located external to the VP, that is, in INFL. The Cases are thus assigned by the categories as shown in (159). For an ergative-absolutive language like Abaza, ergative Case is assigned lower (closer to the verb).

(159)

	nom-acc	erg-abs
transitive V / lower AGR	accusative	ergative
INFL / higher AGR	nominative	absolutive

Such a distribution of Cases is further supported in Abaza by the fact that absolutive Case is not in a one-to-one relation with verbal heads (V°), but it is in a one-to-one relation with predicates (which have tense heads, T°). The fact that there is no one-to-one relation between verbal heads and absolutive Case can be seen both in the fact that verbal heads may occur without absolutive agreement and in the fact that absolutive

---

[69]This ignores the question of whether the verb assigns Case directly or whether this is mediated through an ergative agreement projection immediately above VP.

agreement can occur in constructions lacking a verb. Masdars, nominalized forms of the verb, are the only construction involving a verb root that does not allow certain inflectional material (including T°). Furthermore, masdars are the only construction involving a verbal head which may lack absolutive agreement. This fact remains unexplained if absolutive is licensed simply by VP, since most masdars also involve verbal roots at some level.

That absolutive agreement is not in a one-to-one relation with VP can be seen clearly in nonverbal stative predicates. Examples (160)–(163) show that agreement with the subject of a stative nominal or adjectival predicate is registered in the absolutive series, even though there is no verb involved.

(160) *d-qac'a-b*
    3sr-man-STP
    He is a man.

(161) *wə-s-əsas-b*
    2sm-1s-guest-STP
    You are my guest.

(162) *a-phaspa   d-pʃdza-b*
    DEF-girl   3sr-pretty-STP
    The girl is pretty.

(163) *a-kʷəjʲma   yʔanəzlak'gʲəy   y-kʷəjʲma-b*
    DEF-wolf   everywhere   3si-wolf-STP
    A wolf is a wolf everywhere.   GAL, 104

Such forms demonstrate not only the lack of a one-to-one relation between absolutive agreement and a verb, but they also demonstrate the one-to-one relation between absolutive agreement and tense (TP). There is exactly one absolutive agreement marker in every "predicate complex", regardless of which syntactic category is involved in the predication. Both verb complexes and stative complexes of other categories contain exactly one absolutive.

If absolutive Case is assigned by a functional head associated with an inflectional element, e.g., INFL° or ABS°-T°, then this distribution is accounted for in a straightforward manner, since each verb complex and stative complex has exactly one (set) of these functional heads. If, however, absolutive Case is assigned within VP, it is an accident that only a

2.4 The position of agreement projections

single absolutive may occur, and that in all verb complexes and stative complexes a single absolutive must occur.[70] Furthermore, treating absolutive as assigned within VP fails to explain how and why absolutive Case can be assigned within nonverbal stative predicates (and not within nonverbal projections which are not predicative, thus lacking tense). Clearly, then, absolutive agreement is associated with inflectional material, and not with V. I thus adopt the following licensing condition for absolutive agreement projections:

(164) TP (necessarily) extends to ABSP.

The Mirror Principle (Baker 1985) states that morphological structure mirrors syntactic structure. For Abaza I take this to mean that affixes corresponding to functional heads occur in the order corresponding to the order of movement through syntactic head positions. That is to say, affixes that are closer to the root occur lower in the syntactic structure than affixes which are further away from the root. Since the absolutive prefix occurs external to the ergative prefix, this indicates that ABSP must be higher than ERGP.

The Extended Projection Principle (EPP) (Chomsky 1981, 1986a) was proposed to account for the fact that in English (and other languages) the subject position, taken to be the specifier of IP, must be filled at some point in the derivation. With the decomposition of IP into TP and various AGRPs, the agreement specifiers provide a plausible locus for the EPP.

Abaza predicate complexes always have exactly one instance of absolutive agreement, while they can have zero, one, or two instances of ergative agreement. (Or three, when causatives are involved. See chapter 4.) This points toward the specifier of ABSP as the privileged position for the EPP. I propose, then, that the EPP, (165), holds in Abaza.

(165) Extended Projection Principle:
    The specifier of ABSP must be filled.

In English, if no argument can occupy the subject position, an expletive, i.e., *it* or *there*, is inserted. Expletives, or dummies, are semantically noncontentful elements which can bear no θ-role.

Further evidence for a formulation of the EPP for Abaza as in (165) comes from the fact that Abaza has a small set of verbs which exhibit absolutive agreement that does not register agreement with any

---

[70]Note the similarity to the requirement in some languages, e.g., English, that a particular position external to VP be filled (the specifier of INFL or the specifier of some agreement projection). See the discussion of the EPP in §2.4.2.2.

argument. I take these to involve expletives inserted to satisfy the EPP. In (166) the verb has a single argument, yet the subject is registered in the ergative series, and there is third-person singular irrational absolutive agreement not corresponding to an argument of the verb. In (167) and (168), the subject is registered in the ergative series, a second argument occurs as a benefactive object, and there is third-person singular irrational absolutive agreement not corresponding to an argument of the verb.

(166) y-lə-rxaw-t'
     3si-3sf-get.underway-DYN
     She got underway (to there).   GAL, 113

(167) y-sə-z-č'ə-r-t-t'
     3si-1s-BEN-PV-3p-call-DYN
     They invited me. (lit., They called [it] for me.)   GAL, 113

(168) zurab   a-kolxoz   a-x-brigada-k'
      Zurab   DEF.collective farm   DEF-3-brigade-INDEF

         r-partorganizacia-kʷa   r-sekretar-kʷa
         3p-party.organization-PL   3p-secretary-PL

         y-ʃa-rə-z-č'-i-t-t'
         3si-DIR-3p-BEN-PV-3sm-call-DYN
     Zurab invited the secretaries of the party organizations of the three collective farm brigades   GAL, 113

In verbs having expletives, no argument can move into the specifier of the absolutive agreement projection for reasons discussed in §5.2.1.2. The specifier of the absolutive agreement projection must be filled in order to satisfy the EPP, however, so an expletive is inserted in this position. Agreement with the null expletive is registered on the verb complex with default features.[71] Support for treating third-person singular irrational as the default for features can be seen in that these are the features used to register agreement with clausal arguments.

Jim McCloskey (pers. comm.) has suggested that cross-linguistically it is always the specifier of the highest agreement projection which is

---

[71]Because ergative agreement phrases are freely generated, care must be taken to prevent a simple intransitive verb from registering ergative agreement with the subject and having an absolutive expletive. A simple transitive with two ergative markers registering agreement with the real arguments plus an absolutive expletive must likewise be excluded. This can be accomplished if expletives are used only as a last resort.

privileged with respect to the EPP.[72] If so, then (165) argues that ABSP is structurally higher than ERGP.

2.5 Nesting paths

Having demonstrated the structures and movements involved in Case assignment in Abaza, two sets of questions remain. One is what allows these movements, and the other is what requires these movements. The first of these is discussed in §2.5.1, and the second in §2.5.2.

2.5.1 Allowing movement

There are two separate types of movements involved in this proposal, head movement and the movement of (argument) DPs into the various specifier positions. Head movement is allowed in each of the proposed cases because it is movement from the head of a complement phrase into the head which selects the complement (and is sister to it). There is no relativized minimality violation (Rizzi 1990), since there is no other possible intervening head, and the compound head will always antecedent-govern (and head-govern) the trace of the moved head.[73] (See Baker (1988:51–63) for arguments to this effect.)

The real question is what allows the nesting dependencies seen in the transitive sentence, in which the lower DP (the object) ends up in the specifier of a higher functional projection than the subject. Chomsky (1992) argues that this configuration should be ruled out in principle, and thus proposes a configuration in which the object occupies the specifier of the lower agreement projection. Many working on ergative languages (e.g., Campana 1992, Bittner 1992, Murasugi 1992, Bittner and Hale 1996a, b), however, have argued that the configuration involving nesting dependencies is correct for at least some ergative languages and have

---

[72]But see Kathman (1993) for an analysis of Abkhaz in which a verb may allow absolutive, ergative, or dative expletives, depending on the verb's morphological subcategorization requirements. I am not aware of any similar data in Abaza. Postal and Pullum (1988) argue that object expletives exist in English. It may be that in languages having the possibility of expletives in only one position, this position must be the specifier of the highest agreement projection, while languages allowing expletives in various positions require *at least* the specifier of the highest agreement projection.

[73]The Empty Category Principle (ECP) requires a trace to be either antecedent-governed or head-governed. Relativized minimality is a locality restriction on government, such that no potential governor (of the same type as the actual governor) may intervene between the trace and the actual governor.

proposed various ways to motivate this movement pattern and to allow it in terms of relativized minimality (Rizzi 1990).

Movement of the subject to the lower agreement specifier and of the object to the higher agreement specifier is problematic in terms of relativized minimality.[74] The object necessarily crosses the specifier of VP and the specifier of the lower agreement phrase. If movement to the agreement specifiers is of the same type, the lower agreement specifier is a closer potential governor for the trace of the moved object than the higher specifier itself. This is a violation of relativized minimality.

One proposal to deal with this problem is Campana (1992:48). He proposes that the (transitive) subject moves into the specifier of ERGP, but the direct object *adjoins* to the ABSP.[75] This gives a structure as in (169), adapted from his example (158), with some irrelevant single-bar level nodes omitted.

(169)

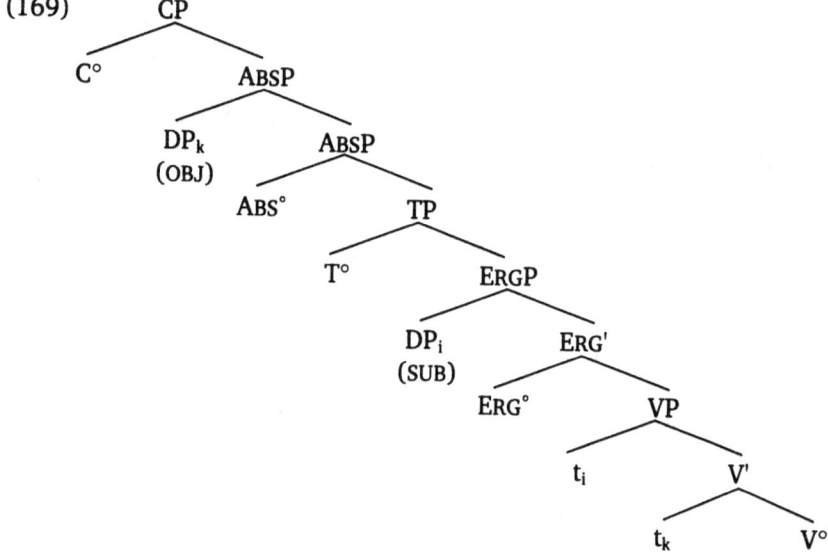

Campana assumes that an adjoined position is an L-bar position, while the specifier of an agreement projection is an L-position.[76] In (169), then, the movement of the subject into the specifier of the agreement phrase is

---

[74]This is problematic not only for the configuration in which the higher agreement specifier is filled by the object, but for any structure having two agreement specifiers.

[75]Campana is thus forced to the position that feature-checking is possible between the agreement head and either (1) its specifier or (2) a DP adjoined to AGRP.

[76]L-positions are defined by Mahajan (1990) as argument positions within VP and specifiers of agreement projections. L-bar positions are non-L-positions. Movement to an L-position is L-movement.

2.5 Nesting paths

L-movement, and the adjunction of the object to the agreement phrase is L-bar movement. The L-bar movement of the object across the subject positions (both d-structure and later) is movement past a position of a different type (L versus L-bar), so there is no violation of relativized minimality.

Campana presents as evidence for his proposal the fact that (many) ergative-absolutive languages do not allow the wh-movement of ergative arguments. Such extractions involve L-bar movement. The higher absolutive argument may extract to a higher position because it does not cross any potential landing sites. The lower ergative argument, however, must cross over the argument adjoined to the absolutive agreement phrase. This results in L-bar movement across an L-bar position, which is a violation of relativized minimality. Campana's system thus accounts directly for the inability of ergative arguments to extract in ergative languages. This set of assumptions is problematic for Abaza, however, since ergative arguments freely extract.

Campana's system is further problematic in that it cannot account for structures involving three arguments. Since there are exactly two phrasal "types" for purposes of minimality, and since the subject and object are each categorized as one of these types, movement of a third argument will necessarily violate minimality with respect to one of these arguments. Either the third argument will move past a specifier of the same type, or it will be of the same type as a higher specifier, thus blocking antecedent-government by the DP in that position since it is a closer potential governor of the same type. In either case, minimality is violated. I conclude, then, that Campana's system is inadequate for Abaza.

The question of allowing this nesting dependency has not been accounted for directly in the literature in terms of relativized minimality. The solution I will adopt can be seen best from the perspective of requiring the subject and object DPs to get to the correct specifier positions. We, therefore, turn to this issue.

2.5.2 Motivating nesting movement

Clearly, the movement of the DPs to the specifier positions of the agreement projections is motivated by the need to get Case. The movement of the verb is motivated both by the need to check the various features, and possibly by morphological requirements as well. Thus, it is relatively clear that movement, in general, is motivated in these structures. A further question, however, is what motivates the particular configuration proposed here. That is, why does a direct object end up in the specifier of AbsP and a (transitive) subject end up in the specifier of ErgP, rather than the other way around. One account of why the verbal arguments end up where they do is that of Murasugi (1992), whose analysis also seeks to provide an answer to what allows the movement of the object across the subject position(s).

Murasugi (1992) proposes to account for the difference between nominative-accusative languages and ergative-absolutive languages in terms of crossing versus nesting dependencies. In her proposal one of the two sources of Case in a transitive clause is "strong", in that it must be checked first, i.e., prior in the derivation to the other.[77] The principle that guarantees that the various arguments end up in the correct position is the requirement that the closest possible DP must be checked by this strong agreement projection.[78] For both agreement projections, which are outside of VP, the subject within VP will always be a closer DP than the object. For nominative-accusative languages, then, the higher agreement projection is strong, and the subject must move to the specifier of the higher agreement projection, as in (170). The object is left with only the possibility of moving to the specifier of the lower agreement projection in order to get Case.

---

[77]Murasugi does not actually utilize agreement projections. She calls the lower "agreement" projection TrP (for transitive phrase) and places the locus of the higher agreement directly in TP (INFL). It is the relative position of these projections that is important to the current discussion, as well as the types of dependencies, and not the labels. Our analyses agree in that the locus of absolutive Case is in the higher of the two positions. Her conclusions do not distinguish between an analysis using agreement projections and an analysis lacking them, and are valid for both analyses so long as the locus of absolutive Case is higher than that of ergative Case. The trees in (170) and (171) reflect my analysis utilizing agreement projections, as does the relevant discussion.

[78]Murasugi defines *the closest possible DP* as the one having the least number of A-positions between the source and the target, where an A-position is a position in which an argument may appear. By this definition, the subject will always be closer than an object to a target position higher in the structure, since the subject appears between the object and that target position. There will always be one more A-position (the subject position) between the object and the target than between the subject and the target.

2.5 Nesting paths

(170)

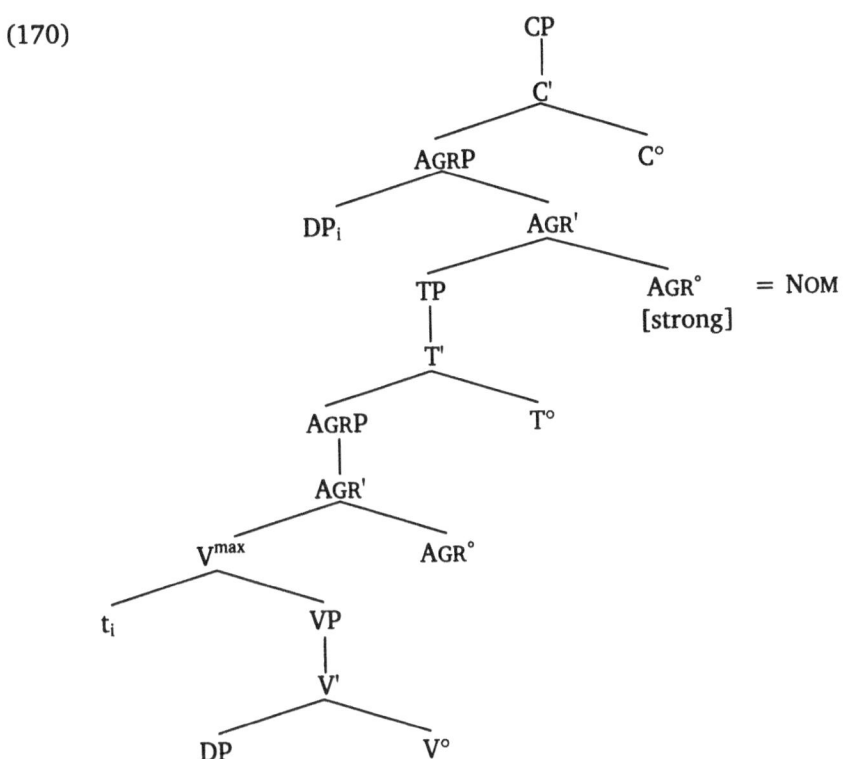

In ergative-absolutive languages, on the other hand, the lower agreement projection is strong, and the subject must move to the specifier of this position, as in (171). This leaves only the specifier of the higher agreement projection open for the object. Regardless of which agreement head is strong, intransitive sentences lack a lower agreement projection entirely,[79] leaving only a single open position for the subject to get Case. The result is that the position of an intransitive subject is the same as that of a transitive subject in nominative-accusative languages, and the same as that of a direct object in ergative-accusative languages, thus accounting for the differing agreement patterns.

---

[79] For Murasugi, the lower projection is actually a TransitiveP. See footnote 75.

(171)

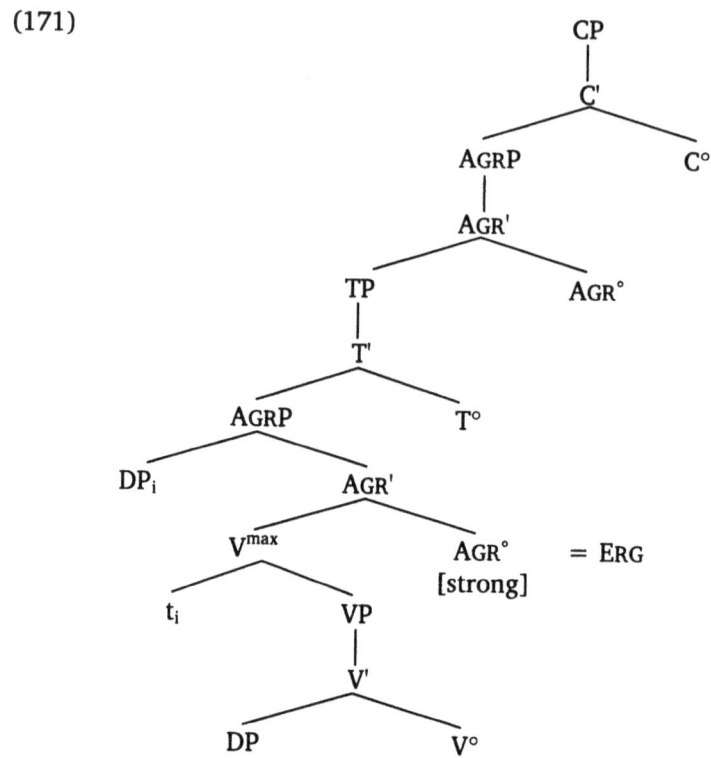

Murasugi presents her analysis using a mixture of concepts from GB and the Minimalist Program (Chomsky 1992). She does not adopt the constraints on the locality of movement from either GB, i.e., relativized minimality, or from the Minimalist Program, i.e., Shortest Move.[80] Instead, she argues for the following constraints on movement:

(172) Principles of Economy for NP Movement:
    1. *Closest Available Source.* At each level of a derivation, a target must take the closest available source NP.
    2. *Closest Featured Target.* At each level of a derivation, a source NP must move to the closest featured target.
    3. *Procrastinate.* An operation must be done as late as possible.
                                          (Murasugi 1992:24)

Murasugi assumes that movement to the specifier of the strong agreement position takes place at s-structure, while movement to the specifier

---

[80]Plus the principle of Domain Extension, as discussed above.

2.5 Nesting paths

of the weak agreement position occurs at LF. Because they do not move at the same level of derivation, they do not interact in terms of locality. For her, then, the Principles of Economy are constraints on movement, rather than on chains.

As Murasugi herself admits, this proposal encounters difficulties with structures having more than two agreement phrases.[81] When there are three movements, two of them must take place at the same level of derivation, either s-structure or LF. For simple cases involving only two movements, she avoids the locality issue by claiming that locality only applies at each level of derivation, so that one movement can occur at each level. With two movements taking place at a single level, as required when there are three movements altogether, however, the issue of locality resurfaces. Neither relativized minimality nor Shortest Move is satisfied in the system Murasugi proposes. Murasugi leaves this issue unresolved.

Further problematic for Murasugi's proposal is the nesting pattern found with ditransitive verbs in Abaza. Ditransitive verbs have a total of three agreement projections. As with transitive verbs, movement to the specifiers of the agreement projections is nested. The highest underlying DP (the subject) moves to the specifier of the lowest agreement projection, the middle underlying DP (the indirect object) moves to the specifier of the middle agreement projection, and the lowest underlying DP (the direct object) moves to the specifier of the highest agreement projection.[82] It is not clear that Murasugi's proposal can account for this pattern.

Applying Murasugi's analysis to Abaza, the lowest agreement projection will be strong and the highest agreement projection will be weak. If the middle agreement projection is strong, when the subject and indirect object DPs move to the agreement specifiers at s-structure, there will be two strong specifiers, making it impossible to determine which one is active first. If, on the other hand, the middle agreement projection is weak, then it is not possible to determine whether the absolutive agreement phrase or the higher ergative agreement phrase is active first for the movement of the direct object and indirect object at LF, since they both share the feature [weak]. A binary feature distinction cannot correctly order a three-way movement pattern.

If we were to adopt a graded scale of strength, such that the lower ergative phrase is strongest, followed by the higher ergative phrase, followed by the absolutive phrase, the generalization about nesting would fail to be captured. It would be purely accidental that the lowest position

---

[81]Murasugi (1992:206–207) cites Abkhaz and Basque specifically as problematic for her system.

[82]Recall that the arguments remain in VP at s-structure and move covertly to the specifiers of the agreement projections at LF.

was always strongest, with increasingly weaker features going up the tree (or presumably down the tree for crossing dependencies). It would be difficult to rule out a configuration in which the middle argument is either weakest or strongest in the hierarchy. This argument is strengthened even more in cases in which there are four agreement phrases, in which the nesting pattern also holds, as in the case of the causative of ditransitives (see §4.1.3).

The two major proposals to account for nesting dependencies in ergative-absolutive languages, Campana (1992) and Murasugi (1992), both fail to adequately account for the nesting dependency in Abaza. Nevertheless, the nesting dependency is well-motivated in Abaza, and underlies much of the basic architecture of the language. I, therefore, propose the Nesting Condition given in (173) for Abaza. (I propose in §5.2 that the Nesting Condition is a default, which can be overridden by lexical requirements.)

(173) Nesting Condition.
    For: α, a DP in the specifier of an agreement projection, and
           β the trace of α, and
           γ, a DP, distinct from α, in the specifier of an agreement projection,
    If α c-commands γ, and
           β does not c-command γ
    Then β does not c-command the trace of γ.

The (abbreviated) structure in (174) is legal according to the Nesting Condition, but the structure in (175) is not.

2.5 Nesting paths

(174)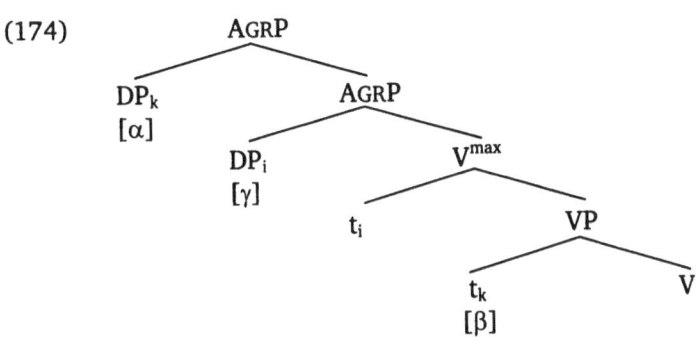

(175)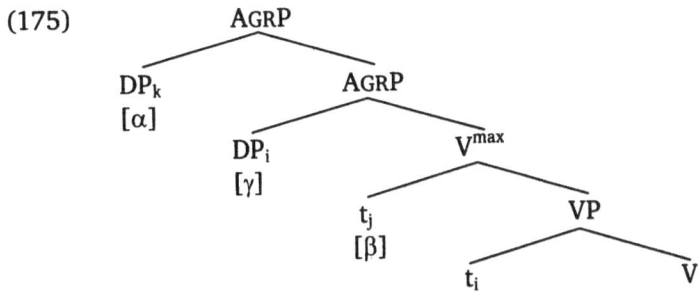

The Nesting Condition is designed specifically to account for movement into agreement specifiers. A possible alternative to the Nesting Condition is the Path Containment Condition, (176), proposed by Pesetsky (1982) as a more general condition on A-bar movement.[83] In spite of the strong similarity between the two principles, I utilize the Nesting Condition for Abaza because it is not clear that such a general condition as the PCC is necessary in Abaza, and as formulated, it may not adequately account for some constructions. (See incorporated postpositions in chapter 6 and wh-movement in chapter 8.)

---

[83] I assume that agreement specifiers in Abaza are A-bar positions. This accentuates the similarities between the Nesting Condition for Abaza and the PCC, which is a condition on A-bar movement.

(176) Path Containment Condition:
If two paths overlap, one must contain the other.[84]

(Pesetsky 1982:309)

As in all analyses involving two or more agreement projections, movement to the specifiers of these projections does not strictly satisfy constraints on the locality of movement.[85] One possible partial solution to the locality problem has been proposed (independent of the facts from ergative languages) in Rizzi (1991), namely that thematic phrases are transparent to minimality effects. Since the subject is thematic, regardless of which specifier position it occupies, it cannot block the movement of the object across it. This analysis provides a partial account for what *allows* the nested dependencies seen in ergative languages, but says nothing about what *requires* nested dependencies in ergative languages. Another possibility is that minimality is sensitive to more distinctions of phrasal type than just the binary A versus A-bar (or L versus L-bar) distinction. I do not pursue this possibility further here. For present purposes, I assume that the specifiers of all agreement projections are A-bar positions, and that the issue of locality can be resolved.

The Nesting Condition in (173) correctly accounts for the movement pattern found with simple clauses in Abaza. This can be seen clearly in the most complex of these simple clauses, i.e., a ditransitive verb; the configuration is shown in (177).

---

[84]Two paths overlap if their intersection is non-null. The definition of path is as follows:
Suppose $\underline{t}$ is an empty category locally A-bar-bound by $\underline{b}$. Then
  (i) for α the first maximal projection dominating $\underline{t}$
  (ii) for β the first maximal projection dominating $\underline{b}$
  (iii) the path between t and b is the set of nodes such that
    $P = \{x \mid (x = \alpha) \vee (x = \beta) \vee (x \text{ dom. } \alpha \;\&\; \neg\, x \text{ dom. } \beta)\}$.

(Pesetsky 1982:289)

[85]The one exception being nominative-accusative systems analyzed within the Minimalist Program (Chomsky 1992). As shown above, though, the Minimalist Program has serious difficulties in dealing with ergative-absolutive languages where the absolutive agreement projection is higher than the ergative agreement projection, and in dealing with more than two agreement projections. I do not consider the locality problem completely resolved within this framework.

2.5 Nesting paths

(177)

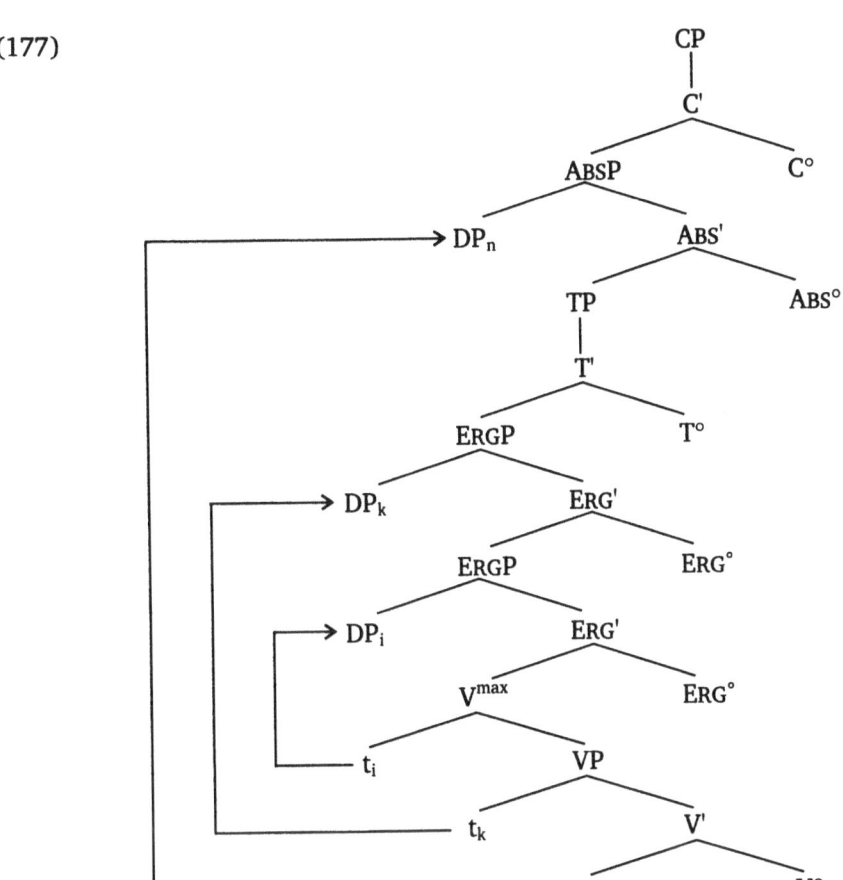

The subject, DP_i, moves to the lowest agreement specifier without interacting with any other movement paths. The next lowest argument is the indirect object, DP_k. It moves to the next highest agreement specifier. This movement obeys the Nesting Condition where the indirect object DP corresponds to α, the trace of the indirect object corresponds to β, and the subject DP corresponds to γ. The moved indirect object c-commands the moved subject, and the trace of the indirect object does not c-command the moved subject. Therefore, the trace of the indirect object may not c-command the trace of the subject, which it does not. This accounts for the observed nesting pattern of movement. The lowest underlying argument is the direct object, DP_n, and it moves to the highest agreement specifier, the specifier of ABSP. This also obeys the Nesting Condition with respect to the movement paths of both the subject and the indirect object, for the same reason as the movement of the indirect object. An examination of more complex constructions in the following chapters will show that the Nesting Condition holds there as well.

Note that the Transitive Subject Condition, (127), does not entirely account for this pattern, (177), since it says nothing about the relation between the direct and indirect objects. The Nesting Condition is thus required for this and other structures involving more than two arguments. As I will argue in chapter 5, the TSC is required for independent reasons. Both principles independently require a transitive subject to move to the specifier of an ergative agreement projection. The overlap is unfortunate, but unavoidable.

2.6 Summary

In summary, with regard to Case assignment, I propose that:

1. Case is assigned, and features are checked, in the specifier-head relationship within AGRP.
2. TP extends to ABSP.
3. Lexical NP and PP extend to ERGP.
4. Lexical VP licenses ERGP* freely within its extended projection.
5. Transitive Subject Condition. The subject of a transitive verb is assigned the feature [+ERG].
6. Unused Agreement Filter. Structures having an agreement projection whose specifier is unoccupied are ill-formed.
7. Closer Agreement Principle. Given two trees structurally identical except for the position of ERGP, both of which satisfy other conditions equally, the structure involving the lower ERGP is used.
8. Movement to agreement specifiers occurs at LF.
9. EPP. The specifier of ABSP must be filled.
10. Nesting Condition.
    For: α, a DP in the specifier of an agreement projection, and
          β the trace of α, and
          γ, a DP, distinct from α, in the specifier of an agreement projection,
    If   α c-commands γ, and
          β does not c-command γ
    Then β does not c-command the trace of γ.

The remaining chapters demonstrate how this basic structure and system accounts for various structures in Abaza more complex than the simple intransitive, transitive, and ditransitive clauses discussed here.

3
Stative Predicates

A fundamental distinction in Abaza is the morphological distinction between dynamic and stative predicates. This contrast is evident primarily in the indicative mood, where different tense morphemes are required by dynamic and stative predications. Compare the stative present indicative form in (178) with the dynamic present indicative form in (179), and the corresponding past forms in (180) and (181). Compare also the past dependent form (182) in the dynamic system. Dynamic predicates are primarily verbal. Stative predicates may be headed by any syntactic lexical category. This chapter is an investigation of stative predicates in Abaza.

(178) *yə-s-taqə-b*
　　　3si-1s-want-STP
　　　I want it.

(179) *yə-s-ga-y-d*
　　　3si-1s-carry-PRS-DYN
　　　I carry it.

(180) *yə-s-taqə-n*
　　　3si-1s-want-PST
　　　I wanted it.

(181) *yə-s-ga-d*
　　　3si-1s-carry-DYN
　　　I carried it.

(182) *yə-s-ga-n*
  3si-1s-carry-DEP
  I was carrying it, and...

Section 3.1 demonstrates that any lexical category can head the predicate of a stative clause, and that it is the entire lexical XP which constitutes the predicate. Section 3.2 presents evidence that, like dynamic clauses, stative clauses are CPs. In addition, AbsP and TP occur in the syntactic structure of stative CPs. Section 3.3 presents my analysis of the stative construction, specifically dealing with how the CP structure at the top interacts with the lexical XP structure at the bottom. I propose a position for the subject of a stative predication parallel to the position for subjects of dynamic verbs. I also demonstrate how the system of Case assignment developed in the previous chapter interacts with the structure proposed here for stative predicates. Finally, the problematic case of the verb *akʷ* 'be' is discussed in §3.4.

3.1 Lexical categories as heads of stative clauses

In Abaza the function of predicate is not limited to the category verb. The examples of dynamic verbs in chapter 2 all involve clauses in which the predicate is headed by a verb. In contrast, stative predications involve predicates which can be headed by any of the lexical categories in Abaza, including N, A,[86] V, and P, although there are restrictions on V and P. The general form of a stative complex consists of a lexical head, with stative morphology designating tense and mood suffixed to it, and with relevant agreement morphology prefixed to it. If the predicate includes structure in addition to the head, the nonhead material occurs to the left of the stative complex, as expected, given the head-final character of the language.

Stative predicates consist of entire lexical XPs. This can be seen in the fact that material included within the lexical projection may occur with statives. This includes possessors in nominal statives, direct objects in verbal statives, objects of postpositions in postpositional statives, and degree modifiers in adjectival statives. With the exception of agreement in certain cases, it is not possible for functional material within the extended projection of the lexical head to be included in statives. Specifically, determiners are not possible with nominal statives.

---

[86] I separate nouns and adjectives here for ease of presentation, although I consider them to form a single lexical category in Abaza.

3.1 Lexical categories as heads of stative clauses

The following sections demonstrate that statives can be headed by any of the lexical categories of Abaza, and that it is the entire lexical projection, and only the lexical projection, which forms the predicate in stative clauses. Stative verbal predicates are discussed in §3.1.1 and stative postpositional predicates in §3.1.2. These two categories allow complements to the lexical head. Stative nominals, which allow specifiers (possessors), are presented in §3.1.3. Finally, stative adjectival predicates are discussed in §3.1.4.

3.1.1 Stative verbs

There is a small class of verbs which take tense and mood suffixes in the stative paradigm instead of the dynamic paradigm. Stative verbs may be transitive or intransitive. Many of the intransitive stative verbs are verbs of position, as in (183)–(185).

(183) a-ǰʷǰʷaxʲa   čʷə-b
      DEF-laundry   hang-STP
      The laundry is hanging.   GAL, 103

(184) y-tdzə   a-day   a-kʷ   a-pnə   y-aʔa-b[87]
      3sm-house DEF-mountain   3si-top   3si-at   3si-be.there-STP
      His house is on the mountain's top.

(185) s-ʃt'a-b
      1s-lie-STP
      I lie, am lying (down).

Stative verbs with two arguments, such as əma 'have', taqə 'want', and cʷəmay 'hate', are more common.[88] The unmarked word order for stative verbs, as for dynamic verbs, is SOV. The agreement pattern for stative transitive verbs is also the same as that of dynamic verbs, with the subject registered in the ergative series and the object registered in the absolutive series.

---

[87]The root aʔa 'be there' is used existentially (*there is an X*) in addition to locationally (*X is there, at that place*).

[88]Note that the antonyms 'love' and 'hate' fall into different categories with respect to the dynamic versus stative contrast. The dynamic verb bzəyba 'love' is a transparent idiom, literally meaning 'see well/good'. On the other hand, the stative verb cʷəmay 'hate' probably derives from the phrase 'be one's enemy' (aya is 'enemy').

(186) a-raxʷxčʲa   bzəy   pʃ-la-k'   y-əma-p'
      DEF-shepherd good   four-eye-INDEF 3sm-have-STP
      A good shepherd has four eyes.   GAL, 103

(187) axʃa-k'   d-s-əma-b
      sister-INDEF 3sr-1s-have-STP
      I have a sister.

(188) a-čkʷən   wandər-k'   y-taqə-b
      DEF-boy car-INDEF   3sm-want-STP
      The boy wants a car.

(189) awəy   d-s-čʷəməy-b
      s/he   3sr-1s-hate-STP
      I hate him/her.

3.1.2 Stative postpositions

Stative predicates can be headed by a postposition. Most postpositions which register agreement with their objects can head the predicate of a stative clause.[89] If the postposition is one which can incorporate into the prefix array in the dynamic verbal system, the form that can occur as the head of a predicate is the same as that which incorporates, as in (190).[90] For postpositions that cannot incorporate, there is only one possible form, and this is used as the head of the predicate, as in (191). A small number of what seem to be stative postpositions do not have any corresponding independent postposition, as in (192).

(190) a-sara   d-rə-c-p'
      DEF-sheep 3sr-3p-with-STP
      S/he is with the sheep.   GAL, 103

(191) məčʲ-k'   də-w-apʃ-b
      little-INDEF 3sr-2sm-like-STP
      S/he looks a little like you.

---

[89]Specifically, this excludes the instrumental postposition, la, which acts like a clitic.

[90]For postpositions which incorporate, there are two lexical entries, a "free" form which cannot incorporate and a "bound" form, which must incorporate. (See chapter 7 for further discussion.) In many cases the free and bound forms differ phonetically. It is the latter (bound) form which is used in stative predications, presumably because the free form would not then be free.

3.1 Lexical categories as heads of stative clauses

(192) qʷbina   d-a-wa-b
      Kubina   3sr-3si-from-STP
      S/he is from Kubina (village). GAL, 103

The entire PP constitutes the predicate in these constructions. This can be seen in the fact that the object of the postposition is present. The head of the PP, P°, occurs in the stative complex, and the complement of P° occurs to the left of the stative complex. At the bottom level of this construction, the phrase structure is identical to that of a simple PP, as in §2.2.2.

The subject of the predication occurs to the left of all the material in PP, as in (193).

(193) wara   marakt   w-a-wa-p'   gʲakʷʷəmma
      you (m)   Marakt   2sm-3si-from-STP   TAG
      You're from the village of Marakt, aren't you? GAL, 172

These postpositional predicates utilize two agreement markers, corresponding to the object of the postposition and the subject of the predicate. The object of the postposition is registered in the ergative series, as in the independent (nonstative) form, and the subject of the predication is registered in the absolutive series like an intransitive verb.

There are some other common stative predicates whose categories are relatively unclear. These are all intransitive, in the sense that they take a single (absolutive) agreement prefix. They all seem to have locative meaning, and Tabulova (1976) classifies them as verbal prefixes.

(194) zač   a-bna   pʃʲə-skʷʃa   də-c'a-n
      Zach   DEF-forest   four-year   3sr-under-PST
      Zach was in the forest four years. GAL, 148

(195) zawər   a-nartəxʷ   də-la-b
      Zawr   DEF-corn   3sr-be.in-STP
      Zawr is in the corn field. GAL, 104

As Tabulova claims, these morphemes occur as verbal prefixes with meanings similar to those they have in the predicative construction. Compare (194) and (195) with (196) and (197), respectively. Like the corresponding roots of stative complexes, these verbal prefixes do not register agreement with a postpositional object.

(196) *c'a-c'a-ra*
　　under-put-MAS
　　to place under

(197) *la-c'a-ra*
　　inside-put-MAS
　　to place inside

I make the claim that all statives are formed from lexical categories. The question for these particular cases is which lexical category they belong to. Verbal prefixes do not independently constitute a lexical category. It is not crucial for my analysis which category these roots are, so long as it is a lexical category. The category of intransitive verbs is one possibility, but the category of (intransitive) postpositions seems to me more likely. The roots in question appear to be transitive in that there is an object, but they are intransitive in the sense that there is no agreement registered with the object. I henceforth refer to them as intransitive postpositions.

Many locatives and temporals in Abaza are licensed independently from the principles discussed here. Specifically, there is never agreement with such phrases. For example, a verb of motion like *ca* 'go' is intransitive, and does not register agreement with the location.

(198) *awǝy　a-tdzǝ　　d-ca-y-d*
　　s/he　DEF-house　3sr-go-PRS-DYN
　　S/he is going to/into the house.

The location in (194) and (195) is likewise not registered by agreement. I take the lack of agreement with the location or temporal phrase in these predicates to be parallel to the lack of agreement with the location phrase in intransitive verbs of motion.

Further support for treating these as intransitive postpositions comes from my analysis of certain verbal prefixes in chapter 7. There, I analyze certain locative prefixes in the verb complex which take agreement as postpositions which incorporate into the verb complex along with their associated agreement. The intransitive locative verbal prefixes, such as those in (196) and (197), occur in the same morphological space as the incorporated (agreeing, or transitive) postpositions. Treating these as intransitive postpositions allows a unified analysis of the agreeing and nonagreeing verbal prefixes.

3.1.3 Stative nominals

Stative predicates can be headed by nouns. Stative tense and mood morphology is suffixed to the noun, and appropriate agreement morphology is prefixed to the noun, with the subject of the predication registered in the absolutive series. Examples can be seen in (199)–(201).

(199) arəy   masa-b
     s/he/it   table-STP
     It is a table.

(200) y-aba   də-ɟʲmaxčʲa-b
     3sm-father 3sr-goatherd-STP
     His father is a goatherd.   NART, 90

(201) a-phaspa-kʷa nap'ə-la yə-nxa-ʕʷə-b
     DEF-girl-PL   hand-AV 3p-work-AGT-STP
     The girls are industrious/skilled with their hands. (lit., The girls are workers with their hands.)

My analysis of NP in §2.2.1 places possessors in the specifier of NP. Since the noun head in the stative predicate projects to NP (like all N° heads), this predicts that possessors should be possible in nominal stative constructions. This prediction is borne out. In such cases, the possessor is registered in the ergative series, as in nonpredicative nominal constructions, and the subject of the predication is registered in the absolutive series, as with postpositional statives. Compare the stative nominal without a possessor in (202) and the corresponding form with a possessor in (203).

(202) d-qac'a-b
     3sr-man-STP
     He is a man.

(203) d-l-qac'a-b
     3sr-3sf-man-STP
     He is her husband.

One noun which frequently occurs in the stative construction with a possessor is čʷə 'belonging'.[91] Tabulova (1976) classifies it as a stative

---

[91] It may be an exception to the generalization that there are no obligatorily possessed nouns.

(inverted) verb, while Tugov (1967) treats it as a verbal affix, although he gives constructions without any overt verb, comparable to the form in (204). I treat it as a noun since this eliminates the need to establish a class of inverted stative verbs.[92]

(204) (y)-y-č'ʷə-b
(3si)-3sm-possession-STP
It belongs to him, it is his possession.

Not surprisingly, in the unmarked order, the subject of the predication precedes the possessor of the noun, as in (205) and (206).

(205) y-an   nartərʕa   d-r-axʃa-b
3sm-mother Narts   3sr-3p-sister-STP
His mother is the Nart's sister.   NART, 90

(206) sara sosrəq'ʷa s-yə-raxʷxč̣a-b
I   Sosruko   1s-3sm-herdsman-STP
I am Sosruko's herdsman.   NART, 72

Not all morphological material possible in independent noun complexes is possible in nominal statives. Specifically, determiner-like material cannot occur in these constructions. Forms including either the definite determiner, a-, as in (207), or the indefinite determiner, -k', as in (208) are ungrammatical. The form in (208), however, is grammatical with the interpretation seen in (210). This correlates with the different interpretations of the simple phrase qac'ak', which means both 'one man' and 'a man'.

---

[92]Further support for treating this root as a noun is that the possessive pronouns, mine, yours, his, hers, etc., are formed from the root č'ʷə plus the corresponding agreement prefix (taken from Serdyuchenko 1956:607):

s-č'ʷə	mine	h-č'ʷə	ours
w-č'ʷə	yours (m)	ʃʷ-č'ʷə	yours (PL)
b-č'ʷə	yours (f)		
y-č'ʷə	his	r-č'ʷə	theirs
l-č'ʷə	hers		
a-č'ʷə	its		

If č'ʷə is a noun meaning 'possession', then this paradigm is accounted for directly. These "pronouns" are simply possessed nouns. If č'ʷə is a verb root, however, this construction is highly unusual, since no other verb root can be combined with just a single ergative agreement prefix and no tense or mood suffix.

3.1 Lexical categories as heads of stative clauses

(207) *d-a-qac'a-b
 3sr-DEF-man-STP
 (He is the man.)

(208) *d-qac'a-k'-b
 3sr-man-INDEF-STP
 (He is a man.)

The fact that determiner-like material (D°) may not occur within the stative complex, while possessors may freely occur here, provides evidence for the claim made in chapter 2 that the possessor does not originate in the specifier of DP. Otherwise, either both determiners and possessors should be able to occur in this construction, or neither should be able to occur.

The impossibility of a determiner head, D°, in the stative nominal construction suggests that DP cannot form the predicate. This is consistent with Stowell's (1991) discussion of the difference between argument and predicate nominal phrases. He argues that argument nominals must include DP structure, while predicate nominals generally do not include DP structure.

Furthermore, the fact that DP does not form the nominal predicate means that some lower XP within the nominal extended projection must form the predicate. Given a nominal structure involving DP, ERGP, and NP, as I assume, the predicate must thus consist of either ERGP or NP. Because agreement with the possessor is registered in the ergative series, as with nonpredicative nominals, there must be an ergative agreement projection in the predicate. The structure of argument nominals in Abaza is thus [DP[ERGP[NP]]], while the structure of predicate nominals is simply [ERGP[NP]].

Although there is no determiner head in predicate nominals, nouns can be numbered in the stative construction. Examples are given in (210)–(211). This requires that numbers not be located within DP in Abaza.[93] This is consistent with standard conclusions drawn on the basis of English.

(209) a. the seven cities
 b. Mike's five children

---

[93]An analysis of the position of numbers within the nominal phrase is beyond the scope of this study. Crucial for our discussion is that they not occur within DP. It is not relevant for present purposes whether they head their own projection, occupy a specifier position, or are adjoined.

As discussed in §1.1.2.2, numbers, which with the exception of -k' 'one' are prefixes, generally require a particular suffix. This is usually -k', but can be the rational plural suffix -čʷa in some circumstances, as in (212). I take the numeral suffix -k' to be distinct from the homophonous indefinite determiner, which cannot occur in the stative construction.[94]

(210) d-qac'a-**k'**-b
    3sr-man-**one**-STP
    He is one man.

(211) y-x-nap'ə-k'ə-z
    AWH-**three**-hand-INDEF-PSP
    having three hands (lit., that which was three hands)   LA, 226

(212) y-ʕʷ-pa-čʷa-p'
    3p-**two**-son-RPL-STP
    They are two sons.

3.1.4 Stative adjectives

Stative adjectives, like stative nouns and postpositions, are formed by adding stative tense and mood suffixes to the adjective and utilizing the absolutive series to register agreement with the subject of the predication.

(213) a-dzə   qʷaʃ'ə-p'
    DEF-water   mud-STP
    The water is muddy.   GAL, 105

(214) awəy   d-mgʷadəw-b
    s/he   3sr-pregnant-STP
    She is pregnant.

Stative adjectival predicates may involve comparative or superlative forms. With the exception of a few suppletive forms, the comparative and superlative forms of adjectives are formed in Abaza by the words *rəc'a* 'more', *raha* 'more', and *rəc'agʲəy* 'most', which occur to the immediate left

---

[94]Further support for drawing a distinction between the indefinite -k' and the "count" -k' comes from the possibility of the latter occurring with the definite determiner. This gives the interpretation, 'the one X', as in a-čʷ-k' 'the one ox' (Tabulova 1976:46). If the suffix associated with numbers were identical to the indefinite determiner, such forms would result in feature clash, producing both the features definite and indefinite on a single form. Therefore, I continue to distinguish the two suffixes.

3.1 Lexical categories as heads of stative clauses

of the adjective.[95] The object of comparison is expressed as the object of a PP headed by the postposition *ack'əs* 'than'. Note that adjectival predicates do not take comparative or superlative morphology *within* the word. Instead, the comparative or superlative adverb is an independent phrase and occurs to the left of the predicate head.[96]

(215) *s-la   selma   y-la   ack'əs   rəc'a-gʲa   y-dəw-b*
       1s-dog   Selma   3sm-dog   than   more-INT   3si-big-STP
       My dog is (even) bigger than Selma's dog.

(216) *a-wap'ə   ack'əs   a-kʷa   rəc'a   y-argʷanə-b*
       DEF-felt   3si.than   DEF-rain   more   3si-near-STP
       Rain is closer than a shepherd's cloak (felt).   AL, 127

(217) *yara   d-duw-n   anaxʲanəy   raha-gʲəy   d-duw-x-b*
       he   3sr-big-PST   other   more-INT   3sr-big-ASP-STP
       He was big, but this one is even bigger.   NART, 88

(218) *anaxʲanat   aynaʒʷ-kʷa   d-gʲ-r-apʃə-m   awat*
       others   giant-PL   3sr-INT-3p-like-NEG   they

       r-ac'k'əs-gʲəy   d-paylʰwan-b
       3p-than-INT   3sr-hero-STP
       He does not resemble other giants (Aynyzh); he is much stronger than they are.   NART, 71

Abney (1987) proposes that comparative and superlative words head their own functional projections in the extended projection of A (and adverb). If this were so in Abaza, it would undermine the claim that stative predicates are formed by lexical projections. However, there is reason to reject this for Abaza. If *rəc'a* 'more' and *rəc'agʲəy* 'most' are taken to be functional heads, then they are the only nonadjoined heads in the language which fail to occur to the right of their complement, AP. Additionally, if the comparative and superlative markers are heads of a DEGP (degree phrase) and the complement of DEG° is AP, one would expect the lexical (adjectival) head to move to the DEG head, and then the A°-DEG° complex to move on in the stative complex, resulting in a construction in which *rəc'a* 'more' and *rəc'agʲəy* 'most' occur between the adjective on the left and the stative morphology on the right. Alternatively, with AP as the

---

[95]This construction is used for the comparison of adverbs as well.
[96]The order in (216) is exceptional in that the comparison PP precedes the subject of the predication. I assume this is due to movement from the canonical order.

complement of DEG°, DEG° could undergo head movement to the next highest head position without A° having incorporated into it. This also predicts forms different from those which actually occur. The adjective head A° cannot skip over the functional head DEG°, on its way to T° as this would result in a violation of minimality. The trace of the lower head must be antecedent-governed by the moved head, but if A° has crossed over DEG° to T°, it will not antecedent-govern the trace because DEG° would be a closer potential governor.

I conclude, then, that the comparative and superlative words in Abaza do not head functional projections within the extended projection of A, but occur as some sort of modifier within AP. The two most likely positions are adjoined to AP and in the specifier of AP. The choice between these two possibilities is not relevant to our current discussion.

Stative predicates can be formed from any lexical category in Abaza. For stative verbs, the agreement pattern is exactly as for dynamic verbs. For stative postpositions, nouns, and adjectives, the subject of the predication is always registered in the absolutive series. Any other arguments, specifically the object of a postposition and the possessor of a noun, are registered in the ergative series. The structure of nonverbal stative predicates is thus identical to the structure of the corresponding nonpredicative phrases. The one obvious difference is that nominal predicates do not have DP. This is consistent with Stowell's observations about the difference between argument and predicate nouns.

Having shown that the bottom part of stative predicate structures consists of lexical XPs plus some of their associated functional projections, we turn to a discussion of the top part of the structure of stative clauses, which I argue involves the same structure as dynamic clauses.

3.2 Statives clauses are CPs

The stative construction shares a number of properties with the dynamic verbal construction. Both constructions morphologically mark mood and tense on the word which heads the construction. In both constructions, I take this word to bear the features of a complex of heads, which are checked as X° raises through the head positions which dominate it. The fact that both constructions mark mood and tense indicates that they share in their clausal projections the functional categories which host these features, CP and TP. In addition, both constructions require exactly one instance of absolutive agreement on the head complex. This indicates the presence of ABSP in each structure. The highest part of the

3.2 Statives clauses are CPs

structure in stative constructions, as in (219), is thus identical to the highest part of the structure in dynamic constructions.

(219)
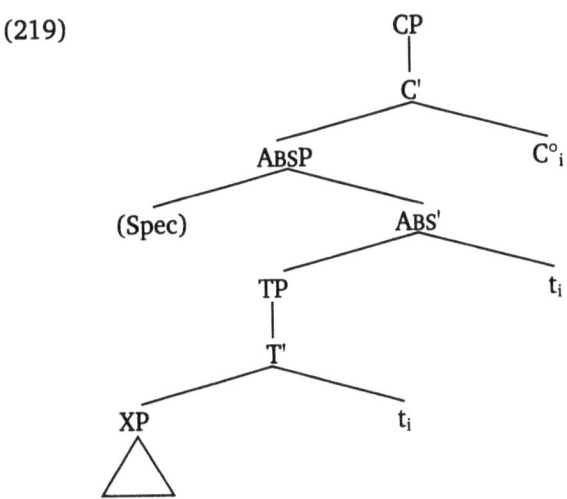

Sections 3.2.1 and 3.2.2 demonstrate that although stative mood and tense morphology is somewhat more limited than that of dynamic verbal complexes, the same categories are involved. Differences in the possibilities are due to the fact that certain values or features are simply impossible for statives. The fact that stative complexes and dynamic verbal complexes extend to the same category makes the prediction that stative phrases should pattern like dynamic verb phrases with respect to their syntactic distribution. This prediction is borne out. Section 3.2.3 shows that stative clauses have the same external distribution as dynamic clauses. Finally, §3.2.4 briefly discusses the problem the Abaza stative data presents for the theory of extended projections proposed by Grimshaw (1991).

3.2.1 Mood

Stative complexes, like dynamic verb complexes, can and must inflect for mood. Some of the possible moods in Abaza include indicative, yes-no interrogative, wh-interrogative (both rational and irrational), imperative, and conditional. Of these, all but the imperative are possible in stative complexes. Of the nonimperative moods, all but the indicative utilize the same suffixes in both the dynamic and stative paradigms. Compare the mood suffixes of the stative forms in (220a)–(224a) with those of the dynamic forms in (220b)–(224b).

(220) a. *də-w-əma-w-ma*
      3sr-2sm-have-PRS-YNQ
      Do you have him/her? (brother)

b. *d-ca-w-ma*
   3sr-go-PRS-YNQ
   Is s/he going?

(221) a. *yə-z-č̣ʷə-w-da*
      3si-EWH-belong-PRS-WHQR
      Who does it belong to?

b. *yə-č̣ʷa-w-da*
   AWH-sleep-PRS-WHQR
   Who is sleeping?

(222) a. *y-wə-xʲəz-ya*
      AWH-2sm-name-WHQI
      What is your name?[97]

b. *yə-ʃʷ-č̣pa-w-ya*
   AWH-2p-do-PRS-WHQI
   What are you doing?

(223) a. *y-s-əma-z-tən*
      3si-1s-have-PST-COND
      If I had had it...   SGSAL, 637

b. *s-čʲa-z-tən*
   1s-eat-PST-COND
   If I had eaten...   SGSAL, 636

(224) a. *sə-bzəyə-nda*
      1s-good-DESID
      If only I were good!   SGSAL, 638

b. *s-čʲa-nda*
   1s-eat-DESID
   If only I had eaten!   SGSAL, 638

Dynamic and stative complexes share not only many of the same mood categories, but the corresponding mood suffixes themselves are identical in many cases. This suggests that an identical treatment for mood is in order for dynamic and stative complexes. The final morpheme (mood suffix) in the dynamic verb forms is taken to involve complementizer, C°, features. I extend this analysis to statives.

3.2.2 Tense

Like dynamic verb complexes, stative verb complexes inflect for tense, although the range of possible tenses for statives is considerably more limited. If the expression of tense is licensed only through a functional tense projection, TP, then stative complexes must contain TP in their clausal projection.

Only past and present tenses can be expressed in stative complexes. This contrasts with at least six tenses for dynamic verbs: three past tenses, present, and two future tenses. For most moods, the present tense suffix is

---

[97] The present tense of some stative forms lacks the present tense suffix, -w, in this mood. See Tabulova (1976:173).

3.2 Statives clauses are CPs

-*w*, as in the dynamic system. In all moods but the indicative, the past tense suffix is -*z*.[98]

(225) *w-bzəyə-w-ma*
2sm-good-PRS-YNQ
Are you well?

(226) *w-bzəyə-z-ma*
2sm-good-PST-YNQ
Were you well?

(227) *yə-w-taqə-w-da*
AWH-2sm-want-PRS-WHQR
Who do you want?

STBMF, 35

(228) *y-s-əma-z-ya*
AWH-1s-have-PST-WHQI
What did I have?

STBMF, 22

Tense is marked in the indicative mood of stative predicates with the suffixes -*n* for the past and -*b* (freely alternating with -*p'*) for the present.[99] In these cases, there is no separate mood suffix. This differs from the dynamic paradigm, in which there is a specific indicative mood suffix, -*d* (alternating with -*t'*), and separate tense suffixes.[100]

(229) *sə-bzəy-b*
1s-good-STP
I am good (well).

---

[98]It is also possible to analyze the *z* in these cases as an aspectual marker, and the tense marker as null. Compare the null aorist (past) suffix in the dynamic system. The choice between these analyses is not relevant to the current discussion. For a fuller discussion of tense and aspect in Abaza see Chkadua (1970).

[99]Note that the past dependent and future definite suffixes in the dynamic paradigm correspond exactly to the two possible stative suffixes in form. It is possible that the dynamic past dependent form is actually the past stative form (many verbs can take either stative or dynamic morphology, with a corresponding difference in meaning), and that the future definite form is actually the stative present form, both of which receive slightly different interpretations in the dynamic system. This latter possibility is strengthened by the fact that this form is not used as a future definite in at least one dialect, but as a "let's" imperative: *h-tsa-b* 'let's go'. It is also possible that these two dynamic tenses developed from the stative suffixes, but the synchronic connection has been lost.

[100]The dynamic paradigm shares with the stative paradigm the fact that the exceptions in the system occur in the indicative mood. Note that the dynamic present tense suffix is -*y* in the indicative, though elsewhere it is -*w(a)*.

(230) sə-bzəyə-n
 1s-good-PST
 I was good (well).

Because the stative indicative suffixes -*b* and -*n* combine the features of mood (indicative) and tense (past or present), I assume that they are portmanteaux, combining T° and C°. In the formation of the word (stative complex) in the lexicon, these suffixes add both tense and mood features to the bundle of features which must be checked in the syntactic derivation.[101] Since tense and mood suffixes are adjacent in the stative paradigm (statives do not have aspectual suffixes which can occur between tense and mood), the order of checking from the inside out is maintained.

Recall that in chapter 2, I argue that the category T extends to AbsP. The presence of TP in the stative clausal structure thus predicts the presence of AbsP in these structures as well. As shown in chapter 2, like dynamic verb complexes, stative complexes require exactly one absolutive prefix (subject to the conditions on null absolutive agreement, plus the extra condition on statives beginning with obstruents discussed in §1.1.2.3). This strengthens the connection between TP and AbsP, in that the same one-to-one correspondence holds between them in two different contexts, within the dynamic verbal extended projection and within the stative extended projection. Furthermore, it provides additional evidence against the association of absolutive Case assignment with the category V, since stative constructions may involve the categories P, N, and A without an occurrence of the category V, yet there is absolutive agreement. If absolutive Case were assigned in association with the category V, there is no straightforward explanation of why absolutive may be assigned in conjunction with the (stative) categories of P, N, or A, just in case there is tense.

3.2.3 Distribution of stative CPs

I have argued that both dynamic verb complexes and stative complexes share the same structure at the highest level, namely a complex of heads involving C° with Abs°, T°, and lower heads incorporated into it. This head projects to CP in both cases. Because phrases headed by stative complexes and phrases headed by dynamic verb complexes are of the same

---

[101] If portmanteaux forms can only be formed from adjacent syntactic heads, this provides support for the placement of TP above AbsP. Nothing in my analysis would change, except that the principle that TP extends to AbsP would be reversed to say that AbsP (and only AbsP) extends to TP.

3.2 Statives clauses are CPs

syntactic category, it is predicted that these two types of phrases should have the same external syntactic distribution. This prediction is accurate.

Stative CPs have the same syntactic distribution as dynamic CPs. The most obvious and common substantiation of this is the fact that both can occur as main clauses, either indicative or interrogative. Indicative and interrogative main clauses have already been exemplified in the preceding sections. Phrases headed by a stative complex can also occur as complements of verbs which select CP complements. This can be seen in (231), where a stative clause is complement to the verb h^wa 'say'. Compare (232) in which a dynamic clause is complement to this same verb. The complement clauses are indicative in both these examples.[102]

(231) sosrəq'"a sosran-y   y-aʃ-č"a-b   r-h"a-y-d
Sosruko Sosran-and 3p-brother-RPL-STP 3p-say-PRS-DYN
They say (that) Sosruko and Sosran are brothers. or They say, "Sosruko and Sosran are brothers."   NART, 97

(232) ahmet s-kʲtab   y-gʲ-s-ʕaw-wa-m   y-h"a-d
Ahmet 1s-book 3si-INT-1s-find-PRS-NEG 3sm-say-DYN
Ahmet said, "I can't find my book."

This pattern holds also for the complement CP of the verb dər 'know', as in (233)–(236), with the complement CP bracketed. In (233) and (234), the CP complements are postposed, while in (235) and (236) the CP complements occur in object position to the left of the verb complex. The CP complements in (233) and (235) are stative CPs, and those in (234) and (236) are dynamic CPs. In all four cases, the form of the head of the complement clause is participial, and includes the manner marker ʃ- 'how'.

(233) wara yə-w-dərə-y-d   [sara pa-k'   də-ʃ-s-əma-wa]
you(m) 3si-2sm-know-PRS-DYN I   son-a 3sr-how-1s-have-PTC
You know that I have a son. (lit., You know how I have a son.)

(234) hara yə-h-dərə-y-d   [a-k"a   ʃ-ʕa-m-k"a-waʃ]
we 3si-1p-know-PRS-DYN   DEF-rain how-DIR-NEG-rain-FUTPTCPL
We know that it won't rain.

---

[102]Note that this construction involves a direct quote. This is most evident in (232). Abaza also allows for indirect quotes.

(235) hara [yə-ʃ-xʲta-wa]   y-h-dərə-y-d
      we   3si-how-cold-PTC 3si-1p-know-PRS-DYN
      We know that it is cold.

(236) aʕʷa-kʷa   zəmʕʷazəgʲa [ʃʲəmta a-mara ʃ-ʕa-cc'a-wa]
      person-PL all   early   DEF-sun how-DIR-rise-PTC

      r-dərə-y-d
      3p-know-PRS-DYN
      Everybody knows that the sun rises in the morning.

Stative clauses may be complement to the postposition *qaz*, which indicates the reason for something, as in (237). Compare (238), in which a dynamic clause is complement to this same postposition. Both complement clauses contain participles.

(237) sa   ʕa-sə-y-d   y-aʔa-yʲnə-wa   a-qaz
      snow DIR-snow-PRS-DYN   3si-LOC-winter-PTC   3si-for
      It snows because it is winter.

(238) sa ʃax s-a-sə-y-d   bzəy y-aʔa-s-ba-wa   a-qaz
      I chess 1s-3si-hit-PRS-DYN good 3si-LOC-1s-see-PTC   3si-for
      I play chess because I like it.

In addition, a stative CP may be conjoined with a dynamic CP, as in (239). Both of these clauses are indicative. This supports the claim that stative complexes and dynamic verb complexes project to the same category, CP, because in general only elements of the same category may be conjoined.

(239) [a-wəs   ʃarda-b]   gʲanagʲa [a-gʷadz   aʃarda-wa
      DEF-work much-STP   but   DEF-wheat much-PTC

      y-aygʷərʸʲə-y-d]
      3p-please-PRS-DYN
      It is a lot of work, but they are pleased there is a lot of wheat.

Such facts provide further evidence that the highest head in stative complexes and the highest head in dynamic verb complexes project to the same category, since this allows for a simpler account of the selectional properties for the heads which subcategorize for these phrases. That is,

3.2 Statives clauses are CPs

there is a single category, CP, which is selected. If stative and dynamic complexes projected to different categories, it would be purely accidental that phrases headed by stative complexes were consistently selected by the same heads which select phrases headed by dynamic verb complexes.

We turn now to the question of how to integrate the CP structure shown to occur at the top of the stative construction with the various lexical categories shown to occur at the bottom. Related to this is the question of where the subject of the stative predication fits into the structure and the question of how Case is assigned to the various arguments involved. These issues will be discussed in §3.3. First, I briefly discuss a difficulty the Abaza data present for the theory of extended projections proposed by Grimshaw (1991).

3.2.4 Extended projections

In §3.1, I demonstrated that the lower portion of a stative predicate structure can consist of any of the lexical projections—NP, AP, PP, or VP headed by a stative verb. Sections 3.2.1–3.2.3 showed that the higher portion of the structure of stative predicates involves the same functional categories as those in dynamic clauses, complementizer (C), tense (T), and agreement (AbsP). Furthermore, §3.3 shows that there is no intervening lexical category between these functional categories and the lexical categories at the bottom of the structure.

Grimshaw (1991) proposed to treat a lexical projection plus the functional projections associated with it as a single extended structure, which she refers to as an extended projection. Specifically, VP-IP-CP forms a verbal extended projection, and NP-DP-PP/KP[103] forms a nominal extended projection. For her, each XP in these extended projections shares the category of the lexical XP at the bottom of the structure. The difference between VP, on the one hand, and IP and CP, on the other, is that the former is a lexical category while the latter are functional categories. Furthermore, the three categories are distinguished from each other in terms of level. Grimshaw compares this distinction with the distinction in bar levels within X-bar theory, i.e., $X°$, X^1 ($=X'$), X^2 ($=XP$). In essence, then, VP is $VP°$, IP is VP^1, and CP is VP^2. Certain features are shared within the extended projection, particularly category features.

Grimshaw's proposal is consistent with the facts of the Abaza dynamic verbal system, in which only lexical verbs may participate. Dynamic verbs can form an extended projection with (dynamic) I and C. Only verbal features are involved. The structure I propose for statives is problematic for

---
[103]KP is the locus of morphological case. In some languages, the category P acts like the highest projection in the nominal extended projection.

Grimshaw's proposal, however, because stative I and C are in an extended projection with members of any of the lexical categories in Abaza, including categories not compatible with V.[104] If Grimshaw's proposal were correct, the observed structure in Abaza, with members of nominal, postpositional, and adjectival categories in extended projections with I and C, should not be possible because the category noun, for example, should extend only to the nominal functional categories, and not to the verbal functional categories, I and C.

Grimshaw allows for functional categories which are unmarked for a particular feature, and which take the feature of whatever extended projection they are in.[105] It would be possible to allow IP and CP to be unmarked for category, taking the features of whatever category headed the extended projection. This is problematic, however, in that it means that there are actually multiple different categories of CP, depending on the head of the extended projection. Furthermore, it becomes more difficult to distinguish nominal CP from (nominal) DP, since both would be maximal nominal functional projections. I conclude that some modification is required in Grimshaw's proposal which allows CP to be at the top of an extended projection headed by a category other than V, but which maintains the basic verbal nature of CP.

3.3 Subject position and case assignment

So far the structure of the predicate (§3.1) and the highest functional categories in the extended projection (§3.2) have been accounted for by the analysis I propose for the stative construction. We turn now to the position of the subject of the predication.

I propose in §3.3.1 that the subject of a stative predication occupies a position parallel to the position I adopt for the subjects of dynamic verbs, i.e., adjoined to X^{max}. The proposed analysis of subjects is integrated into the overall structure in §3.3.2. In §3.3.3 an alternative analysis is contrasted and rejected.

---

[104]The four common categories V, N, A, and P are often distinguished with the two binary features [±N, ±V]. Verbs are [+V, -N], nouns are [+N, -V], adjectives are [+N, +V], and adpositions are [-N, -V].

[105]I assume this analysis for the ergative agreement phrase, since it occurs with any category freely.

3.3 Subject position and case assignment

3.3.1 Subject position

I adopt the preliminary position that the subject of stative predicates is adjoined to the lexical XP, to create a node, X^{max}, parallel to the structure I adopted for dynamic verbs.[106] This produces the positive result that there is a single position for subjects across all constructions requiring them in Abaza. This can be seen in (240). For now, I adopt this structure without argument. It is shown in chapter 4, however, that this structure is necessary because it can accommodate the subject of the complement of the causative verb. Note that the subject must be external to the minimal XP in order to provide a position for the possessor of a noun, which occupies the specifier of N position.

(240)
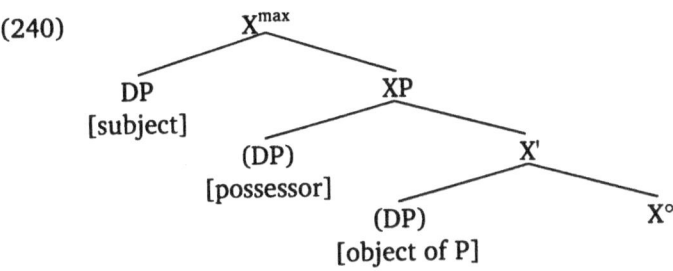

A possible alternative position for the subject is proposed by Bowers (1993). He posits a functional projection, PrP (predicate phrase), directly dominating the lexical projection. The subject occupies the specifier of PrP in his analysis. This structure is problematic for Abaza because the causative verb requires as its complement a saturated predicate (including a subject) which, crucially, does not contain any functional projections.

3.3.2 Integrated phrase structure

In this section, I propose a unified account of the phrase structure of stative predicates. The core issue is how the structure at the top (including the functional projections dominating the configuration) and the structure at the bottom (the lexical projections) fit together.

For those cases in which there is no argument beyond the subject of the predication, the analysis is straightforward. This includes intransitive verbs, stative adjectives, unpossessed stative nouns, and intransitive

---

[106]This will be modified slightly below such that the subject adjoins to the E_{RG}^{max} which immediately dominates a possessed noun or a postposition with an object. In all other cases it adjoins directly to the lexical X^{max}.

stative postpositions. The subject is registered in the absolutive series in this construction. There is a single, independently motivated agreement projection, ABSP, between CP and TP, to which the subject DP moves. There is no other functional material between TP and the lexical projection, so the two parts can be joined directly, i.e., (stative) T° is sister to lexical X^{max}. The underlying structure of the adjectival stative predicate in (214) can be seen in (241).

(241)

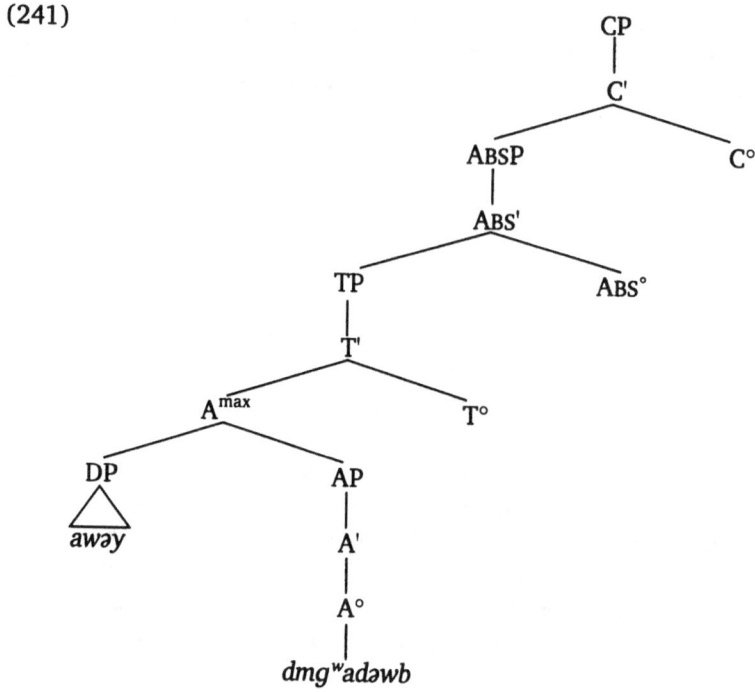

The derivation from this underlying structure proceeds in the usual way, with the A° head raising through all the heads in the extended projection, T° and ABS° in this case, to C°. As in the dynamic construction, the subject moves to the specifier of ABS, where the relevant features are checked.

For a stative transitive verb, the structure is exactly like that of a dynamic verb. The only difference is in the features of tense and mood. Tense and mood heads in the dynamic structure will have some feature, [+dynamic], while tense and mood heads in the stative structure will have the feature [–dynamic]. This is necessary to ensure having the correct types of tense and mood morphology with each lexical category.

3.3 Subject position and case assignment

Presumably, nouns, adjectives, and postpositions have a default setting of [–dynamic]. It is only verbs which can occur in both systems. Crucially, there will be an ergative agreement projection between TP and the lexical XP, as in dynamic clauses. The subject will move to the specifier of this ergative agreement projection in order to have its features checked and have Case assigned, and the object will move to the specifier of the higher, absolutive agreement projection for the same reasons. The movement pattern is nested, as in the dynamic system. As always, the verb head moves up through the heads in the extended projection, ultimately to C°. The resulting structure of (188), repeated here as (242), can be seen in (243).

(242) a-čk"ən wandər-k' y-taqə-b
     DEF-boy car-INDEF 3sm-want-STP
     The boy wants a car.

(243)

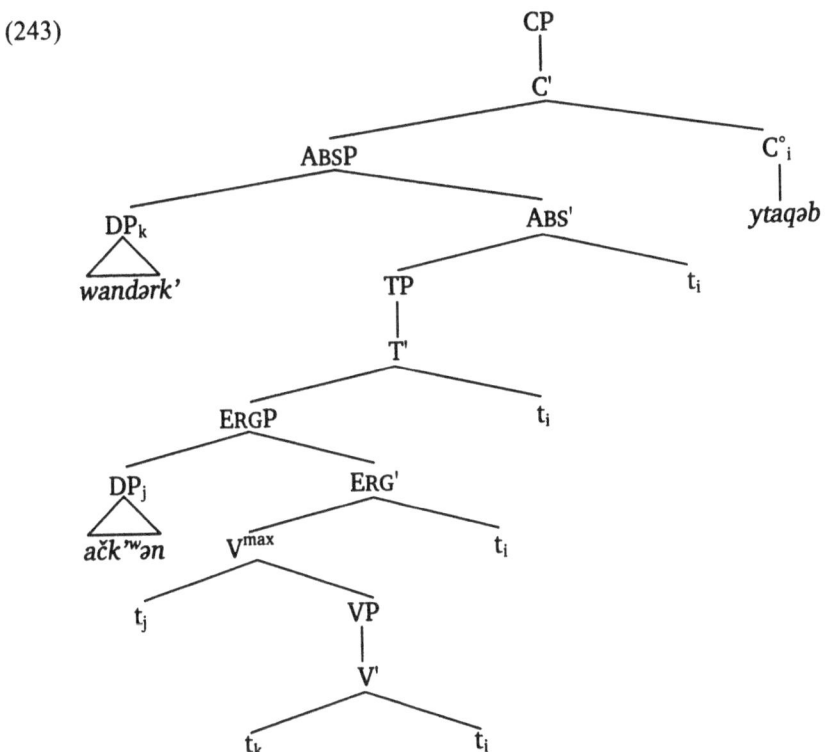

For stative nouns with possessors and postpositions with objects, an ergative agreement projection must be present. This mediates agreement with the possessor and the postpositional object, respectively. The complication with these categories is that the subject of the predication is registered in the absolutive series, while the possessor and postpositional object are registered in the ergative series. This is surprising if the structure is that in (244), since movement to the specifiers of the agreement projections would form a crossing pattern, as indicated, instead of the nesting pattern, expected in accordance with the Nesting Condition. Movement within a postpositional predicate would have the same pattern, but with the object of the postposition moving from the complement position instead of from the specifier position.

(244)

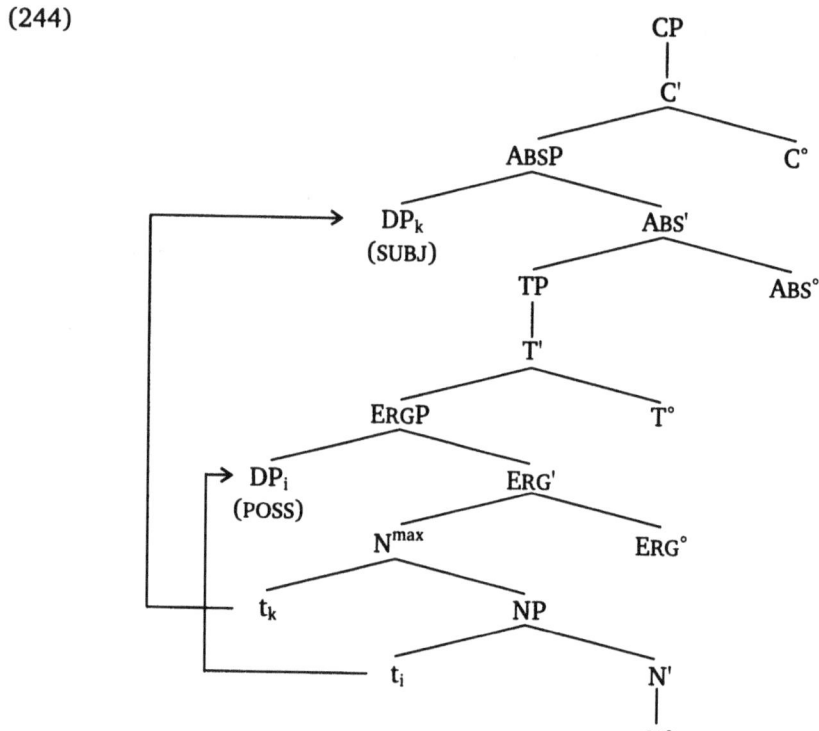

It is therefore necessary to give an account of stative transitive verbs somehow different from that of stative possessed nouns and postpositions. There are two logical possible mechanisms for providing such an account. One is to assign some feature or characteristic to nouns and postpositions which causes them to trigger movement of their possessor and postpositional object to ergative specifiers, resulting in a crossing pattern

3.3 Subject position and case assignment

instead of a nesting pattern. Verbs would lack this feature, so that the Nesting Condition would hold, as in the normal case. The second logical possibility is to propose a phrase structure configuration for stative nouns and postpositions which is different from that of verbs, and which forces movement to the correct specifier positions for each category while still maintaining the Nesting Condition and other principles established in chapter 2.

In Murasugi (1992), as discussed in §2.5.2, there already exists a well-developed account of crossing versus nesting movement based on features of the agreement projections. Her proposal provides a way to account for the distinction in Abaza between verbs and nonverbs by utilizing features which trigger the different kinds of movement. She argues that the nesting versus crossing paths found in ergative-absolutive and nominative-accusative systems, respectively, are accounted for by a feature [strong] on either the lower or higher of the two agreement projections. The (closest) subject must move to whichever of these is strong. If the lower agreement projection is strong, a transitive subject moves there, resulting in a nesting pattern. If the higher one is strong, a transitive subject moves to this position, resulting in a crossing pattern.

In order to adapt her system to the current analysis, we could suppose that the feature [strong] is not inherent to an agreement projection in a particular position, but receives this feature by virtue of the fact that a particular type of head has substituted into the agreement head. This is consistent with assumptions about other factors involved with agreement projections, which are licensed or have other features depending on the nature of the head which substitutes into them. In Abaza, then, an ergative agreement projection would become [strong] only when V° substituted into it. When something other than a verbal head substituted into an ergative agreement projection, then, it would not be strong, and nesting movement would not be forced.[107] This would account for the fact that the absolutive agreement projection is [weak], since it is T° which substitutes into it, and it would account for the movement patterns with possessed nouns and transitive postpositions in the stative construction, since these also do not involve V°. In this way, the featural content of the lexical

---

[107]This assumes that the "default" movement pattern is crossing. An alternative which extends the use of features is to assume that the absolutive agreement head is unmarked for the feature [strong], i.e., [0strong], while nouns and postposition heads trigger the feature [−strong] when they substitute into an ergative agreement head. Crossing movement would then be forced for stative nouns and postpositions because [0strong] on the absolutive head is "stronger" than [−strong] on the ergative head. On the other hand, verb heads would trigger the feature [+strong] when they substitute into an ergative agreement head, forcing a nested pattern of movement because [+strong] on the ergative head is stronger than [0strong] on the absolutive head.

heads would ultimately determine the movement pattern to the specifiers of the agreement projections higher in the structure.

I demonstrated in §2.5.2, however, that Murasugi's system is inadequate for Abaza because of the difficulty in motivating the nesting movement that occurs with three or more agreement projections. Having already rejected this proposal for the dynamic system of Abaza, it is not reasonable to use it for the stative system, especially in light of the fact that there is an adequate alternative account, to which we now turn.

The different movement patterns with verbs and nonverbs in the stative construction can be accounted for in terms of a different phrase structural configuration by assuming that the subject occurs outside of the ergative agreement projection for the relevant nonverbal predicates. That is, the subject is adjoined to the outermost layer of the predication, ERGP, creating ERG^{max}.[108] In such a structure, the subject can only move to the specifier of the absolutive agreement projection, since it cannot move down to a lower specifier position. This leaves the specifier of the ergative agreement projection open for the possessor or the postpositional object. The structure of a stative possessed noun is shown in (245). There is no question of crossing versus nesting movement paths, since the two paths do not interact at all. The Nesting Condition can thus be maintained, since it applies here (vacuously).

---

[108]This analysis is incompatible with Campana's claim that agreement can be checked when the relevant DP is either in the specifier of an agreement projection or adjoined to the maximal projection of an agreement phrase. He makes this assumption solely in order to motivate his analysis that the positions checked by the two agreement projections are of different types with respect to the A/A-bar distinction. Since I have shown (§2.5.1) that his analysis is problematic on independent grounds, I conclude that this (nonstandard) assumption is also not correct.

3.3 Subject position and case assignment

(245)

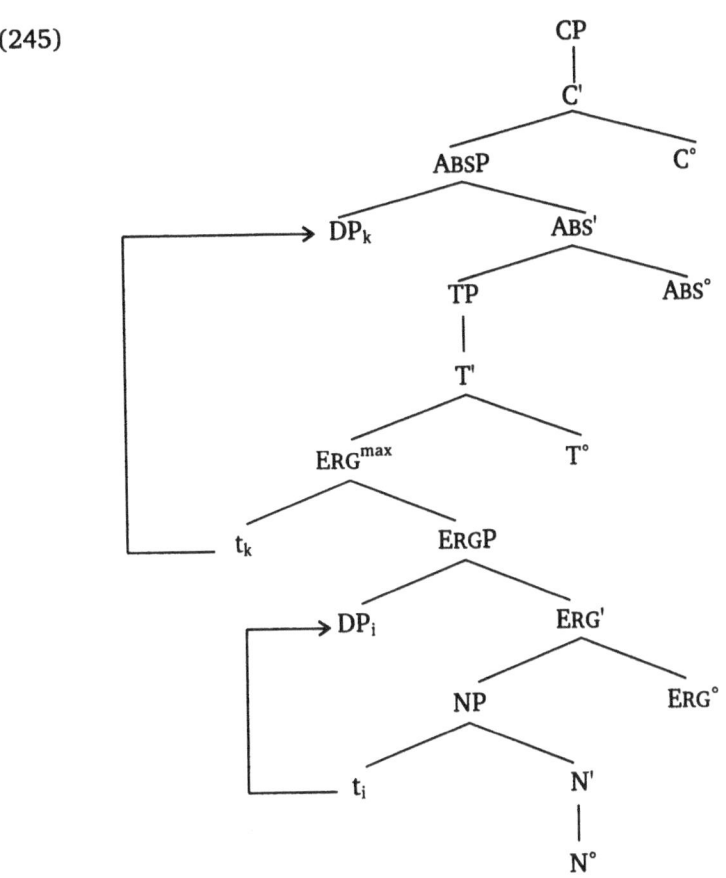

This proposal raises the question of why the subject position is not adjoined to the lexical XP for nonverbal stative predicates as it is for verbs. Part of the distinction must be that subjects of verbs are semantically licensed in a way that is different from the subjects of nonverbal predicates. There are two ways of semantically licensing an argument, through θ-assignment and through predication. (See Williams (1980) for a discussion of predication.) A verb assigns a θ-role to its external argument, the subject. In a nonverbal predicate, the subject does not receive a θ-role from the lexical head of the predicate.[109] For nonverbal predicates, then, the subject must be adjoined to a predicate which is not only saturated

---

[109] I assume that the subject gets its semantic role from the outermost XP of the predicate.

(i.e., it includes all of its internal arguments), but in which all these arguments are capable of being syntactically licensed.[110] I refer to such a predicate as a COMPLETE PREDICATE. The possessor of a noun and the object of a postposition must be able to move to an agreement specifier in order to be syntactically licensed, which means that the ergative agreement projections must be included within a complete predicate.

This analysis is in complete accord with the principles developed in chapter 2, and summarized in §2.6. Specifically, the ergative agreement projection into which the possessor and object of the postposition move in stative predicates occurs immediately dominating NP and PP. This is consistent with the claim that the categories N and P extend to ERGP, and do not license ergative agreement projections freely within their extended projections as verbs do. The position in which these ergative agreement projections occur is the only position licensed by the principles in chapter 2, thus providing confirmation that these principles are correct for Abaza.

3.3.3 A potential alternative analysis

A distinct alternative to my proposal would be to have the subject originate directly in the specifier of ABSP. Having the subject generated in the specifier of ABSP directly accounts for the observed agreement pattern of stative nouns and postpositions. Such a proposal has been made by Doherty (1996), in which he analyzes the modern Irish copular construction. He proposes that the copula is actually a functional head of the inflectional class (I°). The structure for the stative nominal predicate in (199) would be as shown in (246). I assume that the copula would reside in T° under the more articulated INFL structure I am adopting, but nothing crucial rests on this assumption.

---

[110]A syntactic alternative is to base-generate the possessor in the specifier of ERGP, rather than in the specifier of NP. The ergative agreement projection must therefore be present when there is a possessor, and must furthermore be included as part of the (NP) predicate. This structure is more problematic for postpositions, which I assume occupy the complement position within PP for various reasons, including selection, θ-assignment, and (possibly) the nonpercolation of the feature [+wh] within PPs (see chapter 8).

3.3 Subject position and case assignment

(246)
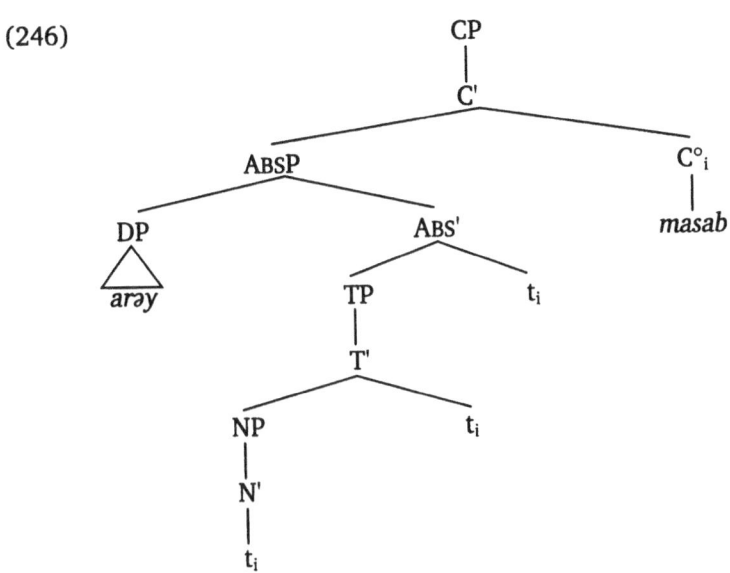

The derivation of this structure proceeds as follows: the head noun, *masa*, raises to the (null) copular head in T°. This N°-T° complex then raises to ABS°. From this position, the relevant features are checked with the subject of the predication in the specifier of ABSP. This complex of heads then substitutes for C°. In contrast to dynamic verbs, where the subject originates within V^{max} (adjoined to VP), the subject of the stative predicate originates in the specifier of ABSP.

Stative predicates having ergative agreement, i.e., nominals with possessors, transitive verbs, and most postpositions, will have an ergative agreement projection between TP and the lexical phrase. This is also consistent with my assumption that it is the lexical categories which allow or license ERGP. The structure for a nominal stative predicate with a possessed noun, as in (206), would be as in (247).

(247)

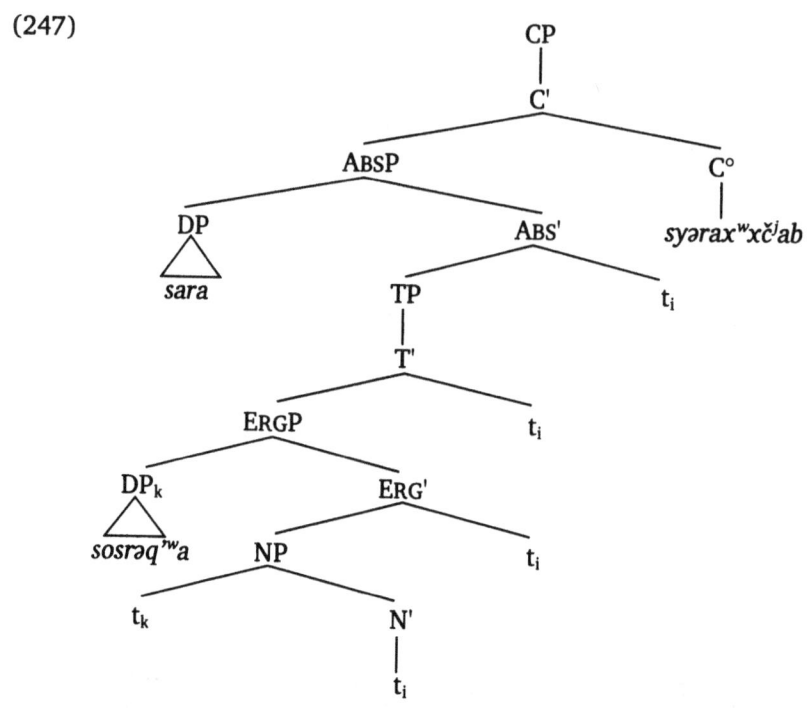

The derivation is parallel to the preceding one, except for the possessor. The possessor originates in the specifier of NP, and raises to the specifier of ERGP in order to get Case, which is checked by the complex of heads as it passes through. One additional difference is that the head noun, N°, passes through one additional functional projection, ERG°, which is thus included in the complex of heads.

This analysis is problematic for Abaza, however, because of the causative construction involving nonverbal predicates. I argue in chapter 4 that the causative verb is a lexical verb which may select as complement a nonverbal predication including a subject. The structure proposed by Doherty does not provide a possible position for the subject within the complement of the causative verb, since it is clearly impossible for an absolutive agreement projection to occur there. Furthermore, it is not possible for the subject of the nonverbal predicate to occur in the absolutive specifier above the causative verb. This would result in a configuration in which the causative verb itself intervenes between the nonverbal predicate XP and the subject of the predication. This results in a nonlocal relationship for purposes of θ-assignment, a violation of general assumptions about the locality of θ-assignment. (See chapter 4 for further details.)

The analysis I propose in which the subject adjoins to lexical XP, or to ERGP in the case of possessed noun or transitive postposition, accounts for nonverbal stative predicates in Abaza in a way consistent with the analysis I give for dynamic verbs. Besides difficulties with the causative construction, Doherty's analysis requires principles distinct from those I utilize for dynamic verbs. My analysis is thus preferable in that it provides a single unified account of both dynamic and stative constructions in Abaza.

3.4 The verb ak'ʷ

I conclude the analysis of stative verbs in Abaza with a discussion of the problematic case of one of the more common stative verbs, ak'ʷ 'be'. This verb is primarily identificational. This function can be seen in (248)–(252).

(248) araʔa y-bzaza-wa   nartərʕa   r-ak'ʷə-n
      there AWH-live-PTC   Narts   3p-be-PST
      It was the Narts who lived there.   NART, 50

(249) d-ʕa-z-rəyə-z   a-haqʷ   a-k'ʷ-b
      3sr-PV-EWH-bear-PSP   DEF-stone 3si-be-STP
      It was the stone which gave birth to him.   NART, 50

(250) c'arak'ʷəʒʷ   s-ak'ʷ-p'
      Ts'arak'wuzh   1s-be-STP
      I am Tsarakwuzh.   IAT, 29

(251) awəy   a-k'ʷ-b   sa   y-ʃ-s-ʕa-z
      this   3si-be-STP   I   3si-how-1s-hear-PSP
      This is what I heard (how I heard it).   NART, 50

(252) nartərʕa r-zaman a-pnə nartərʕa y-rə-wa-ta   rəc'a qac'a-ra
      Narts   3p-time 3si-at Narts   3p-3p-from-AV more   brave-MAS

      dəw z-la-ta   a-təwrəx-kʷa   y-ʕadərba-kʷa-wa   arat
      big EWH-for-AV   DEF-legend-PL   3p-witness-PL-PTC   they

r-akʷ-b totraʃ ɬapʃʷ ʃabantoqʷa aʃamaz q'anʒoqʷa
3p-be-STP Totrash Tlapsh Shabantoko Ashamaz Kanzhoko

sosrəqʷa badinoqʷa ɬabəca bataraz awzərmag agʲə-kʷa
Sosruko Badinoko Tlabitsa Bataraz Uazyrmag other-PL

In the Narts' time, the most brave of the Narts, the bearers of courage, as the legends witness it, were these: Totrash, Tlapsh, Shabantoko, Ashamaz, Kanzhoko, Sosruko, Badinoko, Tlabitsa, Bataraz, Uazyrmag, and others. NART, 49

Note that both terms of the identificational predicate can be expressed. Compare (250) with (253).

(253) sara brian s-akʷə-b
 I Brian 1s-be-STP
 I am Brian.

In addition to the identificational function of this verb, the Anatolian dialect uses it to indicate existence, as in (254).[111] It also seems possible to use this verb to form a postpositional predication when a particular postposition is not one which can host stative morphology, as in (255).[112]

(254) allah y-akʷ-b
 God 3sm-be-STP
 God exists.

(255) a-qəʃʷ a-qaxʲ a-q'apʃə a-kʷ-b
 DEF-yellow 3si-on DEF-red 3si-be-STP
 The red one is on top of the yellow one.

---

[111] I am somewhat hesitant to claim that akʷ can generally be used to indicate existence, since the normal way is with the stative verb aʔa 'be there', as in (i) and the very common (ii). It may be that the form in (254) is a special case because of the Muslim creed.

 (i) čə-k' čada-k' xə-ʒʷ-k'-yʃty wasa ʃarda y-aʔa-p'
  horse-one donkey-one three-cow-one-and sheep many 3p-be.there-STP
  There is one horse, one donkey, three cows, and many sheep.

 (ii) (y)-gʲ-aʔa-m
  (3si)-INT-be.there-NEG
  There isn't any. (lit., It doesn't exist.)

[112] It is possible that the interpretation of (255) is 'It is the red one which is on top of the yellow one.' In this case, the basic identificational nature of the verb is maintained.

3.4 The verb akʷ

For the verb *akʷ*, the argument which is identified, which must be a DP, is registered in the verb complex through the ergative series. I take this to be the subject. The identification of the subject, i.e., the second argument or object, can be expressed with a DP or a PP. It is also very common for the identification to be a headless relative, which can probably be best analyzed as a type of DP. There is no agreement registered with this second argument. A structural configuration in which the subject occurs adjoined to VP and the second (identifying) argument is sister to V° provides positions for the arguments.

One problematic aspect of this construction is the question of how the second argument, is licensed, i.e., gets Case. It is possible that the subject and the object are co-indexed and form a type of chain through which Case can be transmitted, similar to what is often assumed to occur with English *be*. Either the object gets Case through its co-indexation with the subject, or it does not require Case by virtue of the fact that it is predicative.

The truly problematic aspect of this construction is that the subject is registered in the ergative series, while nothing is registered in the absolutive series. This is an apparent violation of the EPP,[113] which requires the specifier of AbsP to be filled. Absolutive agreement is associated with tense, and tense is expressed with the verb *akʷ* as with all other verbs, stative or dynamic. It is therefore reasonable to assume that TP is present in this construction. Since TP is present, AbsP should also be present by the principle that TP extends to AbsP, yet there is no absolutive agreement. The relationship between TP and AbsP is well motivated. It is a true generalization of the facts of the language, with this single exception.

Certain possible analyses can be dismissed. One is that *akʷ* is a normal transitive verb, and the object is always third-person singular irrational or third-person plural, and agreement is always registered with the null absolutive variant. This leaves open the question of why just this particular verb behaves this way. It is also unsatisfactory in that in just this case the null absolutive agreement would obligatorily occur even when there is no corresponding overt argument immediately preceding the verb.

A stronger possibility, but problematic nonetheless, is that the subject of *akʷ* is somehow required to occur in the ergative series. My analysis of lexically inverted verbs in chapter 6 utilizes inherent Case, in that a particular argument is lexically associated with a particular type of agreement projection (ergative). It is possible that the subject of *akʷ* is also specified in this manner. Such an analysis is problematic, however, in that

---

[113]Recall the discussion of the EPP in §2.4.2.2.

the EPP still requires an argument in the absolutive specifier. When there is no argument available to move into the specifier of ABSP, an expletive is inserted, yet no expletive is possible with *akʼʷ*. Inherent Case may be involved in this construction, thus accounting for the fact that the subject is registered in the ergative series,[114] but this cannot be the whole story since it fails to account for the absence of absolutive agreement.

Another possibility is that the licensing conditions for ABSP are more complex than we have assumed to this point, and that they are not met in structures containing *akʼʷ*. For instance, if *akʼʷ* has a defective extended projection, lacking TP, which extends to ABSP, then presumably ABSP would also be absent. The EPP would then be satisfied vacuously, since there would be no specifier of ABSP to fill. Some support for this position comes from the fact that *akʼʷ* seems to lack the ability to express some of the distinctions possible for other stative verbs, for example certain moods.[115] It would still be necessary to account for the observed tense distinctions, which would then occur without the benefit of TP.[116]

I leave the question of the verb *akʼʷ* open, noting that an analysis of it is problematic primarily because of its lack of an absolutive agreement prefix. In many languages, the verb *be* has exceptional properties.

---

[114]Recall the Transitive Subject Condition from §2.2.3.

[115]The evidence I have for this claim is not strong. The overwhelming majority of occurrences of the verb *akʼʷ* in texts are either past or present indicative forms. A few cases in the yes-no question mood also occur, mostly in a frozen tag marker, *ygʲakʼʷəwmma* 'right?' (lit., isn't it?)', but content questions, conditionals, and masdars are completely lacking. I am uncertain whether this is simply a gap in the data I have, whether it is a real gap due to the semantics and function of this verb, or a real morphological gap because of the lack of certain functional projections. I leave this as an area for further research.

[116]The observed tense distinctions may be available here, in spite of the absence of TP, because the relevant suffixes are portmanteaux if the presence of just one of the functional projections associated with the features of these portmanteaux, i.e., CP, is sufficient to license the suffixes. This is not entirely consistent with my assumptions concerning the checking of features of portmanteaux (see §3.2.2).

4

Causatives

I have developed a unified framework for Case assignment in Abaza. Chapter 2 has shown how this system accounts for dynamic verbs, and chapter 3 extended the analysis to stative predicates. Both of these constructions involve a single lexical head and a single extended projection. We turn now to more complex constructions involving more than a single lexical head. This chapter deals with the causative construction, which, following Baker (1988), I analyze as consisting of two clauses, one headed by the causative verb and one a complement to the causative verb. I demonstrate that the system of Case assignment developed thus far accounts for the causative data, as well.

Abaza has a highly productive morphological causative construction. The causative morpheme, *r-*, is prefixed to the immediate left of the lexical root. Agreement with the causative subject, i.e., the subject of the causative VP which causes the action of the complement VP, is registered in an ergative series to the immediate left of the causative prefix. Agreement registered with other arguments generally occurs in the same pattern as in noncausative forms, but to the left of agreement with the causative subject. Consider the causative of the intransitive verb *čʲa* 'eat', in which the causative subject to the immediate left of the causative prefix is in bold.

(256) *yə-**lə**-r-čʲa-y-d*
3si-**3sf**-CAUS-eat-PRS-DYN
She caused it to eat (i.e., she fed it).

Section 4.1 presents data for the causatives of dynamic verbs and an analysis in which the causative prefix is treated as a verb head that selects a VP complement. Section 4.2 discusses reflexives, presenting first a basic analysis, and then discussing the interaction of the reflexives with causative verbs. Section 4.3 presents causative data for stative lexical categories, and extends the analysis of the causative verb by expanding its selectional properties. In §4.4, we return to a discussion of the details of the subject position. The causative data supports the position proposed by Koopman and Sportiche (1988, 1991), which I have adopted without argument to this point. Section 4.5 discusses more limited data on double causatives in Abaza.

4.1 The causative of dynamic verbs

The causative construction can be used with all dynamic verbs regardless of the transitivity of the verb. The causative of intransitive dynamic verbs is discussed in §4.1.1. I propose a basic analysis of the causative construction here, demonstrating how both phrase structure and Case assignment operate. This analysis is extended to transitive dynamic verbs in §4.1.2 and supports the claim made in chapter 2 that ergative agreement projections may be freely generated. In §4.1.3, I show how this analysis works for the causative of ditransitives, as well. The nesting movement pattern to the agreement specifiers is especially evident in these cases.

4.1.1 The causative of intransitive dynamic verbs

The formation of the causative of intransitive dynamic verbs is discussed in §4.1.1.1. In §4.1.1.2, I propose that the causative morpheme is actually a verb head, which selects a dynamic VP complement. This analysis follows Baker's (1988) analysis of causatives. Section 4.1.1.3 demonstrates how Case assignment operates in these constructions within my overall analysis for Abaza.

4.1.1.1 Data. The causative of simple intransitive dynamic verbs is formed by adding the causative prefix, *r-*, directly to the verb root. Without the causative prefix, an intransitive verb registers agreement with its subject in the absolutive series. This is true also with the causative prefix; the subject of the base verb is registered in the absolutive series. The causative subject is registered in the ergative series. This produces a form having the agreement pattern of a normal simple transitive verb, with the

4.1 The causative of dynamic verbs

(causative) subject registered in the ergative series and the object, i.e., base subject, registered in the absolutive series. Compare (257) and (258).

(257) d-qʷəc-i-t'
    3sr-think-PRS-DYN
    S/he thinks.
                                GAL, 178

(258) d-a-r-qʷəc-i-t'
    3sr-3si-CAUS-think-PRS-DYN
    It makes him/her think.
                             GAL, 178

In the noncausative (257) the third-person singular rational subject of the intransitive verb $qʷəc$ 'think' is registered in the absolutive series, and there are no other arguments registered. The causative of (257) is seen in (258), and the third-person singular irrational causative subject is registered in the ergative series, and the subject of 'think' is registered in the absolutive series. The same pattern can be seen in the causative of $qʷaʃa$ 'shatter' in (259), where the first-person singular causative subject is registered in the ergative series, and the subject of 'shatter' is registered in the absolutive series.

(259) y-s-rə-qʷaʃa-t'
    3si-1s-CAUS-shatter-DYN
    I broke it into smithereens.
                             GAL, 179

The causative construction usually provides an easy way to identify intransitive verbs with separable preverbs,[117] since the causative prefix and the ergative series occur between the preverb and the root.[118] This can be seen in the causative of the intransitive roots ʃaqčʷal 'squat' in (260) and adgəl 'approach' in (261).

(260) y-ʃaq-yə-r-čʷal-t'
    3si-PV-3sm-CAUS-**squat**-DYN
    He made it squat.
                             GAL, 179

---

[117] Recall the discussion of complex roots having separable preverbs in §1.1.2.3.
[118] The causative prefix apparently does not split all preverbs. Tabulova (1976) claims that the root $qʷaʃa$ in (259) is separable. This distinction is apparently lexically determined, though it seems to me that it is much more common for the causative morpheme to split the root and preverb.

(261) apxʲarta w-gʲ-ad-də-r-gəl-waʃə-m
school 2ms-INT-PV-3P-CAUS-**approach**-FUT-NEG
They won't allow you into school.   GAL, 180

The causative prefix and the agreement with the causative subject also separate an intransitive root from one of the optional nonagreeing locational prefixes.[119]

(262) də-ʕʷna-sə-r-čʷʼa-tʼ
3sr-home-1s-CAUS-sit-DYN
I seated him/her in the house.   GAL, 180

The basic word order places the causative subject to the left of the base subject in (263).

(263) sara a-čə   sə-rə-ʕʷə-y-d
I   DEF-horse 1s-CAUS-run-PRS-DYN
I ride the horse. (lit., I cause the horse to run.)

4.1.1.2 The causative morpheme as verb.

My analysis of the causative construction in Abaza follows Baker (1988) in treating the causative morpheme as a lexical (verb) head, which selects a VP (V^{max}) complement. In keeping with my assumptions about word formation, I assume that the causative verb head is phonologically null, but featurally contentful. The fully inflected head of the V^{max} complement substitutes for the causative verb head, where the appropriate features are checked, and this head then substitutes for the head of the next highest projection in the usual way. I propose, then, that the syntactic structure of a causative verb is biclausal, as in (264).

---

[119] Recall the discussion of these prefixes in §1.1.2.3.

4.1 The causative of dynamic verbs

(264)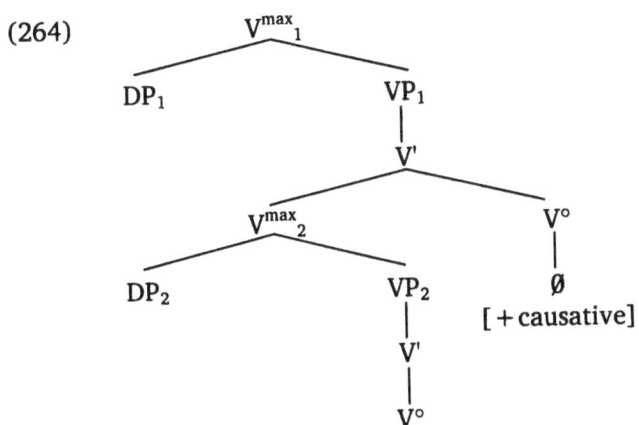

In this structure VP$_1$ is the phrase headed by the causative verb. DP$_1$ is the causative subject, which occurs in the usual position for subjects, adjoined to VP. The complement of the causative verb is V^{max}$_2$. The subject of VP$_2$, DP$_2$, also occupies the normal subject position with respect to VP$_2$. This correctly accounts for the basic word order.

4.1.1.3 Case assignment. Case assignment in these constructions operates very much like Case assignment in simple transitive verbs. The verbal functional projections dominate the higher VP$_1$ in (264), resulting in the complete structure in (265). AbsP is present as the extension of TP. ErgP is present since such projections may be freely generated within the extended projection of V, in accordance with the principles established in chapter 2.

(265)

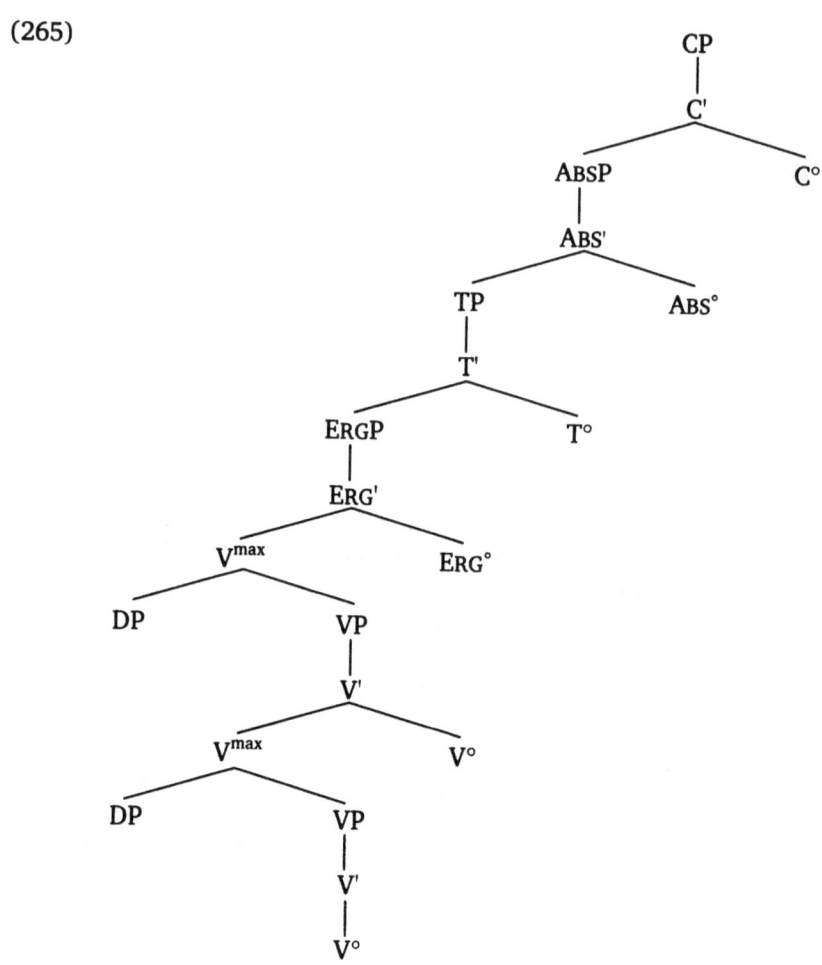

From this structure, the higher (causative) subject moves into the specifier position of the ergative agreement projection, and the lower subject moves into the specifier of the absolutive agreement projection. This obeys the Nesting Condition. The lowest verbal head substitutes for the causative verbal head, and then the ergative agreement head, the tense head, the absolutive agreement head, and finally C°. This is identical to the primary pattern already discussed. The resulting structure is given in (266).

4.1 The causative of dynamic verbs

(266)

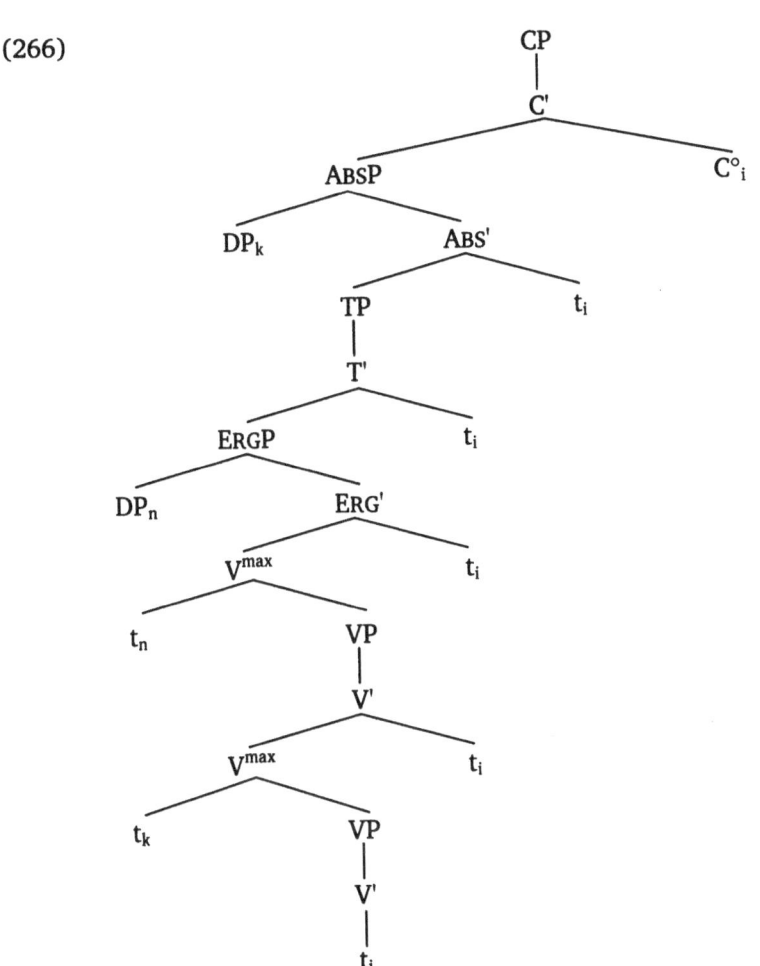

The question arises as to why the ergative agreement phrase occurs above the causative VP rather than dominating the lower VP (complement to the causative verb). The Closer Agreement Principle predicts that the lower position should be used unless there is a reason to eliminate one of the possibilities. I argue that the structure with the ergative agreement projection between the two VPs should be ruled out on independent principles.

Li (1990) argues that head movement is restricted such that a functional head may not incorporate into a lexical head. All other combinations are possible: lexical into lexical, lexical into functional, and functional into functional. Each of these legitimate types of incorporation is, in fact, attested in the structure in (266). The lexical verb head incorporates into the head of the lexical causative verb, the (lexical) causative verb head incorporates into the head of the (functional) ergative agreement phrase, and the heads of the functional categories, ERG°, T°, and ABS°, incorporate into the heads of the functional categories dominating them.

If the ergative agreement projection were to occur dominating the complement of the causative verb, Li's Generalization would be violated. The lower V°, which is lexical, could incorporate into ERG°, but when this head incorporated into the causative V°, it would be a case of a functional head incorporating into a lexical head. The two configurations [ERGP[VP[VP]]] and [VP[ERGP[VP]]], therefore, do not satisfy all conditions equally. This means that the Closer Agreement Principle does not apply to compare these two structures, since the latter is ruled out independently by Li's Generalization. The configuration [ERGP[VP[VP]]] is thus used as the one having an ergative agreement phrase in the lowest possible position.[120]

Note that this structure is consistent with the order of morphemes. If the ergative phrase were between the two VPs, the movement of the lower V° to ERG° would require the agreement features associated with this head to be checked first and the corresponding morphology to occur close to the root. The subsequent movement to the higher V° should place the causative morpheme further from the root than the ergative prefix, but the causative morpheme occurs between the ergative agreement and the lower verb head. The structure in (266) correctly accounts for the order of morphemes, since the lower V° incorporates first into the causative V°, and then this complex incorporates into ERG°.

I adopt Li's Generalization, (267), for Abaza and show that this generalization is valid for other structures in Abaza, including the potential construction (chapter 5) and incorporated postpositions (chapter 7).

(267) Li's Generalization:
    A functional head may not incorporate into a lexical head.

4.1.2 The causative of transitive dynamic verbs

Like intransitive dynamic verbs, transitive dynamic verbs can host the causative construction. Section 4.1.2.1 discusses data involving the causative of transitive verbs, and extends the analysis of the causative of

---

[120]The Transitive Subject Condition, §2.2.3, also accounts for this pattern since the causative subject must occur in the specifier of an ergative projection. For transitive verbs, the TSC cannot rule out a structure with an ergative projection below the causative VP.

4.1 The causative of dynamic verbs

intransitive verbs. Section 4.1.2.2 shows how this data supports the claim made above that ergative projections may be freely generated. Section 4.1.2.3 discusses the dissimilation of the third-person plural ergative agreement morpheme, r-, from the causative morpheme, turning into d-.

4.1.2.1 Data. As with the causative of intransitive verbs, the causative of transitive verbs is formed by attaching the causative prefix to the verb root, and registering the causative subject in the ergative series to its immediate left. The object of the base verb is registered in the absolutive series, as in noncausative transitive verbs. The subject of the base verb is registered in an ergative series which occurs to the left of the ergative series registering the causative subject. Compare the simple transitive verb in (268) with the causative of this form in (269). Another causative form is given in (270). The basic word order places the causative subject first, followed by the base subject and the base direct object, as in (271).[121]

(268) *yə-l-hʷa-t'*
    3si-3sf-say-DYN
    She said it.   GAL, 178

(269) *yə-l-də-r-hʷa-t'*
    3si-3sf-3p-CAUS-say-DYN
    They made her say it.   GAL, 178

(270) *yə-l-sə-r-sa-t'*
    3si-3sf-1s-CAUS-cut-DYN
    I had her cut it.   GAL, 179

(271) *a-qac'a   a-phʷəspa   a-la   l-y-r-ʃʲə-d*
    DEF-man   DEF-girl   DEF-dog   3sf-3sm-CAUS-kill-DYN
    The man made the girl kill the dog.   SSAVC, 157

As with intransitive verbs, the causative prefix and the agreement prefix which registers agreement with the causative subject occur between the preverb and the root of transitive verbs with separable preverbs.[122] Contrast the noncausative in (272) with the causative in (273). In both cases, the preverb *ʃa* and the root *aw* are separated by the first-person

---

[121]Note that the third-person agreement marker in (269) is phonetically [d] instead of the normal ergative [r]. This dissimilation is discussed in §4.1.2.3.

[122]As with intransitive verbs, the causative affix occurs just to the left of the preverb, which must then be immediately adjacent to the root of some transitive verbs with separable preverbs. This distinction is entirely lexical.

singular prefix, *s-*, registering agreement with the subject of *find*. In (273), the causative prefix also occurs between the preverb and the root.

(272) *y-ʕa-s-aw-t'*
3si-PV-1s-**find**-DYN
I found it. GAL, 179

(273) *y-ʕa-s-d-r-aw-t'*
3si-PV-1s-3p-CAUS-**find**-DYN
They made me find it. GAL, 179

4.1.2.2 The free generation of ERGP. As with the causative of intransitive verbs, the causative of transitive verbs can be analyzed in terms of a causative verb selecting a V^{max} complement. The transitivity of this complement is not restricted.

The causative of a transitive verb involves three arguments. This requires two ergative agreement projections plus the obligatory absolutive agreement projection in order to license all of the arguments. It is possible for there to be two ergative phrases because they may be freely generated within the verbal extended projection. Under the assumption that the lower V° must incorporate into the higher (causative) V°, both of these ergative projections must occur above the causative VP in order not to violate Li's Generalization, as in the intransitive case. This results in the following underlying structure: [CP[ABSP[TP[ERGP[ERGP[V^{max}[V^{max}]]]]]]]. This structure correctly accounts for the basic word order.

In the causative of transitive verbs, the prefix which registers agreement with the causative subject occurs closer to the verb root(s) than the prefix which registers agreement with the base subject. As elsewhere, I assume that this indicates a position structurally lower in the tree for the causative subject. This means that the causative subject, DP_1, moves into the specifier of the lower ergative agreement projection, $ERGP_2$. The subject of the base verb, DP_2, is also registered in an ergative series, so it moves into the specifier of the higher ergative agreement projection, $ERGP_1$. The direct object of the base verb, DP_3, moves into the specifier of the absolutive agreement projection. This again results in the familiar nesting pattern of movement, motivated by the Nesting Condition. The resulting tree can be seen in (274). (Head movement is not shown.)

4.1 The causative of dynamic verbs

(274)

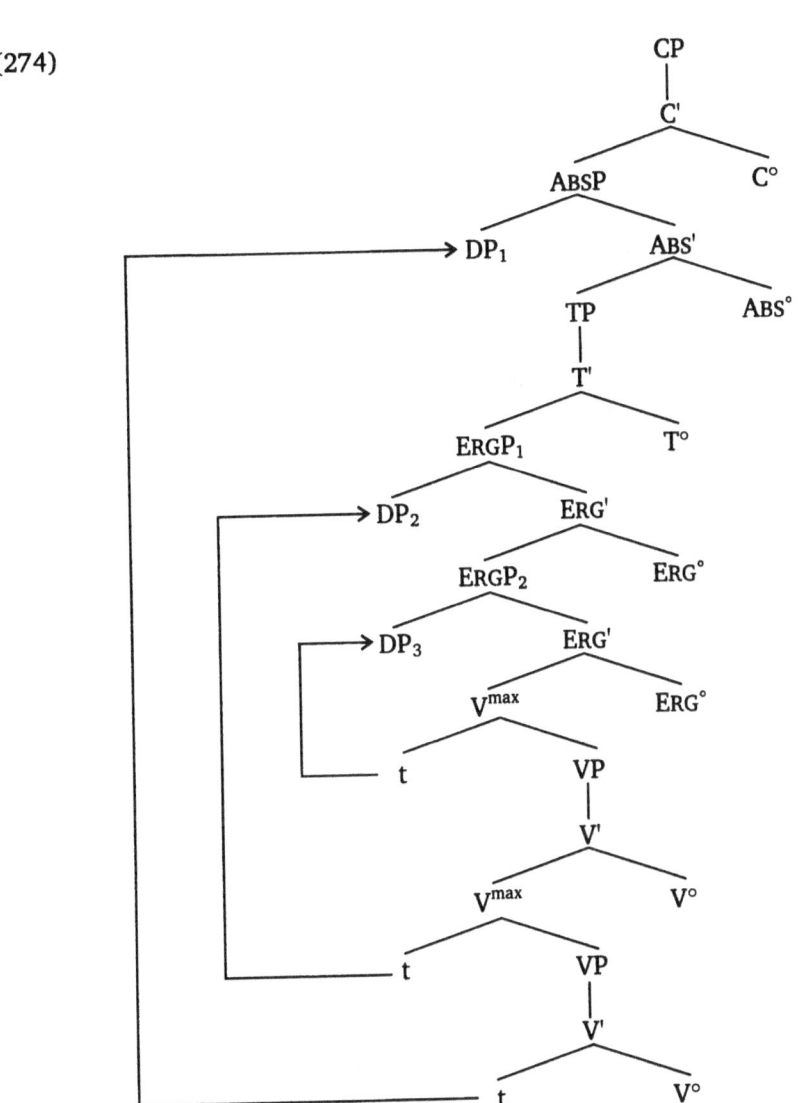

This structure embodies the claim that ergative agreement projections may be freely generated within a verbal extended projection. Two such phrases are required in order to provide Case and the configuration for feature-checking sufficient for all three arguments in this structure. If agreement projections were licensed only in positions (directly)

dominating a lexical phrase, such an underlying structure could not occur.[123] Furthermore, the presence of the higher ergative agreement projection in (274) cannot be attributed directly to the transitivity of the VP complement to the causative verb.[124] This would require a nonlocal licensing relationship for ERGP, both in the sense that the agreement phrase and the licensing head have material intervening between them, and in that the licensed agreement phrase occurs in a different extended projection from the VP which licenses it. Such nonlocal licensing relationships are in general disfavored. The simplest and most direct way to account for the presence of the higher ERGP in this construction is to allow such phrases to be generated freely.

A common pattern found in languages with causative constructions is that the subject of a lower transitive clause is treated syntactically as the indirect object of the complex predicate formed through causativization. This is true for Abaza insofar as the agreement which registers agreement with the transitive subject of the complement of the causative verb is registered in the same way as the indirect object of a simple ditransitive verb. Compare (275) and (276).

(275) *də-l-sə-r-ga-y-t'*
3sr-3sf-1s-CAUS-carry-PRS-DYN
I make her carry him/her.   SGSAL, 624

(276) *də-l-sə-tə-y-d*
3sr-3sf-1s-give-PRS-DYN
I gave him/her to her.

The fact that in Abaza the lower subject behaves like the indirect object of a ditransitive verb has no basis in grammatical relations in my analysis. Instead, it is the result of the architecture of the clause. The fact that ergative projections may be freely generated and the fact that no functional projections may intervene between the two VPs (because of Li's Generalization) conspire to produce identical configurations of agreement projections for both simple ditransitive clauses and the causatives of transitives. The underlying position of transitive subject is between the causative subject and the direct object, and the indirect object of a ditransitive verb likewise occurs structurally between the subject and

---

[123]The one configuration in which each of the three agreement projections directly dominate the phrase which licenses it, i.e., AbsP over TP and two instances of ERGP over V^{max}, has already been shown to be impossible because of Li's Generalization.

[124]Such an argument could feasibly be made for simple ditransitive verbs. That is, they project two ergative agreement phrases because they are ditransitive.

4.1 The causative of dynamic verbs

direct object. These facts, in conjunction with the Nesting Condition, require these two arguments to end up in ergative specifiers in the same structural position with respect to other arguments and agreement phrases.[125]

4.1.2.3 Ergative-causative dissimilation. There is a morphophonological rule which operates only in the context of the causative prefix. The causative prefix is phonetically [r], as is the third-person plural ergative agreement prefix. When the causative subject is third-person plural, the agreement marker dissimilates to [d].[126] Compare the noncausative form in (277) with the causative form in (278) having a third-person plural causative subject.

(277) d-čaɜʷ-y-c'a-t'
    3sr-horseback-3sm-place-DYN
    He put him on the horse.   GAL, 182

(278) d-čaɜʷ-s-**də-r**-c'a-t'
    3sr-horseback-1s-3p-CAUS-place-DYN
    They caused me to put him on the horse.   GAL, 182

This is true regardless of whether the complement VP to the causative verb is transitive or intransitive. Example (261), repeated here as (279), demonstrates an intransitive base verb.

(279) a-pxʲarta   w-gʲ-ad-**də-r**-gəl-waʃə-m
    DEF-lesson   2sm-INT-PV-3p-CAUS-arrive-FUT-NEG
    They won't allow you into the lessons.   GAL, 180

A peculiar aspect of this rule is that it affects not only a third-person plural causative subject, but also a third-person plural subject of a base transitive verb. Compare the noncausative transitive form having a

---

[125] Judith Aissen (pers. comm.) has suggested that the adoption of a double VP structure for ditransitives similar to Larson (1988), except with the indirect object as the subject of the lower VP shell, would result in a greater parallel between these two constructions. The lower VP shell of ditransitives would be identical structurally to the complement of the causative verb, with the indirect object and (lower) subject in the same position. This would also allow subjects to be in a specifier position, rather than adjoined. It is unclear whether this move is advantageous, since it removes the similarity between verbal (dynamic) subjects and the subjects of stative predications, which must be adjoined since the specifier of NP is already occupied by the possessor. (See §3.3.)

[126] Lomtatidze (1945:96) claims that this dissimilation takes place because the two prefixes have the same origin, a plural affix. The dissimilation occurred in order to distinguish the various functions of the two affixes.

third-person plural subject in (280) with the causativized form in (281) having the same argument structure in the base verb. Example (282) shows the dissimilation with a different intervening agreement prefix.

(280) *yə-r-ba-t'*
   3si-3p-see-DYN
   They saw it.

(281) *y-d-yə-r-ba-t'*
   3si-3p-3sm-CAUS-see-DYN
   He showed it to them. (lit., He caused them to see it.)   GAL, 179

(282) *y-ʕa-sə-kʷ-d-wə-r-c'a-t'*
   3si-DIR-1s-on-3p-2sm-CAUS-place-DYN
   You made them place it on me.   GAL, 180

If both the causative subject and the base subject are third-person plural, they both dissimilate from the causative affix.

(283) *čə-nqʷ-d-də-r-ga-wn*
   REFL-PV-3p-3p-CAUS-look.after-PST
   They made them look after themselves.   GAL, 180

It is not possible for a third-person plural ergative agreement prefix to dissimilate from the causative prefix if the ergative prefix registers agreement with an oblique argument.[127] The goal argument in (284) is expressed with the goal prefix, *a*, plus ergative agreement to its immediate left. When this form is causativized, as in (285), the ergative prefix registering agreement with the third-person plural goal argument does not dissimilate from [r] to [d].

(284) *y-r-a-r-hʷ-t'*
   3si-3p-GOAL-3p-say-DYN
   They said it to them.

(285) *y-r-a-d-d-rə-hʷ-t'*
   3si-3p-GOAL-3p-3p-CAUS-say-DYN
   They made them tell it to them.   GAL, 180

---

[127]See chapter 7 for an analysis of these as incorporated postpositions.

4.1 The causative of dynamic verbs

This dissimilation occurs only between the causative prefix and a third-person plural ergative agreement prefix. Elsewhere when two occurrences of /r/ are juxtaposed, there is no dissimilation. Normally, a single /r/ is pronounced as a flap [ɾ], as in (286). Two adjacent /r/ segments may merge into a short trill, as in (287).[128]

(286) [yəz'dəɾit']
    yə-s-dər-y-t'
    3si-1s-know-PRS-DYN
    I know it.

(287) ['dəra]
    dər-ra
    know-MAS
    to know, knowing

This set of facts suggests that agreement with the causative subject and agreement with the base subject in the causative construction share some property not shared with other ergative agreement projections. My analysis provides an easy account of what this property is. The ergative projections in which dissimilation occurs are those which immediately dominate the causative VP, or immediately dominate an ergative projection which immediately dominates the causative VP. This structure results in head movement (substitution) of the causative V° into ERG°, and then into a second ERG° if there is one. Ergative-causative dissimilation thus occurs when (1) the ergative projection is headed by third-person plural features, and (2) a causative V° incorporates (substitutes) into it, either directly or after first incorporating into an intervening ERG°.[129] This accounts for why the dissimilation can be nonlocal, since it is a result of the causative head incorporating into a particular type of agreement projection, and not a linear requirement on a string of phones.

If this analysis of causative-ergative dissimilation is correct, it provides further support for the position of the ergative agreement projection which mediates agreement with the base subject as higher than the causative verb. This in turn provides additional support for the free generation of ergative agreement phrases, since there is nothing which could directly

---

[128] I normally transcribe this phoneme as [r], even though it is generally a flap [ɾ]. The transcriptions in (286) and (287) are narrower.

[129] The transparency of an intervening ERGP for this dissimilation is reminiscent of the claim that the features of an inflectional head disappear once checked (Chomsky 1992).

license one in this position if specific heads license agreement projections based on their transitivity or some other feature.[130]

4.1.3 The causative of ditransitive dynamic verbs

It is unusual for a language to allow the morphological causative of a ditransitive verb, yet Abaza does. The primary difficulty in allowing the causative of a ditransitive verb is that there is insufficient means to assign Case to all the arguments. My analysis for Abaza, however, allows the free generation of ergative agreement projections, so that enough agreement phrases can be generated to license all four arguments in this construction. The analysis, thus, correctly predicts that Abaza should allow the causative of ditransitive verbs.

Section 4.1.3.1 presents the relevant data and the corresponding underlying structure. The analysis is presented in §4.1.3.2. The causative of a ditransitive verb involves four arguments, all of which must move to agreement specifiers. This movement is nested, which provides further support for the Nesting Condition.

4.1.3.1 Data. The ditransitive verb, t 'give', can occur with the causative prefix. In a noncausative ditransitive, the direct object is registered in the absolute series, the subject is registered in the ergative series closest to the root, and the indirect object is registered in the second ergative series, as in (288). The causative from this is formed in the usual way. The causative prefix is added to the immediate left of the verb root, and the causative subject is registered in the ergative series to the immediate left of the causative prefix. The direct object is registered in the absolute series. The subject and indirect object of the base verb are registered in the ergative series to the left of the ergative series which registers agreement with the causative subject, in the same order as they occur in simple ditransitives. This can be seen in (289).

(288) yə-l-rə-tə-t'
   3si-3sf-3p-give-DYN
   They gave it to her.

---

[130]If ergative agreement projections were, in fact, licensed only by particular heads having sufficient argument structure to require them, then the causative verb must somehow be able to license two ergative agreement projections, even though it is "only" transitive, selecting a VP complement.

4.1 The causative of dynamic verbs

(289) *yə-l-d-sə-rə-ta-t'*
3si-3sf-3p-1s-CAUS-give-DYN
I made them give it to her.

My framework predicts an underlying structure for the causative of a ditransitive in which three ergative agreement projections dominate the causative VP. The free instantiation of ergative agreement phrases allows there to be three ergative phrases. They must all be higher than the causative verb, for the same reasons as discussed above, namely morpheme order and Li's Generalization. The underlying structure for the causative of a ditransitive is thus as in (290).[131]

---

[131] Unfortunately, I have no examples of the causative of a ditransitive with overt arguments to verify the word order predictions of this structure.

(290)

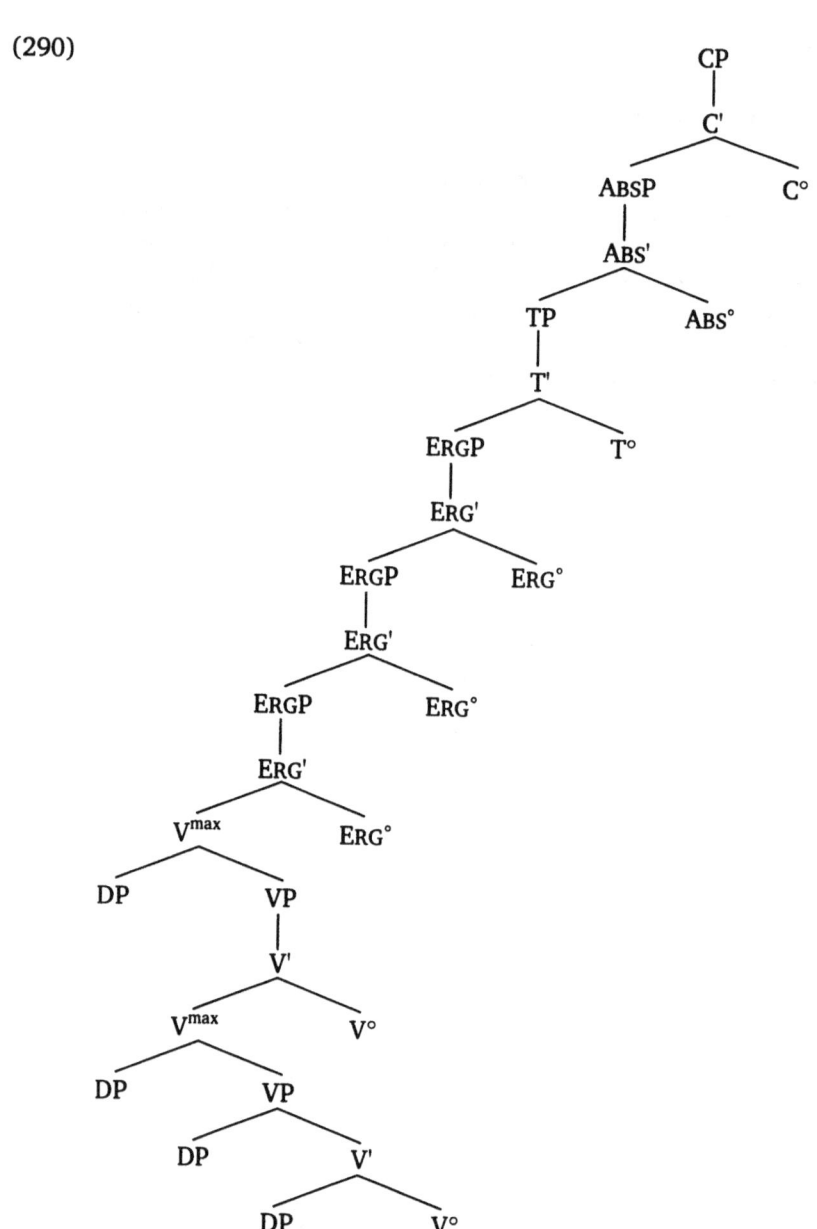

4.1.3.2 Nesting paths. In chapter 2 I argued that the absolutive agreement projection is higher than the ergative agreement projection. In a normal transitive verb, this requires a pattern of movement in which the subject's path to the specifier of the ergative agreement projection is nested within the path of the direct object's movement to the specifier of the agreement projection. This pattern is supported by the case of simple ditransitives and by the case of the causative of transitives, in which there is nested movement to three agreement specifiers. The nested movement of four arguments in the causative of ditransitives, as in (291), provides still further support for the Nesting Condition.

(291)

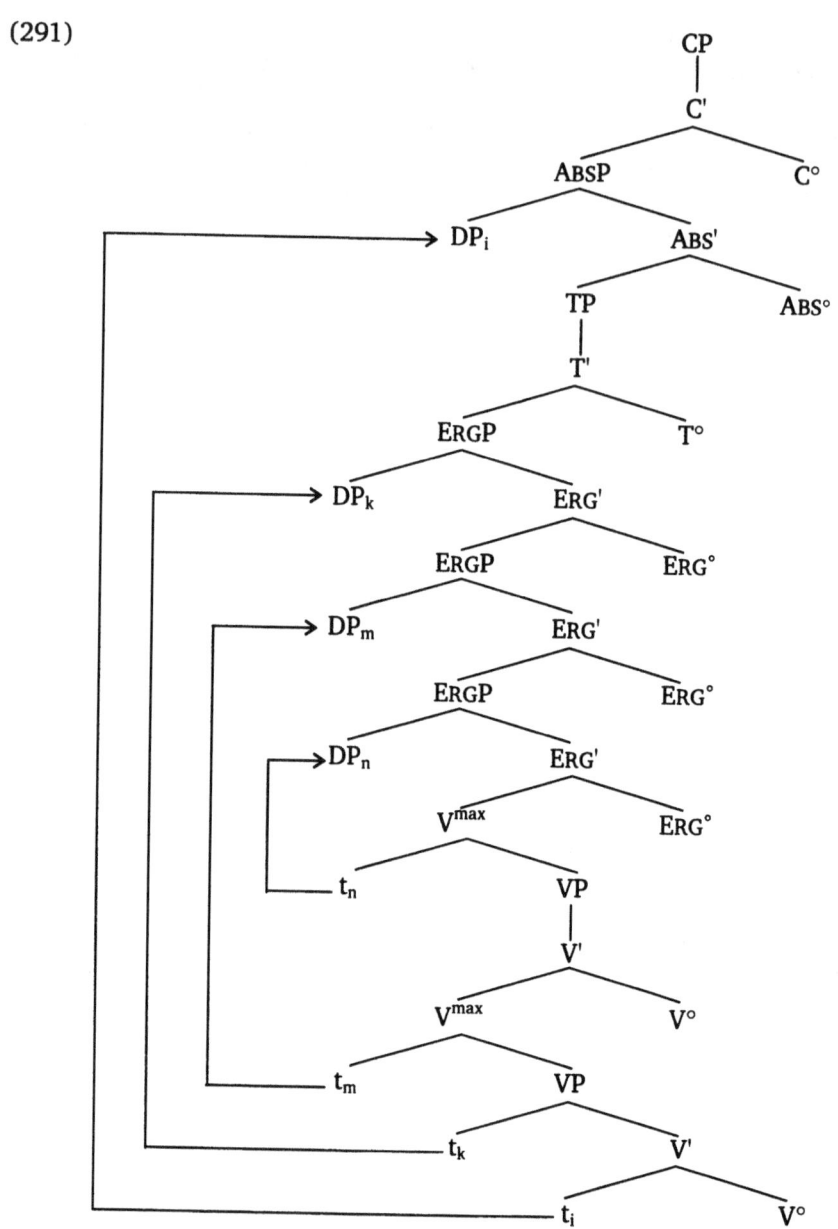

In the underlying lexical structure of (290), it is in principle possible to turn the order of the agreement projections upside down, with three ergative agreement projections at the top, and an absolutive agreement

4.1 The causative of dynamic verbs

projection at the bottom of the range of functional phrases. The movement of the DPs to their respective agreement specifiers would thus be crossing, but each movement would be across three argument positions, either underlying or the specifier of an agreement projection. The paths would be as follows:

$[_{\text{ERGP}} \text{DP}_1 \, [_{\text{ERGP}} \text{DP}_2 \, [_{\text{ERGP}} \text{DP}_3 \, [_{\text{ABSP}} \text{DP}_4 \, [_{\text{V}_{\max}} t_1 \, [_{\text{V}_{\max}} t_2 \, [_{\text{VP}} t_3 \, [_{\text{V}'} t_4 \, \text{V}°]]]]]]]]$.

I argued in chapter 2 against the Minimalist Program position (Chomsky 1992) which claims that the locus of ergative agreement is higher than the locus of absolutive agreement. Chomsky's original motivation for proposing this relationship was to allow the legal movement of both subject and direct object in terms of his Shortest Path requirement. Having three, or even four, arguments which must move to agreement specifiers poses a serious difficulty for such a system. With more than two agreement projections, the first two which move "fill up" all of the available specifier positions, so domain extension will not allow the third (or fourth) argument to move across these lower specifier positions.[132] This removes an important argument used in favor of positing the ergative agreement projection higher than the absolutive agreement projection.

The causative data strengthens this argument. It could be argued for the simple ditransitive cases that the indirect object receives Case in some way other than through movement to an agreement specifier, such as by inherent Case within VP. This would have made it possible to maintain the constraints on movement found within the Minimalist Program. With the causative of a ditransitive verb, however, it is much more difficult to maintain that all but two of the arguments receive inherent Case, and are licensed *in situ*. Both the base subject and direct object, as well as the causative subject, should receive Case in the normal way, i.e., in the specifiers of agreement projections, which requires at least two DPs to move out of the lower VP across the higher VP's subject, an impossibility under current Minimalist assumptions.

Note that the indirect object is structurally higher than the direct object in its underlying position. This is in contrast with the proposal made by Bowers (1993), in which the direct object is structurally higher than the indirect object. For an analysis with complete nesting, as I propose, or for an analysis with complete crossing (in which the highest argument ends up in the highest agreement specifier, the second highest argument in the second highest agreement specifier, and so on), positing the indirect object higher than the direct object allows for the movement patterns to be

---

[132]Recall the discussion in §2.4.2.1.

completely consistent. If the direct object is higher, as Bowers proposes, this requires a movement pattern to agreement specifiers which is neither crossing, in a way that mirrors the underlying hierarchy, nor nesting. All relationships except that between the direct and indirect object would be nesting, and that between the two objects would be crossing. It is unclear how to motivate this difference in a principled way. I take this as strong evidence for the phrase structure having the indirect object higher than the direct object, as opposed to the reverse.

4.2 Reflexives

The behavior of reflexives in Abaza supports the analysis of the causative construction as syntactic, rather than as purely morphological. Section 4.2.1 gives an account of the general morphological reflexive construction in Abaza. Section 4.2.2 shows how the reflexive facts interact with the causative construction, and how this supports a syntactic analysis.

4.2.1 General account

Normal transitive verbs in Abaza may be reflexivized morphologically.[133] This is accomplished through the use of the reflexive prefix, č-, which occurs in the position normally occupied by the absolutive agreement series. This reflexive prefix replaces agreement with the object. There is no overt (syntactic) object allowed in reflexive constructions. Reflexive verbs are syntactically and morphologically transitive, as the subject is registered through ergative agreement. The reflexive prefix, č-, may occur with subjects of any and all person and number combinations.[134]

---

[133]There is also a syntactic reflexive, in which the position to be reflexivized is occupied by the lexical word qa 'head', obligatorily possessed by the antecedent. Normal third-person singular irrational agreement is registered with this DP.

    s-qa   y-a-s-tə-y-t'
    1s-head 3si-3si-1s-give-PRS-DYN
    I give it to myself.

This construction will not be discussed further here. It is generally used in cases where the morphological reflexive is unavailable.

[134]These reflexive forms historically developed from a form in which the reflexive prefix occurred between the absolutive and ergative prefixes, e.g., s-čə-s-ba-d for (292a), with the subsequent loss of the absolutive prefix (Sergei Pazov, pers. comm.). Such forms are still found in Abkhaz (see Hewitt 1989:77).

4.2 Reflexives

(292) a. čə-s-ba-d   I saw myself.
     b. čə-b-ba-d   You (f) saw yourself.
     c. čə-w-ba-d   You (m) saw yourself.
     d. čə-l-ba-d   She saw herself.
     e. čə-y-ba-d   He saw himself.
     f. č-a-ba-d   It saw itself.
     g. čə-h-ba-d   We saw ourselves.
     h. čə-ʃʷ-ba-d   You (PL) saw yourselves.
     i. čə-r-ba-d   They saw themselves.

Transitive verbs select an object (many of them obligatorily), and they assign a θ-role to this complement position. In order to fulfill both syntactic and semantic (θ-role) selectional restrictions, there must be a DP in the normal complement (object) position of a reflexive verb. Because of the indexing properties of this DP, it must be an anaphor, and because there is never an overt object, this element must be null. I therefore conclude that there is a null (reflexive) anaphor in Abaza which occupies the object position, i.e., sister to V°, in reflexive constructions.

There are at least three possible accounts of the reflexive prefix in Abaza compatible with these assumptions.[135] These include analyses in which (1) the reflexive prefix is the head of an anaphoric DP and this head incorporates into the C° complex from the specifier of ABSP; (2) the reflexive prefix is the head of an anaphoric DP and this head incorporates into V° from the underlying object position; and (3) the reflexive prefix is an absolutive agreement prefix. The first two of these are clearly problematic for Abaza, as I now demonstrate.

One possible account of reflexives is that the reflexive prefix is itself the anaphor, in the form of an overt clitic, or X°, č-, which adjoins to the [[ABS°-[[ERG°-V°]-T°]]-C°] complex. The phrase headed by the reflexive anaphor must be in a position c-commanded by the subject at s-structure in order to satisfy the Binding Conditions. Generating the anaphor in object position satisfies this condition, and selectional and theta requirements as well. One possible route for the anaphor head to the position adjoined to the complex of verbal heads is for the whole object DP to first move to the absolutive specifier, and then for its head to incorporate into the verb complex from this specifier position.

The problem for this analysis is how to prevent overt absolutive agreement from co-occurring with the reflexive prefix. Obligatory null absolutive agreement is a possible way to accomplish this. Recall that the

---

[135]An analysis in which reflexives are lexically derived intransitives is inadequate for Abaza since the subject is registered in the ergative series.

conditions for null absolutive agreement are that the XP registered by null absolutive agreement (1) be either third-person singular irrational or third-person plural and (2) occur overtly to the immediate left of the complex on which absolutive agreement is registered. In this construction the reflexive clitic would necessarily be to the immediate left of the verb complex, and it is possible that the anaphor is registered by (possibly default) third-person singular irrational features. The conditions for null absolutive agreement, however, would not be met at the appropriate level. Movement of an anaphoric DP to the absolutive specifier, like the movement of all arguments to agreement specifiers, occurs at LF, yet the conditions for null absolutive agreement cannot make reference to LF positions. Null absolutive agreement, therefore, cannot be used to rule out overt absolutive agreement if the reflexive head cliticizes from the specifier of AbsP position. I reject this proposal because it does not account for the complementarity of the reflexive prefix and the absolutive prefix.

A related possibility also treats the reflexive prefix as an anaphor which incorporates into the verb complex, but instead of incorporating after the object moves to the specifier of AbsP, it incorporates directly from the underlying object position. The anaphor head thus cliticizes to V° before V° has moved from its underlying position, and then raises with V° as it moves through the series of heads in its extended projection by substitution. This requires a meaningful distinction between head movement by adjunction (for clitics) and head movement by substitution (where the word is formed in the lexicon and the relevant features are checked in each position). As in the related analysis, overt absolutive agreement would be excluded because the object, as a clitic, is always to the immediate left of the verb complex, making null absolutive agreement obligatory.[136] In order to satisfy the EPP, and possibly for Case reasons,[137] the empty (i.e., lacking overt specifier and complement, and headed by a trace) object DP, out of which the head, č-, has moved, must move to the specifier of AbsP.

One difficulty with this analysis is that ECP issues concerning the licensing of the trace of D° arise. A second problem with this analysis is that it wrongly predicts that the reflexive prefix should correspond only to an anaphor in direct object position, since head movement from a specifier position, specifically from subject position, is ruled out in general (see Travis 1984, Baker 1988). The reflexive prefix, however, can correspond

---

[136] Both of these analyses falsely predict that absolutive agreement should be possible between the reflexive prefix and the rest of the verb complex in extremely slow speech.

[137] It is possible that the object DP receives Case through the incorporation of its head. See Baker (1988) and Rizzi and Roberts (1989). Movement to the specifier of AbsP would thus be motivated entirely by the EPP.

4.2 Reflexives

to an anaphor in subject position, specifically the lower subject of the causative of an intransitive verb, as in (293). I reject this analysis since it makes false predictions.[138]

(293) a-sabəy-kʷa   y-an-qʷmar-wa   č-də-r-p'ayə-y-d
      DEF-child-PL   3p-when-play-PTC   REFL-3p-CAUS-dirty-PRS-DYN
      The children get dirty while playing.

The final possible analysis treats the reflexive prefix as built into the verb complex in the lexicon. This prefix adds to the verb complex a feature, say [+REFL], which must be checked during the derivation as with other similar features. The null anaphor is the only lexical element having this feature, so it alone can satisfy this checking requirement. The question arises as to where the checking of the feature [+REFL] occurs. Such features are generally checked in the specifier-head relationship within a functional projection. The Mirror Principle applies to Abaza such that morphology more distant from the root is associated with structurally higher syntactic structure. Because the reflexive prefix is always the outermost prefix in the verb complex, the functional projection which mediates the checking of the feature [+REFL] must be higher than other projections associated with prefixal morphology. I adopt the natural solution that checking of the feature [+REFL] takes place within the absolutive agreement projection. I assume that φ-features are those features mediated by agreement projections, which means that [±REFL] is a φ-feature, parallel to the other agreement features in the absolutive paradigm. This not only accounts for its high position structurally, since ABSP is the highest projection involved in prefixal morphology,[139] but it also

---

[138]This argument does not go through under Chomsky's (1986a) definition of L-marking, in which the specifier of an L-marked category is itself L-marked. The causative V° L-marks its complement, VP, so the specifier of VP is L-marked as well. D° can move from the specifier of the complement VP to the higher (causative) V°, since DP is not a barrier by virtue of being L-marked. This analysis is not available if the subject position adjoined to VP is not a specifier position.

[139]Only CP is higher, and it is associated with suffixal morphology.

accounts for the fact that the reflexive prefix is in complementary distribution with the absolutive agreement prefixes.[140]

Reflexive φ-features are never associated with an argument registered in an ergative series. I take this to be a morphological gap in the ergative series. For evidence that this is a morphological gap, and not subject to purely syntactic principles, see the discussion of subjects of the complement of the causative verb in §4.2.2 and the discussion of lexical inverted verbs in chapter 6.

This analysis requires that the Binding Conditions apply at s-structure, since at LF the c-command relations will be reversed, so that at LF an anaphor which originates as the complement of a simple transitive verb will c-command its antecedent which originates as the subject of that verb, in clear violation of the Binding Conditions.

4.2.2 Reflexives and the causative construction

As already seen in (293), the causative of an intransitive verb can be reflexivized. In such cases, the causative subject is registered in the ergative series, as usual, and the base subject is registered with the (absolutive) reflexive prefix. The two arguments are necessarily co-indexed. Further examples can be seen in (294)–(296), where the causative and reflexive prefixes are in bold. The first two of these examples are causatives of stative forms.

(294) č-ʃa-y-rə-pʃdza-wa   d-alaga-d
      REFL-DIR-3sm-CAUS-pretty-PTC 3sr-begin-DYN
      He began to get ready.   NART, 63

(295) b-gʷə   bə-m-rədzə-n   s-hʷa-n
      2sf-heart   2sf-NEG-lose-DEP   1s-say-NEG.IMP

---

[140]The single exception to this complementarity is that the reflexive prefix may occur with (nominal) masdars, where absolutive prefixes are not possible. I would argue, however, that the reflexive of (nominal) masdars is formed lexically. Evidence for this is that a reflexivized masdar may be possessed, and the ergative series which registers agreement with the possessor occurs *outside* the reflexive marker. This is completely impossible in all forms which allow normal absolutive agreement, as in the following example..

s-č-kʷʼaba-ra
1s-REFL-wash-MAS
my self-washing

4.2 Reflexives

    č-ʕa-sə-r-qac'a-t'
    REFL-DIR-1s-CAUS-courage-DYN
    "Don't lose heart," I said and plucked up my courage.

(296) alkaʃ   yə-ʕʷza-čʷ-i   yar-i   pʃa-qənhʷə-ta
       Alkash 3sm-friend-RPL-and 3sm-and wind-twist-as

    č-d-rə-dz-x-t'
    REFL-3p-CAUS-disappear-again-DYN
    Alkash and his friends disappeared [again] as a whirlwind. GAL, 186

With the reflexive form of the causative of a transitive verb, the reflexive prefix in the absolute position registers agreement with the base direct object, the inner ergative registers agreement with the causative subject, and the outer ergative registers agreement with the base subject, exactly as in nonreflexive causative forms. Crucial for our purposes, a reflexive direct object can only be co-indexed with the subject of the base verb, and not with the causative subject. This can be seen in (283), repeated here as (297), and in (298) and (299).

(297) čə-nqʷ-d-də-r-ga-wn
       REFL-PV-3p-3p-CAUS-look.after-PST
       They made them$_i$ nurse themselves$_i$.
       *They$_i$ made them nurse them$_j$/themselves$_j$. GAL, 180

(298) č-y-s-rə-psʃ'a-t'
       REFL-3sm-1s-CAUS-rest-DYN
       I made him$_i$ rest (himself$_i$).   čpsʃ'a 'rest' (lexically reflexive)

(299) č-y-s-rə-kʷ'aba-t'
       REFL-3sm-1s-CAUS-wash-DYN
       I made him$_i$ wash himself$_i$.
       *I$_i$ made him wash me$_i$/myself$_i$.

The fact that a reflexive base direct object must be bound by the base subject supports my analysis of causatives as syntactically involving two VPs. The reason is that according to Binding Condition A, the reflexive anaphor must be bound in its Governing Category.[141] If the VP complement to the causative verb counts as a Governing Category, the co-indexation possibilities are accounted for directly. But the VP complement of the causative verb

---

[141] Recall the discussion from §1.2.6.

can only count as a Governing Category if it is a syntactic complement to the causative verb, and not if the causative is lexicalized.[142]

Further support that causatives are not lexically formed monoclausal ditransitive verbs can be derived from the fact that reflexivized simple ditransitive verbs have indexing distinct from that in reflexivized causatives of transitives. The direct object is necessarily co-indexed with the subject, registered by the inner ergative prefix, not with the indirect object, registered by the outer ergative prefix, as in (300) and (301).[143] This differs from the causative of a transitive verb, in which the reflexive is co-indexed with the argument registered by the outer ergative prefix.

(300) č-yə-y-t-d
REFL-3sm-2sm-give-DYN
He submitted to him. (lit., He$_i$ gave himself$_i$ to him$_{j/*i}$.)
(*He gave him$_i$ to himself$_j$.)

(301) allah č-yə-ʃʷ-t
God REFL-3sm-2p-give
Submit to God! (lit., [You$_i$] Give yourself$_i$ to God!)
(*Give God$_i$ to himself$_i$!)

It is possible for the subject of an intransitive VP complement to the causative verb to be registered with the reflexive prefix, as in (293)–(296). It is not possible for the subject of a transitive VP complement to the causative verb to be registered with a reflexive prefix, as in (302).

(302) *d-č-s-rə-kʷʼaba-tʼ
3sr-REFL-1s-CAUS-wash-DYN
(I made myself wash him/her.)

---

[142] A Governing Category (GC) for an element, α, is the minimal domain containing α and a governor for α. In Chomsky (1986b), the "minimal domain" of the GC must be a Complete Functional Complex (CFC), in which all of the grammatical functions compatible with a head (the lexical governor of α) are realized. Under this interpretation, the VP complement to the causative verb is a GC. In Chomsky (1981), the GC must also contain an accessible subject for α. Under this interpretation, the complement VP of a causative verb is not a GC, since the subject is not an accessible subject, which is a subject in the specifier of INFL. I therefore adopt the definition of GC as a CFC from Chomsky (1986b), since it correctly accounts for the Abaza data.

[143] The reflexive of the verb t 'give' is used idiomatically to mean 'submit'. This same reflexive verb without an indirect object, i.e., 'to give oneself', is used euphemistically for 'commit suicide'.

Since the two subject positions are in the same structural configuration with respect to the binding conditions, the impossibility of reflexive transitive subjects, as opposed to the possibility of intransitive reflexivized subjects, cannot be attributed simply to configurational differences. The presence of an object within the complement VP will not affect the governing category of the subject of that VP. The main difference between these two types of subjects is that one is registered in the absolutive series and one is registered in the ergative series. This supports the claim that there is a morphological gap in the ergative series such that there is no reflexive form.

4.3 The causative of statives

Section 4.1 demonstrates that the causative verb may select as complement a saturated dynamic lexical verb phrase, including a subject plus all the other arguments of the verb, regardless of how many there are. It is also possible in Abaza to form causatives from stative predications. The formation of the causative of stative predications is like the formation of the causative of dynamic verbs. The causative prefix, *r-*, is prefixed to the lexical root, and the causative subject is registered in the ergative series to the left of this prefix. As in the causative of dynamic verbs, the remaining agreement pattern is basically unchanged from the corresponding noncausative pattern.

I propose an analysis for the causative of stative predications parallel to that given above for the causative of dynamic verbs, namely that the causativized predication is complement to the causative verb. The only modification this requires in the analysis I have developed is the simple extension of the categories that the causative verb may select, from dynamic verbs to all (saturated) predicates, i.e., lexical X^{max}. Note, however, that causativized predications of nonverbal predicates having an argument, i.e., possessed nouns and transitive postpositions (cf. §3.1.2), are not possible. I argue that this falls out from the same principles and structure which cause the apparently distinct pattern of agreement for these two constructions in the simple stative construction.

Stative predicates having no internal argument are discussed in §4.3.1. Their analysis is straightforward. Stative verbs, which behave in exactly the same way as dynamic verbs, are discussed in §4.3.2. Nonverbal predicates with an argument are impossible as complement to the causative verb; this is discussed in §4.3.3.

4.3.1 The causative of intransitive stative verbs

The causativization of stative predications having a single argument is highly productive. It is possible with stative adjectives, nouns, and verbs, plus those categories I treat as intransitive postpositions. As with dynamic verbs, the causative of statives is formed with the causative prefix r-, which occurs to the immediate left of the lexical root. The causative subject is registered in the ergative agreement series to the immediate left of the causative prefix. For stative predicates having no internal argument, the subject of the predication is registered in the absolutive series in both causative and noncausative forms. Compare the stative adjective in (303) with the causative form in (304).

(303) a-dzə   qʷaʃə-p'
DEF-water   mud-STP
The water is muddy.   GAL, 105

(304) a-dzə   d-rə-qʷaʃ-d
DEF-water   3p-CAUS-mud-DYN
They muddied the water.   GAL, 105

Compare also the stative intransitive verb in (305) with its corresponding causative form in (306).

(305) d-čʷ'a-p'
3sr-sit-STP
S/he is sitting.   GAL, 179

(306) d-yə-r-čʷ'a-t'
3sr-3sm-CAUS-DYN
He seated him/her.   GAL, 179

The causative of a nominal stative is shown in (307).[144]

---

[144]Note that 'I caused him to be a smith' with the interpretation that 'I taught him to be a smith' requires the use of the factitive construction, as in the following example. An analysis of the factitive construction is beyond the scope of this study.

ӡʲəy-ta   d-y-sə-r-čʲpa-t'
smith-FAC   3sr-3sm-1s-CAUS-do-DYN
I caused him to be a smith. (= I taught him work as a smith.)

4.3 The causative of statives

(307) d-sə-r-ʒʲəy-t'
   3sr-1s-CAUS-smith-DYN
   I caused him to be a smith. (=I gave him work as a smith.)

As can be seen from these examples, a causative verb complex formed from a stative predicate requires dynamic verbal tense, aspect, and mood morphology. This is directly accounted for by my analysis, since the head of the verbal extended projection is the dynamic causative verb. The stative predication is merely a complement to this lexical head, and does not affect the dynamicity of the head which selects it.

I propose to account for the causativized intransitive stative predications by modifying the selectional properties of the causative verb to select any lexical X^{max}, including stative X^{max} as well as dynamic V^{max}. X^{max} must be a saturated predicate, including a subject. The underlying structure of the causative of an adjectival stative predicate is given in (308). Causatives of intransitive stative predicates of other categories are identical except for the category of the complement of the causative verb.

(308)

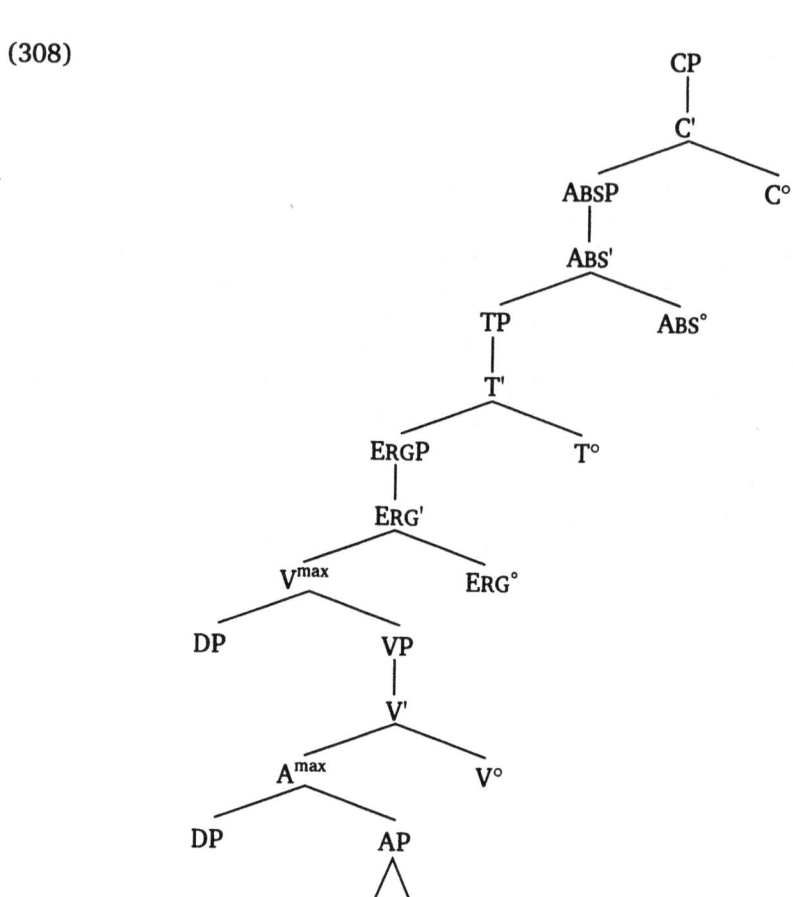

From this structure the causative subject moves into the specifier of the ergative agreement projection, and the subject of the adjectival predication moves into the specifier of the absolutive agreement projection, consistent with the Nesting Condition.

4.3.2 The causative of transitive stative verbs

The causative may have as complement a transitive stative V^{max}, and the construction is identical to the causative of transitive dynamic verbs.[145] Examples can be seen in (309) and (310). The unmarked word order is exactly what is expected in the proposed structure, with the causative subject first, followed by the base subject, and the base object closest to the verb complex.

(309) axč^ja   l-d-r-taqə-y-d
      money 3sf-3p-CAUS-want-PRS-DYN
      They cause her to want money.

(310) awəy hara wandər-k' hə-y-r-əma-y-d
      s/he   we   car-INDEF 1p-3sm-CAUS-have-PRS-DYN
      He causes us to have a car.

Nothing further needs to be said to account for these. The extension of the selectional properties of the causative verb to include lexical X^{max} irrespective of category or dynamicity was discussed above. The selection of X^{max} should not make reference to the internal structure of XP, to see whether there is a complement to $X°$, so it is predicted that transitive stative verbs should be able to occur in this construction just as freely as intransitive stative verbs.

The agreement pattern is accounted for in the same manner as the agreement for the causative of transitive dynamic verbs. That is, two ergative agreement phrases are generated in the extended projection of the causative verb. The causative subject moves into the specifier of the lower of these, the base subject moves in the specifier of the higher one, and the base object moves into the absolutive specifier. Again, this follows the familiar nesting pattern, in observance of the Nesting Condition.

---

[145]Even though examples of causatives of transitive stative verbs are possible, they are quite rare and pragmatically strange. Much more natural is the use of the causative with a stative verb which has been dynamicized with the suffix *-xa*. The more natural counterparts of (309) and (310) are (i) and (ii), respectively.

  (i) axč^ja   l-d-r-taq-xa-y-d
      money 3sf-3p-CAUS-want-become-PRS-DYN
      They cause her to want money.

  (ii) awəy hara wandər-k' hə-y-r-əma-xa-y-d
      s/he   we   car-INDEF 1p-3sm-CAUS-have-become-PRS-DYN
      He causes us to have a car.

4.3.3 Possessed nouns, transitive postpositions, and the causative

The causative verb selects lexical X^{max}. This accurately accounts for the fact that it may take as complement any dynamic V^{max} (§4.1), a stative X^{max} of any category so long as there are no arguments within XP (§4.2.1), and a stative V^{max} regardless of the internal structure of VP (§4.2.2). This covers all categorial possibilities of X^{max} except the nonverbal categories of X^{max} having arguments internal to XP, i.e., nouns with possessors and postpositions with objects. These are not possible as complements to the causative verb. I show now that this is predicted by the analysis presented in chapter 3.

Possessed nouns and transitive postpositions may not host causative morphology. A possessed nominal stative predicate is possible, as in (311), but this cannot be causativized, regardless of whether the ergative prefix registering agreement with the possessor occurs before or after the causative prefix, as in (312) and (313).[146] Likewise, a postposition with its object is a legitimate stative predicate, as in (314), but it cannot be causativized, regardless of the position of the ergative series registering agreement with the object of the postposition with respect to the causative prefix, as in (315) and (316).

---

[146]In order to express the causative sense of these forms, one of the factitive constructions in (i), (ii), or (iii) must be used. Compare these to the construction in footnote 143.

(i) *pa-ta də-s-čʲpa-t'*
    son-FAC 3sr-1s-do-DYN
    I made him my son.

(ii) *pa-ta d-y-sə-r-čʲpa-t'*
    son-FAC 3sr-3sm-1s-CAUS-do-DYN
    I caused him to become my son.

(iii) *də-s-pa-ta d-y-sə-r-čʲpa-t'*
    3sr-1s-son-FAC 3sr-3sm-1s-CAUS-do-DYN
    I caused him to become my son.

The use of the dynamicizing suffix *-xa* cannot make a possessed noun into a stative predicate which can be causativized, as in (iv). This follows from the fact that this suffix cannot be used with possessed nouns in general.

(iv) **d-lə-r-s-pa-xa-t'*
    3sr-3sf-CAUS-1s-son-BECOME-DYN
    (She caused him to become my son.)

4.3 The causative of statives

(311) *də-s-pa-b*
3sr-1s-son-STP
He is my son

(312) **də-sə-r-s-pa-t'*
3sr-1s-CAUS-1s-son-DYN
(I caused him to become my son.)

(313) **də-sə-s-r-pa-t'*
3sr-1s-1s-CAUS-son-DYN
(I caused him to become my son.)

(314) *a-sara   d-rə-c-p'*
DEF-sheep   3sr-3p-with-STP
S/he is with the sheep.   GAL, 103

(315) **d-y-r-rə-cə-y-d*
3sr-3sm-CAUS-3p-with-PRS-DYN
(He causes him/her to be with the sheep.)

(316) **d-d-y-rə-cə-y-d*
3sr-3p-3sm-CAUS-with-PRS-DYN
(He causes him/her to be with the sheep.)

Recall from §3.3.2 that exactly these two constructions have an apparently exceptional agreement pattern with respect to the Nesting Condition. I argued there that the subject is predicated of a COMPLETE predicate in these cases, so that it adjoins to ERGP, and that this accounts for the fact that agreement with the subject of the predication occurs outside of agreement with the possessor or postpositional object, since the resulting movement paths will not interact at all.

If the causative verb selects an N^{max} or a P^{max} which has an internal argument, i.e., a possessor or object, then the selected X^{max} will necessarily contain an ERGP because of the requirement that a subject adjoin to a complete predicate to form a nonverbal stative predication. This configuration, however, is ruled out within the general framework I have adopted. The reason is that the lexical head incorporates into ERG°, and this complex head then incorporates into the causative head, V°. This is a violation of Li's Generalization, in that a functional head, ERG°, is incorporating into a lexical head, V°. The fact that possessed nouns and postpositions with objects cannot be causativized thus falls out from my analysis.

4.4 Subject positions

In chapter 2, I adopted without argument the Koopman and Sportiche (1988) analysis of subjects for both dynamic verbs and stative predicates of any category. In this analysis the subject occurs in a position adjoined to the lexical XP, creating a node X^{max}. Koopman and Sportiche claim that this type of adjoined position is not an A-bar position. We return now to an account of why this is the optimal configuration for subjects in Abaza.

Li's Generalization is a restriction on head movement based on the lexical versus functional distinction. Lexical heads may incorporate into either lexical or functional heads, but functional heads may incorporate only into other functional heads. The movement of a functional head into a lexical head is forbidden. This generalization is well motivated for Abaza. It accounts for the nonoccurrence of various forms in Abaza which might otherwise be expected on purely structural grounds, and it accounts for the relative ordering of particular constituents as reflected in the morphology. Specifically, I showed in §4.3.3 that Li's Generalization accounts for why transitive postpositions and possessed nouns cannot be causativized. In chapter 5, Li's Generalization is shown to account for the possible relative order of the causative and potential prefixes. In chapter 7, Li's Generalization is used to motivate movement so as to allow the incorporation of a functional head into another functional head instead of into a lexical head.

The causative construction involves a lexical head selecting a saturated predicate as a complement. The saturated predicate must include a subject. This means that structurally, the subject must be within the maximal phrase of the predication, whatever that maximal phrase is. It would be a violation of the locality of θ-assignment if, for example, the subject of the predicate were located above the causative verb which has the predication as its complement.

In the causative construction, the head of the complement of the causative verb incorporates into the causative verb head. Under the Koopman and Sportiche analysis in which the subject is adjoined to the lexical XP, the incorporation of the head of the causative complement into the causative head is movement of a lexical head to another lexical head, which is allowed under Li's Generalization.

Partly in order to bring the position of subjects in line with more standard assumptions about X-bar structure, various alternatives have been proposed in which the subject occupies the specifier of some functional head immediately dominating the lexical XP (e.g., Bowers 1993 proposes a Predicational phrase, PrP, and Kratzer 1994 proposes a Voice phrase). If there is some functional projection (regardless of the category label) dominating the lexical XP, however, the Abaza causative facts become problematic. The reason is that the resulting structure would require the lexical head of the complement of the causative verb to incorporate into the functional head of the projection which provides the specifier position for the subject. This is allowed according to Li's Generalization. The resulting complex of heads, however, is functional, and this functional head then must incorporate into the lexical causative verb, in violation of Li's Generalization. I conclude, then, that the Koopman and Sportiche analysis is correct for Abaza.

4.5 Double causatives

If the causative prefix *r-* corresponds to a lexical verb which selects a lexical XP, then the prediction is made that double causatives, i.e., the causative of a causative, should be possible in Abaza. This prediction appears to be true. Consider the forms in (317)–(319). The first of these is a simple intransitive dynamic verb. The next is a single causative form based on the simple intransitive form. The final form is a double causative based on the single causative form. The two causative markers occur together to the immediate left of the root.[147] The subject of the outer causative is registered in the ergative series to the immediate left of the causative prefixes, and the subject of the inner causative is registered in a second ergative series to the immediate left of that. As with other causative constructions, the subject of the intransitive base verb is registered in the absolutive series.

(317) *y-k'aʃʷa-t'*
 3si-fall-DYN
 It fell (down).

---

[147]Note that the two causative morphemes do not dissimilate. They both remain [r] in spite of being adjacent. A third-person plural subject agreement prefix, however, does dissimilate, as seen in (319).

(318) y-k'a-y-rə-ʃʷ-t'
  3si-PV-3sm-CAUS-fall-DYN
  He threw it (down). (lit., He caused it to fall.) GAL, 181

(319) y-k'a-y-də-r-rə-ʃʷ-t'
  3si-PV-3sm-3p-CAUS-CAUS-fall-DYN
  They caused him to throw it (down). GAL, 181

It would be possible to give a syntactic analysis for these double causative constructions in which the higher causative verb selects the lower causative verb, which in turn selects its intransitive VP complement. Two ergative agreement projections would be generated above the higher causative verb, and the subject of the higher causative would move into the specifier of the lower ergative agreement projection while the subject of the lower causative verb would move into the specifier of the higher ergative agreement projection. The subject of the intransitive base verb would move into the specifier of the absolutive agreement projection. This movement to the specifiers of the agreement projections follows the familiar nesting pattern, and the underlying structure of these complex causatives corresponds exactly to the underlying structure of simple causatives.

Nevertheless, for the verbs which can host the double causative construction, I choose to treat the single causative in these constructions as a lexicalized form. One reason is that unlike the single causative, the double causative is not highly productive. It occurs only with certain intransitive roots, the single causative of which are common to the degree that it is not unreasonable to treat them as lexicalized. A second reason is that there is independent reason to believe that these are lexicalized forms, namely, their meaning is often noncompositional. That is, there are cases in which the simple verb root, X, plus the causative affix does not mean 'cause to X'.

The combination of simple root plus causative prefix can differ from a pure causative interpretation of the simple root. In (320) and (321), for example, the simple root $qʷəx$ means 'snatch (from the fire)', but the simple root plus the causative prefix $rqʷəx$ means 'check, examine'.

(320) y-sə-r-qʷəx-t'
  3si-1s-CAUS-snatch-DYN
  I checked it. GAL, 181

4.5 Double Causatives

(321) *y-s-də-r-r-qʷəx-t'*
   3si-1s-3p-CAUS-CAUS-snatch-DYN
   They caused me to check it.   GAL, 181

Furthermore, some cases of what appear to be simple intransitive roots plus the causative prefix do not actually correspond to any intransitive root. Consider, *rčqʷa* 'praise', for which there is no corresponding root *čqʷa*. Such a verb may host what looks like the double causative construction, as in (323).

(322) *d-sə-rčqʷa-t'*
   3sr-1s-praise-DYN
   I praised him/her.   GAL, 181

(323) *d-s-də-r-rčqʷa-t'*
   3sr-1s-3p-CAUS-praise-DYN
   They caused me to praise him/her.   GAL, 181

Tabulova (1976) lists several additional verbs which she considers to constitute frozen causatives, including: *rəyy* 'pull down (into pieces), grind', *rəfa* 'wind, twist', *rʃʷʃʷa* 'shake, wag (tail)', *rčap'a* 'smash, crush', *rqʷʷč'* 'crumble, press, knead', *rč'aÿʲ* 'repair', *rÿʲa* 'condemn, doom, slander'.

A number of verbs used commonly with the causative also allow a double causative. Consider the causative of *ca* 'go', which is *rca* 'lead', as seen in (324).[148] Various forms of 'fall' are causativized to produce verbs meaning 'drop' or 'throw', as in (318) or (325).

(324) *a-larÿʲ   a-dzqa   y-w-sə-r-r-ca-waʃ-t'*
   DEF-gray   DEF-water.source   3si-2sm-1s-CAUS-CAUS-go-FUT-DYN
   I will have you lead the Gray (horse) to the watering place. GAL, 181

---

[148]The reflexivized form of *rca* means 'behave oneself':

   bata   zak'gʲi   yə-m-hʷa-wa   č-d-yə-r-r-ca-t'
   Bata   nothing   3sm-NEG-say-PTC   REFL-3p-3sm-CAUS-CAUS-go-DYN
   Bata, without saying anything, caused them to behave themselves.   GAL, 186

Based on the few examples I have, it seems that a reflexivized double causative always results in coreference between the lower causative subject and the base subject, which is registered in the absolutive series. This is consistent with either a syntactic analysis or a lexical analysis of the double causatives.

(325) y-pha-gʲə-y   yʲaʃaʒʷ-gʲə-y   a-gʲadaʃ
     3sm-daughter-INT-and Ghashazh-INT-and   DEF-hen.house

   y-ta-d-yə-r-rə-ʃʷ-t'
   3p-in-3p-3sm-CAUS-CAUS-fall-DYN
   He caused them (servants) to throw his own daughter and
   Ghashazh into the hen house.   GAL, 181

In addition to lexicalized causative forms from intransitive verb roots, there are also lexicalized causative forms from nominal and adjectival roots. These also can have interpretations which are not entirely compositional. Consider *rbza* 'lick (off)' from *bzə* 'tongue', as in (326), and *rdzagʷa* 'grow dull, blunt' from *dzagʷa* 'toothless, dull', as in (327). Example (328) shows a causative of *rc'abərg* 'justify' from *c'abərgə* 'true', which appears to be a double causative.

(326) acxa   nqʷə-z-ga-wa   yə-mačʷ   yə-r-bzə-y-t'
      honey   PV-EWH-bear-PTC   3sm-finger   3sm-CAUS-tongue-PRS-DYN
      Whoever has something to do with honey, licks his fingers.   GAL, 182

(327) a-rəcha   y-kʷʼaya   a-baya   yə-r-dzagʷa-y-t'
      DEF-pauper 3sm-ax   DEF-rich   3sm-CAUS-dull-PRS-DYN
      The rich man dulls the ax of the pauper.   GAL, 181-2

(328) l-aʒʷa   l-ʃʷə-r-r-c'abərg-t'
      3sf-word   3sf-2p-CAUS-CAUS-true-DYN
      You made her justify her words.   GAL, 181

Although, a syntactic account of these double causatives is possible and relatively straightforward, I analyze them as the (single) causative of a lexicalized form of the (single) causative. The reasons are threefold. The double causative is not at all productive, which would be expected if this were a syntactic process reflected in the morphology. Second, all of the roots which may host the apparent double causative are intransitive, which requires a nonlocal selection by the higher causative head. Finally, some of the forms which host the double causative show independent evidence for treatment as lexicalized verbs in that their meaning is not purely compositional.

Nothing in my overall analysis of Abaza hinges on the assumption that these are lexicalized causatives, however, and a straightforward account can be given for them in terms of the analysis I propose here for causatives in general, although some sort of ad hoc feature may be required to ensure that only the correct intransitive roots may host the double causative.

4.6 Conclusion

The highly productive morphological causative in Abaza can be easily accounted for within the framework established in chapter 2. The primary analytical point is that the causative morpheme corresponds to a V° which selects an X^{max} complement. This analysis provides additional support for Li's Generalization, since no functional elements may occur between the causative verb and its lexical complement. It provides additional support for the free generation of ergative phrases, since an adequate number of agreement phrases is required to license all the arguments which can occur in this construction. Finally, this analysis provides additional support for the Nesting Condition, since in every instance the highest underlying argument ends up in the specifier of the lowest agreement projection, and the lowest underlying argument ends up in the specifier of the highest agreement projection.

We turn now to other complex constructions: derived inverted verbs in chapter 5 and lexically inverted verbs in chapter 6. These also are accounted for within the basic set of assumptions described in chapter 2 plus minimal additional assumptions. Both of these constructions can be causativized, and the interaction of each of these with the causative is accounted for within my framework without any additional assumptions or machinery.

5

Derived Inversion

The causative construction discussed in the previous chapter is a complex construction involving two VPs, but the agreement patterns of the component VPs are the same as in simple VPs. In this chapter we turn to a discussion of certain prefixes in the Abaza verbal complex which cause a rearrangement of the agreement pattern. I refer to this as DERIVED INVERSION.[149] Derived inversion is exemplified here in verbs having the most common of these prefixes, the potential. (The prefix of unintentionality, *mqa-*, behaves like the potential, with the same agreement patterns.)

The potential prefix, *z-*, indicates that the subject is able to carry out the action of the verb.[150] This includes physical and cognitive ability, as well as permission. The potential prefix is added to both stative and dynamic

---

[149]Derived inversion contrasts with lexical inversion, in which simple forms exhibit inversion without any additional affixes. (See chapter 6 for discussion.) Tabulova (1976) also categorizes the reciprocal construction as inverted. Reciprocals have a complex paradigm with many lexically determined irregularities. A full treatment of the reciprocals is beyond the scope of this study. The class of benefactives, instrumentals, locatives, and comitatives are also sometimes considered to trigger inversion, since they introduce an additional "indirect object." I analyze these in chapter 7 as incorporated postpositions.

[150]Tabulova (1976) claims that there are a few forms which have a frozen potential prefix, but which lack a potential meaning. For example, *ayk^w* 'make up one's mind about something' is used only with the potential form:

y-g^j-s-z-ayk^w-wa-m
3si-INT-1s-POT-decide-PRS-NEG
I cannot make up my mind about it.   GAL, 201

verbs.[151] It may be used with any tense and mood except the imperative (Tabulova 1976). It is used frequently with interrogatives, negation, and the subjunctive mood.

The potential prefix triggers inversion in transitive and ditransitive verbs in that the ergative prefix which registers agreement with the subject occurs further to the left than in corresponding nonpotential forms. Compare the normal and potential ditransitive forms in (329) and (330); the root and subject agreement are in bold. For the potential of an intransitive verb, the subject is registered in the absolutive series. There is no reorganization of the argument structure. Compare the normal and potential intransitive forms in (331) and (332).

(329) *yə-lə-y-ta-t'*
      3si-3sf-**3sm-give**-DYN
      He gave it to her.

(330) *y-sə-z-lə-**ta**-t'*
      3si-**1s**-POT-3sf-**give**-DYN
      I was able to give it to her.

(331) **d-ʕay**-y-d
      3sr-come-PRS-DYN
      S/he comes.

(332) *y-čʲa-nəs   yə-z-taqə-w   də-z-ʕay-y-d*
      AWH-eat-INF   3si-EWH-want-PRS   **3sr**-POT-**come**-PRS-DYN
      Whoever wants to eat may come.

Stative morphology is possible with the potential prefix, even if the base verb is an underlying dynamic verb, as seen in the intransitive (333) and the transitive (334). This is unsurprising since ability is a state. This use of stative affixation can be accounted for either if the potential is itself designated as possibly stative, or if the use of stative morphology with dynamic verbs is freely allowed when the semantics warrant. (Recall that a number of verbs optionally occur with either stative or dynamic morphology, with a corresponding difference in meaning. The potential auxiliary verb belongs to this class as well.)

---

[151] Stative verbs thus form a natural class with dynamic verbs to the exclusion of statives of other categories. This provides evidence that stative verbs and dynamic verbs are of the same lexical category, V.

5.1 The potential of ditransitive verbs

(333) s-zə-qʷmar-b
1s-POT-play-STP
I can play.

(334) sə-z-pxʲa-z   a-kʲtab-kʷa   zəmʕʷa   a-ck'əs   rəc'a
1s-EWH-read-PSP DEF-book-PL   all   3si-than   more

y-bzəyə-w   arəy   a-kʲtab   a-kʷ-ta   y-s-zə-hʷa-b
AWH-good-PTC this DEF-book   3si-on-FAC   3si-1s-POT-say-STP
I can say that this is the best book I have ever read.

Section 5.1 presents the inverted agreement pattern which results when the potential morpheme is prefixed to a ditransitive verb and analyzes the potential prefix as an auxiliary (modal) verb in the extended verbal projection. This analysis shows that the Nesting Condition can and should be maintained, even in structures which, on the surface, seem to violate it. The Transitive Subject Condition, (127) in §2.2.3, which requires the subject of a transitive verb to be assigned the feature [+ERG], is motivated by the inverted agreement pattern in ditransitive constructions. Section 5.2 shows how this analysis extends to the potential prefix with transitive and intransitive verbs, where inversion is less obvious. Section 5.3 briefly discusses reflexivization of derived inverted forms. Section 5.4 deals with the interaction of the potential prefix and the causative prefix; this interaction supports Li's Generalization.

5.1 The potential of ditransitive verbs

The effect of the potential prefix on agreement can be seen most clearly in ditransitive verbs. In a normal ditransitive verb, as in (329), repeated here as (335), the subject is registered in the ergative series to the immediate left of the root, the indirect object is registered in another ergative series to the left of that, and the direct object is registered in the absolutive series. With the potential prefix, the order of affixes is rearranged as in (330), repeated here as (336), so that agreement with the indirect object is registered in the ergative series to the immediate left of the verb. To the left of that occurs the potential prefix, and the ergative series which registers agreement with the subject occurs to the left of the potential prefix. As in the nonpotential case, agreement with the direct object is registered in the absolutive series.

(335) *yə-lə-y-ta-t'*
3si-3sf-3sm-give-DYN
He gave it to her.

(336) *y-sə-z-lə-ta-t'*
3si-1s-POT-3sf-give-DYN
I was able to give it to her.

This pattern is surprising in that it is an apparent violation of the Nesting Condition. Agreement with the subject is registered further from the verb root than agreement with the indirect object. This indicates that the subject is located in an agreement specifier higher than the one in which the indirect object is located. Thus, the highest underlying argument, the subject, ends up in the specifier of a higher agreement projection than the indirect object, whose underlying position is lower than the subject, resulting in an apparent crossing pattern of movement, rather than nesting.

The agreement pattern in the potential of ditransitive verbs is further puzzling in that the potential prefix heads its own projection in the verbal extended projection, as I argue below. The reason this is a problem is that the relative position of the prefixes places the projection headed by the potential lower than the higher ergative agreement projection, in apparent violation of the Closer Agreement Principle, which ensures that ergative agreement projections occur as low as possible in the structure (see §2.2.4).

One possible analysis of these facts is one in which the grammatical relations are themselves rearranged.[152] In such an analysis, the underlying subject becomes an indirect object, while the underlying direct object becomes the subject. Such an analysis is unsatisfactory in some respects. Most notably, it does not account for the basic, unmarked word order in clauses with a potential verb. Consider (337), in which the underlying subject occurs sentence initially. If *hara* were the indirect object and *ala* were the subject, we would expect the reverse order. This suggests that the underlying subject remains the surface subject, and that the different morpheme order in the potential cases is not due to the realignment of argument structure.

---

[152]Traditional Russian analyses of Abaza, e.g., Serdyuchenko (1955) and (1956), Klychev and Tabulova-Malbakhova (1967), Tabulova (1976), Klychev (1991), and Pazov (pers. comm.), analyze the potential in this way. This is also similar to analyses that might be given in the theories of either Relational Grammar or Lexical Functional Grammar.

5.1 The potential of ditransitive verbs

(337) hara   a-la   g^j-ha-zə-m-ba-z-d
we   DEF-dog INT-1p-POT-see-ASP-DYN
We could not see the dog.

An analysis in which the argument structure is rearranged in the potential construction has further difficulty in accounting for why an intransitive subject fails to become an indirect object, considering that there are repair strategies in the language which would allow the specifier of ABSP to be filled in order to satisfy the Extended Projection Principle, such as inserting an expletive, when the only argument is forced to occupy a different position.[153] Additionally, it is unclear how to motivate this rearrangement of argument structure.

I propose a different analysis for the potential, in which the basic argument structure of the verb remains unchanged. Specifically, I propose that the potential prefix heads a functional projection, AUXP, in the extended projection of the verb.[154] For ditransitive verbs, the relative order of morphemes is accounted for if AUXP occurs between the two ergative agreement projections. The underlying structure is given in (338).

---

[153]Recall the discussion of the EPP in §2.4.2.2. Expletives are discussed there, and in §6.3.
[154]This projection must be functional in nature, and not lexical, because of Li's Generalization. See the discussion in §5.4.

(338)

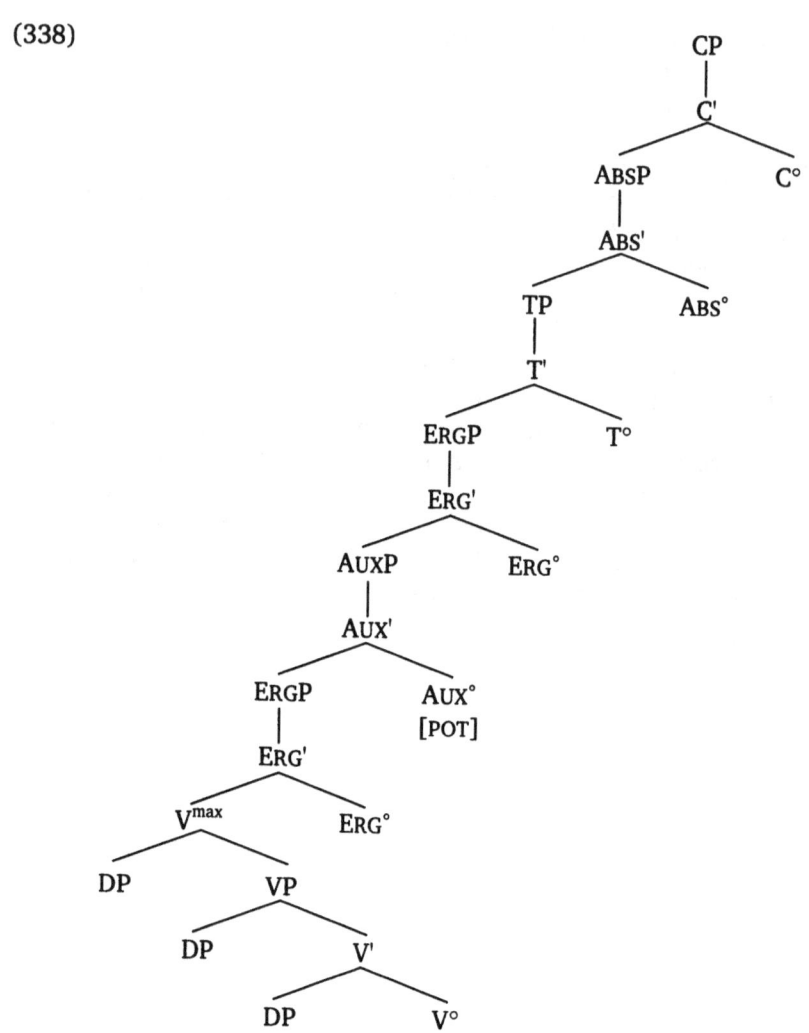

The structure in (338) directly reflects the order of morphemes in the potential of a ditransitive. This tree raises a number of questions, however. These include: (1) what licenses the agreement projections in these positions?, (2) what forces this configuration of agreement projections, as opposed to other possible configurations, e.g., with both ergative projections above, or both below, AuxP?, and (3) why does the subject end up in the specifier of the higher ergative specifier, in apparent violation of the Nesting Condition, rather than in the lower ergative specifier?

5.1 The potential of ditransitive verbs

The first question has a straightforward answer in terms of the framework I have already developed. Lexical VP licenses unlimited ergative agreement projections within its extended projection. The ditransitive verb in (338) thus licenses both agreement projections in this structure. Both positions are within the extended projection of the ditransitive verb. In accordance with the Unused Agreement Filter, no more than two ergative agreement projections are licensed since only two are used.

The question of why the ergative projections occur one above VP and one above AUXP has a partial answer within the framework I have developed thus far. The two alternatives are for both agreement projections to occur between TP and AUXP or for both to occur between AUXP and VP. The configuration in which both occur above AUXP is ruled out by the Closer Agreement Principle, which states that given two structures differing only in the relative position of an ergative agreement projection, and meeting all other conditions equally, the structure having the lower ERGP is used. The structure in (338) and the structure having both ergative projections above AUXP differ only in the position of one ergative projection. They satisfy all other conditions equally. The structure in (338) is chosen over a structure having two ERGPs above AUXP because it has the lower ergative projection.

The structure in (338) and the structure having both ergative projections below AUXP are likewise identical except for the position of one ERGP. The Closer Agreement Principle (CAP) should apply to differentiate between these two structures. According to the CAP, (338) should be disfavored because it has a higher ERGP. This is not the case, however. I argue that the CAP does not apply here because other conditions are not satisfied equally. This can be seen in the answer to the third question, namely, why the subject ends up in the higher ergative specifier, to which we now turn.

Given the order of affixes in (336), and the resulting structure in (338), we are faced with the question of how the arguments end up in the correct agreement specifiers. All things being equal, the Nesting Condition should force the subject into the lowest agreement specifier, the indirect object into the next lowest one, and the direct object into the highest (absolutive) specifier as in simple ditransitive clauses. The question is what aspect of the potential prefix triggers the observed movement pattern, or inversion.

Observationally, an ergative agreement prefix external to the potential prefix may register agreement with only one argument, the subject, and this occurs only if there is a direct object registered in the absolutive series, as in the transitive (334) and the ditransitive (336). If there is no direct object, as in the intransitive (332), the subject is registered in the absolutive series. In either case, the subject must be registered in a series external to the potential prefix. This observation suggests that the subject is somehow forced into a position higher than AUX°.

I propose that the subject must move to the specifier of AUxP, prior to the movement of any of the arguments into their respective agreement specifiers.[155] This produces a configuration in which the subject must move to an agreement specifier higher than the auxiliary. The indirect object, on the other hand, can still move to an agreement specifier lower than the auxiliary. The result is that the LF movement to agreement specifiers of the subject and of the indirect object is neither nesting nor crossing, since these two movements do not interact at all.[156] These movements can be seen in (339). The direct object is nested with respect to both other arguments, so the Nesting Condition is maintained.

---

[155]The easiest way to guarantee this ordering is to have movement to the specifier of AUxP occur in the overt syntax. Movement to agreement specifiers occurs at LF (on independent grounds). It is difficult to determine, for sure, whether the subject has moved in the syntax, since such movement would be string-vacuous.

[156]I argue that the movement of the subject to the specifier of AUxP is A-movement, while movement to the specifier of an agreement projection is A-bar movement. The A-movement of the subject will thus not interact with the Nesting Condition at all. See below for further discussion.

5.1 The potential of ditransitive verbs

(339)

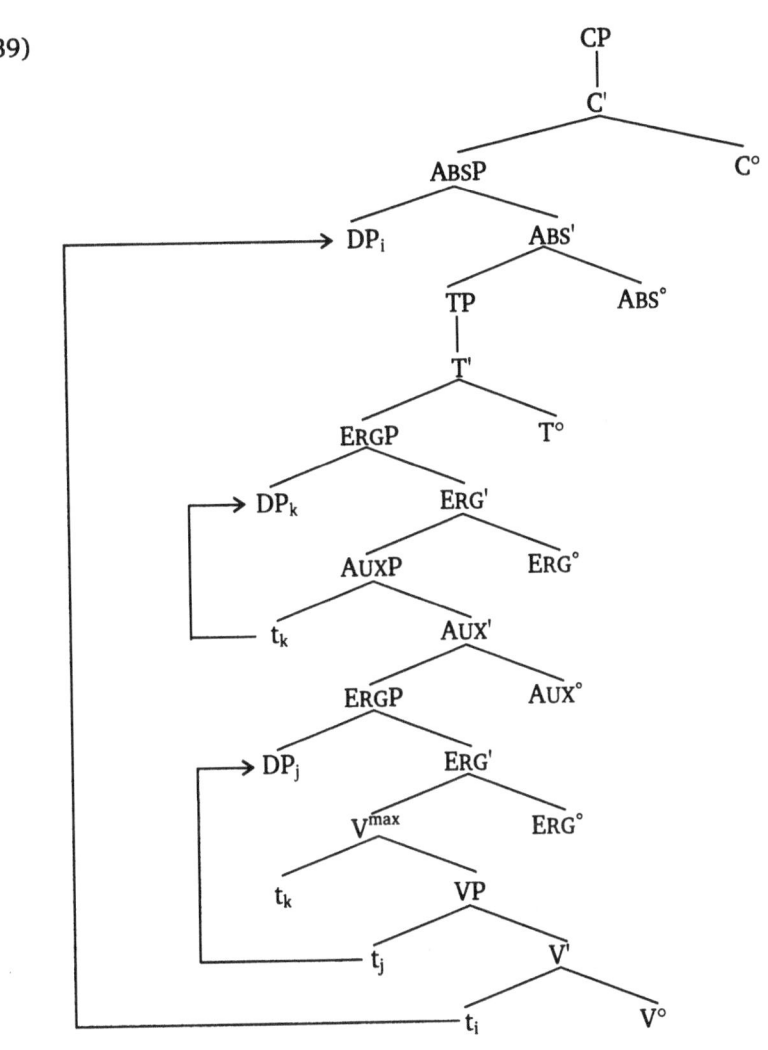

What then forces the subject to occur in the specifier of AUXP? The potential head plus the VP form a predicate distinct from the VP predicate, with the interpretation 'can VP'. If every predicate requires a subject, then the specifier of AUXP must be filled. In these cases, the potential plus VP combination is always predicated of the subject of the VP predication. This indicates that the subject of the VP must occupy the subject (specifier) position of AUXP. This can be accomplished either through movement of the subject from its VP-internal position to the specifier of the auxiliary (raising), or through base-generation of a subject in the specifier of AUXP which is linked to a null element in the VP-internal subject position (control).

An analysis in which the overt subject is base-generated in the specifier of the auxiliary, with a null subject, perhaps PRO, in subject position of the VP, directly accounts for the fact that the overt subject (which eventually gets Case) is in the specifier of the auxiliary. The question arises as to how to ensure that the subject of the VP is the correct null element, since it could be independently licensed in terms of both theta theory and Case theory.[157] The possibility exists for the subject of the verb to be overt and distinct from the subject of the auxiliary, as well as for there to be separate agreement with the subject of the verb. Neither of these ever occurs.

An analysis in which the subject originates in V^{max} and moves to the specifier of AUXP requires no stipulations limiting what can occur in the subject position of VP. Movement is forced by the need for the potential predicate to have a subject. This analysis raises the question of why it is necessarily the subject which moves to the specifier of AUXP. One possible account is that the closest possible DP must move into this position.[158]

Both the raising and control analyses account for the presence of the subject in the specifier of AUXP, although both require an account of why the subject of the lower clause is targeted. Because subjects of transitive verbs behave differently from the subjects of intransitive verbs (see below), I adopt the raising analysis, since this directly accounts for why the subject in the specifier of AUXP behaves as a transitive subject if the lexical verb is transitive and as an intransitive subject if the lexical verb is intransitive.

The movement analysis raises the additional question of how to rule out a derivation in which the subject originates in the lower subject position, moves into the specifier of an ergative agreement projection below AUXP, and then moves into the auxiliary specifier.[159] For the subject to count as a potential antecedent-governor for the trace of the DP which moves to the specifier of AUXP, these two positions must be of the same type. Since the

---

[157]Nothing in the framework I have developed would prevent a third ERGP from occurring in the structure into which the base subject could move.

[158]This restriction can possibly be motivated through relativized minimality. Any nonsubject argument must cross over the underlying subject position to get to the auxiliary specifier. If both the underlying subject position and the specifier of AUXP are A-positions, the subject of VP would be a closer potential governor for the trace of the moved argument, leading to a minimality violation. An appeal to minimality is somewhat problematic, however, in that movement of arguments to the specifier positions of agreement phrases is incompatible with relativized minimality.

[159]This is somewhat similar to the focus movement I propose in chapter 8, except that the final target position here is an A-position, and the target of focus movement is an A-bar position.

5.1 The potential of ditransitive verbs

subject position is an A-position by definition, the subject of the potential must, therefore, also be an A-position. I have assumed that the specifier of an agreement projection is an A-bar position. The movement of the subject into the specifier of ERGP and then further into the specifier of AUXP would thus be ruled out as improper movement. Movement from an A-bar position into an A-position is prohibited in general.

We return now to the question of why the higher ergative agreement projection in (338) occurs above AUXP, rather than below it as predicted by the CAP which requires agreement projections to occur as low as possible. The starting point for the movement of the subject to an agreement specifier is the specifier of AUXP. The subject cannot move into an ergative specifier lower than AUXP because of the general prohibition on downward movement. This requires the presence of an ergative phrase above AUXP. The structure in (338) is not subject to a comparison with a structure having two ergative agreement projections below AUXP, in accordance with the CAP, because the two structures do not equally satisfy other conditions, since the subject cannot move into the specifier of an ergative projection from the specifier of AUXP if there are no ergative projections above AUXP. The principles established in chapter 2, plus the added requirement that the subject move into the specifier of AUXP prior to movement into agreement specifiers, thus account for the agreement pattern found in the potential of ditransitives.

Before moving on to the structure of the potential with transitive and intransitive verbs, we address one problematic issue. I argued that a structure having two ergative projections below AUXP was not valid because the subject must move into an ergative specifier higher than the auxiliary specifier, thus making the CAP irrelevant for distinguishing between this structure and the actual structure. A different movement pattern is possible, however, in a structure having both ergative projections below AUXP. Specifically, the subject could move from the specifier of AUXP to the absolutive specifier, while the direct and indirect objects move into the ergative specifiers below AUXP. The Nesting Condition would be maintained in this configuration, so long as the direct object ended up in the higher of the two ergative projections. The subject would not interact with either of these movements.[160] This faulty LF movement of the arguments into their respective agreement projections can be seen in (340).

---

[160]This possibility exists also for the potential of transitive verbs, minus the indirect object, of course. See below.

(340)

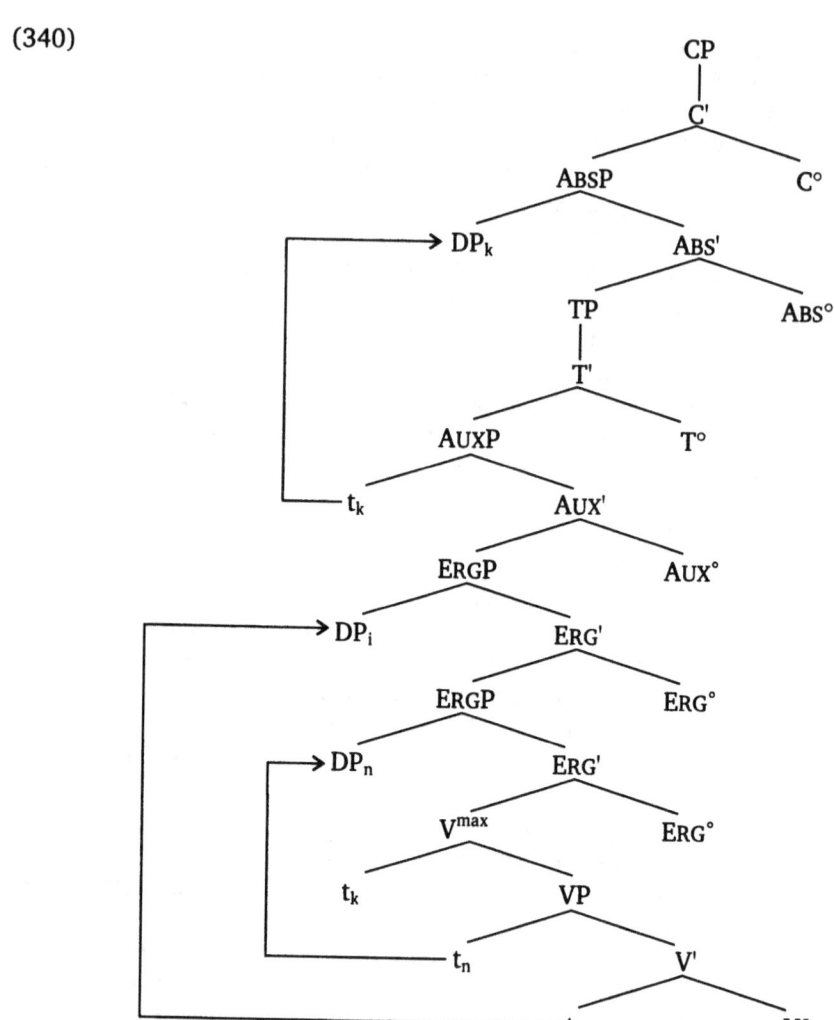

How is the structure in (340) ruled out? The subject moves from the specifier of AuxP into the specifier of an ErgP when the base verb is either transitive or ditransitive. When the base verb is intransitive, the subject ends up in the specifier of AbsP. This is the same pattern found in normal (nonpotential) forms. This suggests that there is something inherent which forces the stability of these types of agreement for the different arguments. Woolford (1993), following Mahajan (1989), Harbert and Toribio (1991), and Bok-Bennema (1991), argues that ergative is an inherent (lexical) Case. In a system making use of agreement projections, I

5.2 The potential of transitive and intransitive verbs

assume that inherent Case is realized in that the lexical head, which has traditionally been assumed to assign inherent Case directly, actually assigns a feature requiring the lexically Case-marked argument to occur in a certain type of agreement specifier.[161] Assigning inherent ergative Case is thus equivalent to assigning a feature, [+ERG], which requires the element which has it to occur in the specifier of an ergative agreement projection. I adopted the Transitive Subject Condition (TSC), repeated here as (341), in chapter 2 without argument. The subjects of transitive (and ditransitive) verbs are registered in an ergative series, even where there is an alternative position available leading to a preferable structure based on different principles (the CAP). This provides motivation for treating the movement of transitive subjects to the specifier of ERGP as a result of more than just the Nesting Condition. I take this as evidence for the TSC.

(341) Transitive Subject Condition:
The subject of a transitive verb is assigned the feature [+ERG].

This accounts for the observed movement pattern as follows. From the underlying structure in (338), the subject moves to the specifier of AUXP. At LF, the subject, which is marked [+ERG] by the TSC, must move to the specifier of the ergative agreement projection immediately dominating AUXP. The direct and indirect objects likewise must move to agreement specifiers, nesting into the two open positions, the specifier of ABSP and the specifier of the lowest ERGP. As already observed, the movement of the subject and indirect object do not interact, and the movement of the subject and direct object obeys the Nesting Condition. This set of assumptions forces exactly the configuration seen in (339).

5.2 The potential of transitive and intransitive verbs

Inversion is less clear for the potential with transitive verbs than it is for the potential with ditransitive verbs. Consider the simple transitive verb in (342), and the form in (343), which differs only in that it has the potential prefix. Nevertheless, the analysis presented in the previous section accounts directly for the potential of transitive verbs without additional modification.

---

[161]See the discussion in chapter 6.

(342) y-gʲ-rə-m-ga-t'
   3si-INT-3p-NEG-take-DYN
   They didn't take it.   GAL, 197

(343) y-gʲə-r-zə-m-ga-t'
   3si-INT-3p-POT-NEG-take-DYN
   They were not able to take it.   GAL, 197

For transitive verbs, the potential prefix occurs to the left of the verb root, as with ditransitives. The direct object is registered in the absolutive series, as in the nonpotential form. The subject is registered in an ergative series to the left of the potential marker. Examples can be seen in (344)–(347).

(344) hara   a-la   gʲ-ha-zə-m-ba-z-d
   we   DEF-dog   INT-1p-POT-see-ASP-DYN
   We could not see the dog.

(345) sa   y-s-zə-fa-r-ma
   I   3si-1s-POT-eat-SUBJ-YNQ
   May I eat it?

(346) y-s-zə-hʷa-y-t'
   3si-1s-POT-say-PRS-DYN
   I can say it.   GAL, 116

(347) yə-z-zə-čʲpa-z
   3si-EWH-POT-do-PSP
   that which could do it

The relative position of ergative agreement and the preverb demonstrates more clearly that the subject series for normal transitives is truly different from the subject series for the potential. In a simple transitive with a preverb, as in (349), ergative agreement separates the verb and preverb. In a transitive verb with the potential prefix (348), the potential prefix occurs to the left of the preverb, so that the preverb and root are not separated.

(348) yə-r-zə-ʃt'ə-x-y-t'
   3si-3p-POT-PV-lift-PRS-DYN
   They can lift it.   GAL, 116

5.2 The potential of transitive and intransitive verbs

(349) a-čʷa   ʃtʼə-r-x-tʼ
     DEF-hay   PV-3p-lift-DYN
     They picked up the hay.   AOD, 305

Given my account of the potential of a ditransitive verb in the preceding section, the structure of a potential of a transitive verb should likewise require the subject to move to the specifier of the auxiliary prior to movement into the agreement specifiers. As in the ditransitive structure, this requires an ergative agreement projection higher than AUXP, since the transitive subject is marked [+ERG] as in the ditransitive case. This accounts also for the observed order of morphemes, with ergative agreement to the left of the potential prefix. The subject moves to the specifier of AUXP in the overt syntax as in (350).

(350)

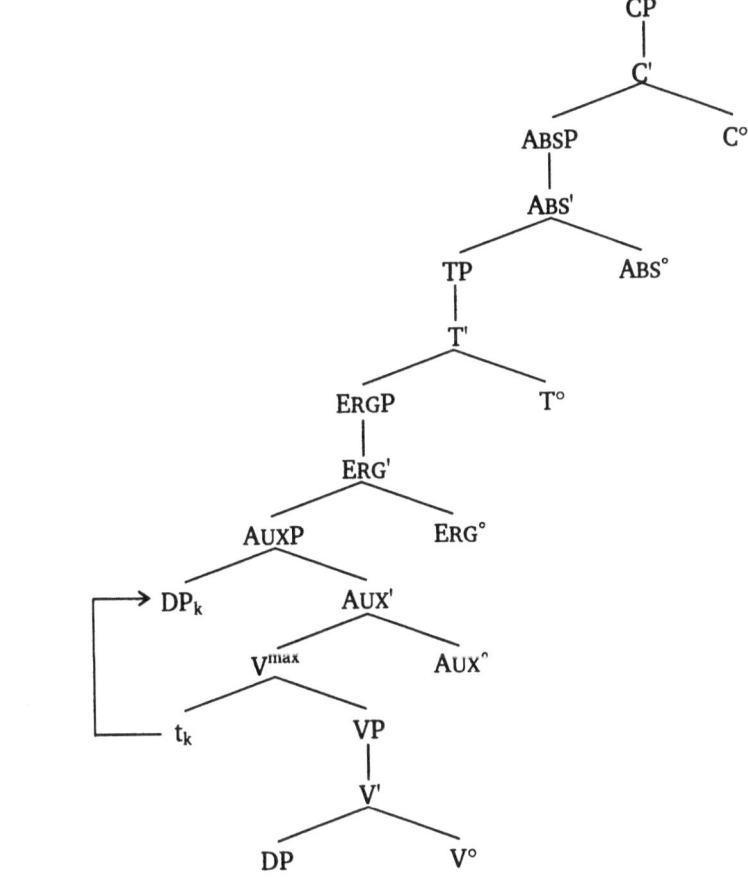

At LF the subject moves into the ergative specifier from the specifier of AUXP, and the object moves directly to the absolute specifier from its underlying position. This is entirely consistent with the Nesting Condition.[162] The resulting structure is given in (351).

(351)

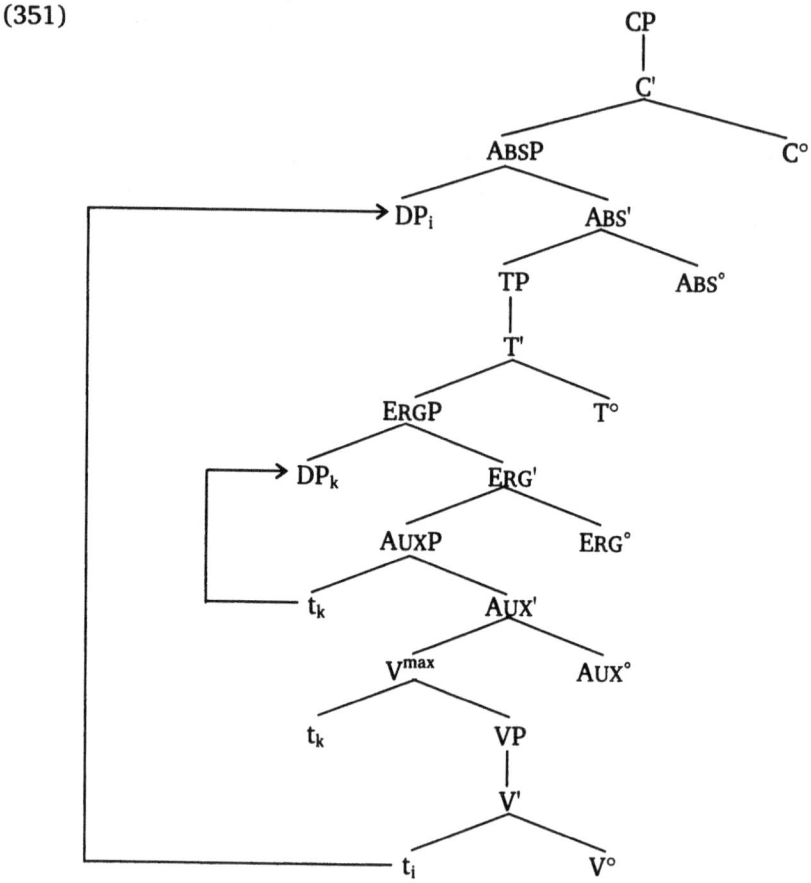

For intransitive verbs, there is no difference in the agreement pattern between forms with and without the potential prefix. In both cases, the subject (and sole argument) is registered in the absolutive series. Intransitive verb examples can be seen in (352)–(356).

---

[162]But inconsistent, as in the general case, with relativized minimality.

5.2 The potential of transitive and intransitive verbs

(352) sa   s-zə-č^ja-y-d
      I   1s-POT-eat-PRS-DYN
      I can eat.

(353) sa   s-zə-č^ja-r-ma
      I   1s-POT-eat-SUBJ-YNQ
      May I eat?[163]

(354) sa   s-zə-q^wmarə-r-ma
      I   1s-POT-play-SUBJ-YNQ
      May I play?

(355) sə-z-nayə-r-ma
      1s-POT-come-SUBJ-YNQ
      May I come?

(356) s-g^jə-z-nay-rə-m
      1s-INT-POT-come-SUBJ-NEG
      I can't come.

One of the difficulties in an account which rearranges the argument structure is understanding why the potential prefix triggers inversion only for transitive and ditransitive verbs. Specifically, the subject becomes something like an indirect object in the potential construction just in case the main verb is transitive or ditransitive. In the case of an intransitive verb, the argument structure remains unmodified. This results in two distinct analyses for a single construction, depending on the transitivity of the verb involved.

My proposal, on the other hand, provides a single analysis that accounts for all forms in the construction. With intransitive verbs, the subject still must raise to the specifier of AuxP, as in the other cases. The intransitive verb has a single argument, and thus a single agreement projection, which must be absolutive in accordance with principles already discussed. AbsP, however, by virtue of being an extension of TP, is necessarily higher in the structure than AuxP. Movement from the specifier of AuxP to the specifier of AbsP is straightforward, as in (357). The subject is not required to move to an ergative agreement specifier as in the transitive and ditransitive cases because an intransitive verb does not mark its subject [+ERG].

---

[163]Abaza has distinct roots for obligatorily transitive 'eat', *fa*, and obligatorily intransitive 'eat', *č^ja*. Compare (345) and (353).

(357)

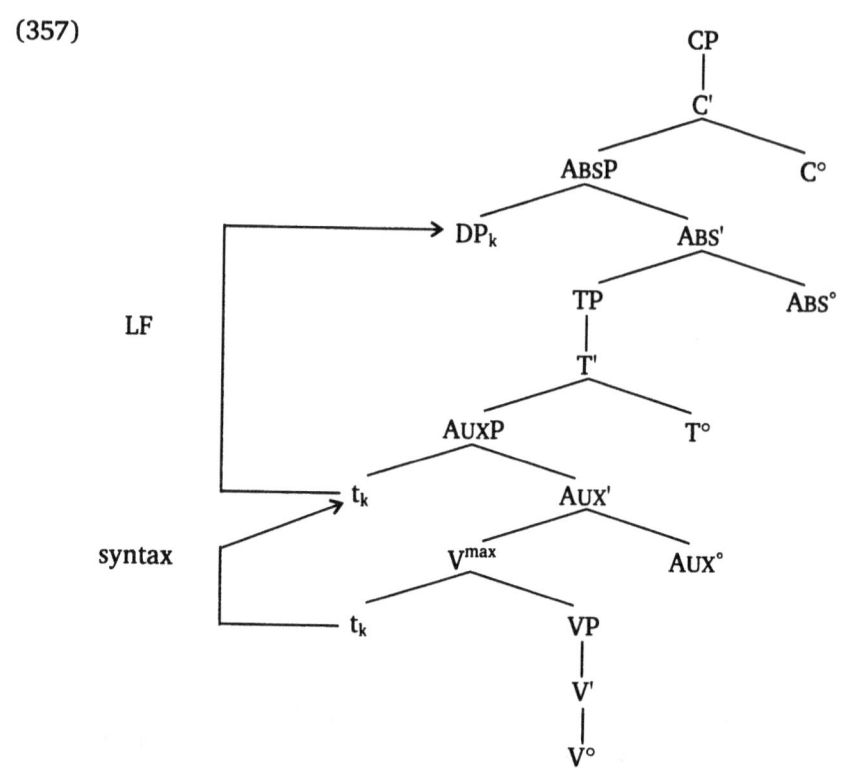

In summary, my analysis differs from an analysis in which the potential prefix causes the grammatical relations of transitive and ditransitive verbs to be reorganized so that the underlying subject becomes an indirect object. Instead, I propose that the subject moves first to the specifier of an auxiliary projection, headed by the potential prefix, and then to the specifier of an agreement projection. Since morphological structure reflects syntactic structure, the fact that the subject must pass through the specifier of AuxP on its way to an agreement specifier directly accounts for the fact that the ergative series which registers agreement with the subject occurs to the left of the potential prefix. My analysis is preferable to an account which restructures grammatical relations because it correctly accounts for the unmarked word order in these constructions. Furthermore, my analysis applies uniformly to the potential of any verb, regardless of transitivity. This analysis integrates easily within the overall framework I have developed for Case assignment.

5.3 Reflexives and derived inverted verbs

In this section we briefly address the issue of the reflexivization of verbs with derived inversion. The data here support an analysis in which the argument structure of a verb clause containing a derived inverted verb is not different from that of a clause containing a noninverted verb..

A form having a potential prefix can be reflexivized, as in (358). The reflexive prefix occurs in the usual absolutive position, registering reflexive agreement with the direct object. The subject is registered in an ergative series to the left of the potential prefix, as in nonreflexive forms.

(358) č-gʲə-y-zə-k'-wa-m
REFL-INT-3sm-POT-restrain-PRS-NEG
He cannot restrain himself. GAL, 201

My analysis correctly predicts such forms. The direct object is a reflexive anaphor, bound by the subject. The subject moves to the specifier of AUXP, as usual. At LF, the subject moves into the specifier of ERGP, and the anaphor object moves into the specifier of ABSP. All conditions are satisfied. The transitive subject is in an ergative specifier, in accordance with the Transitive Subject Condition. The movement paths of the two arguments obey the Nesting Condition. The specifier of ABSP is filled, satisfying the Extended Projection Principle. And the DP bearing the feature [+REFL] is in a position where this feature can be checked.

Such forms are quite problematic for an analysis in which the argument structure is rearranged. If the underlying direct object becomes a subject, and the underlying subject becomes an indirect object, then the prediction is made that such forms should be impossible. The derived subject could not be the reflexive anaphor, because Binding Condition A would be violated. The indirect object could not be the reflexive anaphor because it ends up in an ergative specifier, and the feature [+REFL] could not be checked.[164] I take this as further evidence against an analysis of derived inversion in which argument structure is rearranged.

---

[164]Exactly this configuration rules out reflexives with lexically inverted verbs. See §6.4. Traditional Russian analyses of Abaza (e.g., Serdyuchenko 1955 and 1956, Klychev and Tabulova-Malbakhova 1967, Tabulova 1976, Klychev 1991, Pazov, pers. comm.) treat derived inverted verbs and lexically inverted verbs as a single class of intransitive verbs. The reflexive data demonstrate that this cannot be so, since derived inverted verbs may reflexivize but lexically inverted verbs may not.

5.4 Interaction of the potential and causative

In chapter 4, I analyzed the causative as a lexical verb which selects as complement a lexical X^{max}. Here, I have analyzed the potential prefix as the head of an auxiliary phrase in the extended projection of a lexical verb. This predicts that the potential prefix should be able to occur in conjunction with the causative. The potential prefix may, in fact, occur in the extended projection of the causative verb, but it may not occur in the extended projection of the complement to the causative verb. Both of these facts are accounted for in my analysis, with no additional machinery required. We address first the cases in which the potential and causative prefixes occur together, before turning to an account of the impossible patterns.

When both the potential and causative prefixes occur in the same verb complex, the potential prefix is always morphologically external to the causative. If the causative splits a preverb-root combination, as in (359), the potential prefix still occurs external to the preverb, as in (360).

(359) y-gʲ-aca-na-mə-r-pa-t'
 3si-INT-PV-3si-NEG-CAUS-change-DYN
 It did not change it. GAL, 197

(360) y-gʲ-a-z-aca-mə-r-pa-t'
 3si-INT-3si-POT-PV-NEG-CAUS-change-DYN
 It was not able to change it. GAL, 197

Agreement with the causative subject is registered in an ergative series to the immediate left of the potential prefix, as in noncausative transitive and ditransitive forms. The absolutive series registers agreement with either the base subject, in the case of the causative of an intransitive, or the base direct object, in the case of the causative of a transitive or ditransitive. Example (361) is a simple intransitive verb. The causative from this form is shown in (362), and the potential of (362) is given in (363).[165]

(361) d-ca-t'
 3sr-go-DYN
 S/he went.

---

[165] The intervention of the potential prefix between the ergative agreement series and the causative prefix calls off third-person plural dissimilation.

5.4 Interaction of the potential and causative

(362) *d-də-r-ca-t'*
3sr-3p-CAUS-go-DYN
They made him/her go.

(363) *də-r-zə-r-ca-t'*
3sr-3p-POT-CAUS-go-DYN
They were able to make him/her go.

The pattern of the potential of the causative of an intransitive verb is thus identical to the pattern of the potential of a simple transitive verb, with the base subject moving to the absolutive specifier like the direct object in the noncausative form. The structure is as follows:

(364)

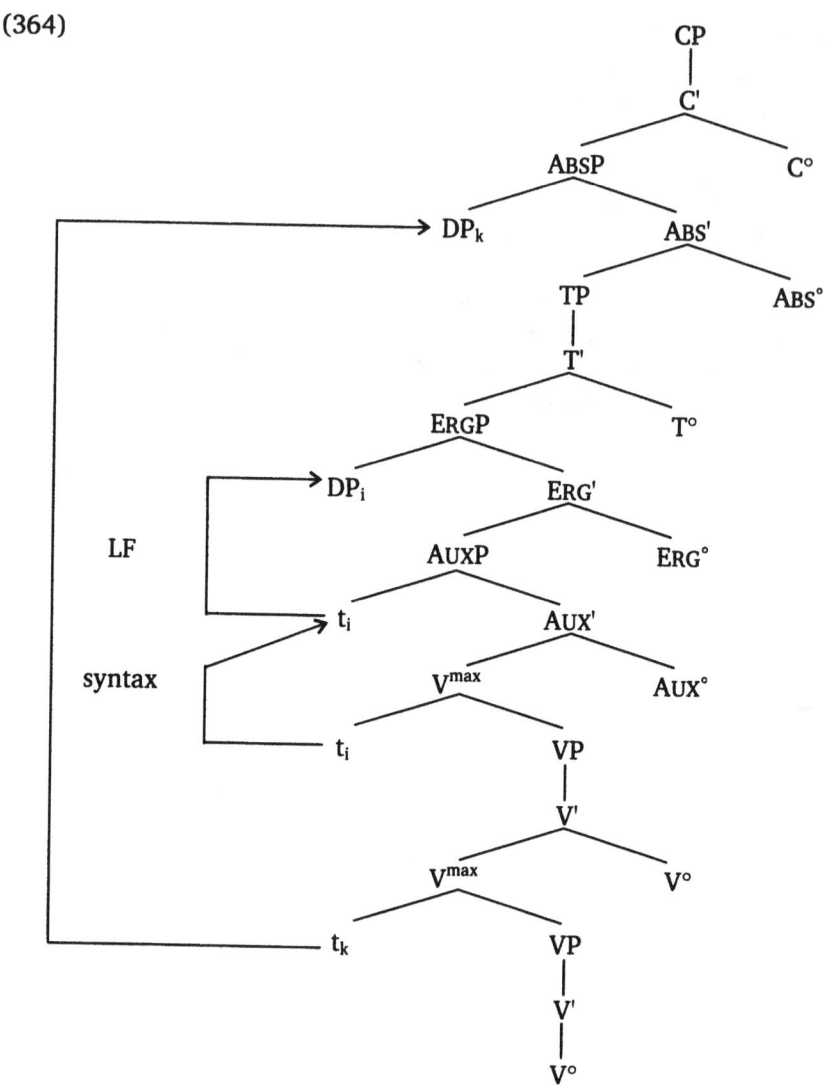

For the potential of the causative of a transitive verb, the causative subject is registered in the ergative series to the left of the potential prefix, the base subject is registered in the ergative series between the potential prefix and the causative prefix, and the base object is registered in the absolutive series. For presumably pragmatic reasons, examples with both

5.4 Interaction of the potential and causative

causative and potential prefixes are more unnatural or difficult to construct for transitive verbs, yet these forms are fully grammatical.[166] Example (365) shows causative forms of the transitive verb *fa* 'eat', and (366) shows the potential form based on (365).

(365) *yə-l-s-rə-f-t'*
3si-3sf-1s-CAUS-eat-DYN
I made her eat it.

(366) *yə-s-zə-l-rə-f-t'*
3si-1s-POT-3sf-CAUS-eat-DYN
I was able to make her eat it.

The structure for a form like (366) is given in (367). The base subject moves to an ergative specifier lower than the potential, in accordance with the Closer Agreement Principle (recall (139) in §2.2.4), and consistent with the fact that it is registered in an ergative series to the right of the potential prefix. Both the causative subject and the transitive base subject are registered in an ergative series, in accordance with the TSC.[167] This structure is similar to the potential of a simple ditransitive verb, with the base subject in the place of the indirect object.

---

[166]It appears possible to have the potential of the causative of a ditransitive verb, as in the example below. I find this form suspect because (1) Sergei Pazov (pers. comm.) claims that it is not possible for ditransitive verbs to host both potential and causative prefixes in the same complex; (2) the agreement pattern is different from the expected; (3) Allen, himself, seems unsure of the status of this elicited form; and (4) this is the only such example I have. In this construction, the causative subject is registered in the ergative series to the left of the potential, as expected. The base subject and indirect object are registered in ergative series between the potential prefix and the verb root, also as expected, but the order of these two is reversed from what one expects. One would expect the interpretation to be 'The old man couldn't make the girl give the boys her dog.' The direct object is registered in the absolutive series.

  a-ləgaʒʷ *a-č'ʲkʷʼən-čʷa-kʷa* *l-la* *a-phʷəspa*
  DEF-old.man DEF-boy-RPL-PL 3sf-dog DEF-girl

  y-gʲ-y-z-d-m-l-rə-t-x-d
  3si-INT-3sm-POT-3p-NEG-3sf-CAUS-give-again-DYN
  The old man couldn't make the boys give the girl her dog back. SSAVC, 139

[167]Both the TSC and the Nesting Condition play a role in getting these arguments into ergative specifiers.

(367)

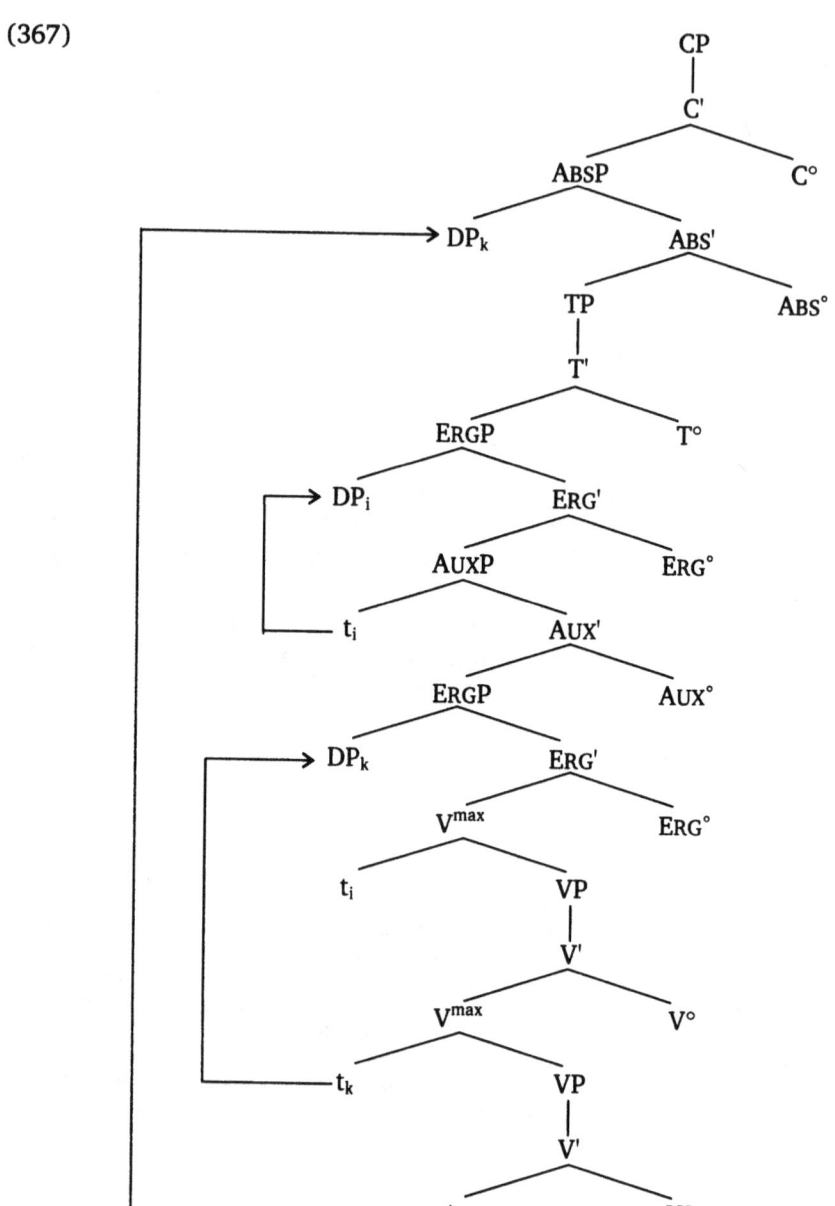

In verb complexes with both potential and causative prefixes, the potential prefix always occurs to the left of the causative prefix, giving the reading, 'X is able to cause Y'. This indicates that the auxiliary phrase is

5.4 Interaction of the potential and causative

structurally higher than the causative verb. Given these building blocks, the interpretation, 'X causes Y to be able to Y', is logically possible. Such a construction should correspond to a structure in which the auxiliary headed by the potential occurs in the extended projection of the complement to the causative verb. Such forms are completely impossible, however.

I argue that the causative verb selects a lexical X^{max}, but that AuxP is a functional projection. Evidence for this comes from Li's Generalization and the fact that ERG° may incorporate into AUX°. Since the ergative head is functional, the auxiliary head must also be functional, in order to avoid the incorporation (substitution) of a functional head into a lexical head, in violation of Li's Generalization. The same principle rules out the structure in question. Because AUX° is a functional head, it may not incorporate into a lexical head. Specifically, it may not incorporate into the lexical causative V°. Any configuration in which the potential is structurally lower than the causative verb will necessarily result in a violation of Li's Generalization when this head incorporates (as it must) into the higher structure.

The analysis I have developed makes certain predictions about the interaction of the potential and causative prefixes, namely that the potential should be possible in the extended projection of the causative verb. This is not only possible, but it results in the agreement patterns predicted by my analysis. This analysis also correctly predicts that the potential should not be possible in the extended projection of the complement of the causative verb, because of Li's Generalization. The framework developed in chapter 2 thus accounts for both simple and complex structures involving derived inversion. A minimum of added machinery, specifically the requirement that the subject move to the specifier of AuxP prior to the LF movement of arguments to agreement specifiers, is needed to account for derived inversion. This analysis provides a single unified account of this construction, in spite of the apparently different behavior of the subjects of intransitive verbs and the subjects of transitive and ditransitive verbs in the potential construction.

6
Lexically Inverted Verbs

Besides derived inversion, which is caused by the addition of certain affixes, a small class of two-argument verbs in Abaza exhibits an inverted pattern of agreement without the addition of any special affixes. I refer to these as lexically inverted verbs. In these verbs, as in (368), the subject (*spa*) is registered through the absolutive series and the object (*səmač'ʷ*) is registered through the ergative series. The word order in clauses having lexically inverted verbs is the same as that in clauses having normal transitive verbs, namely SOV.

(368) *s-pa   sə-mač'ʷ   d-a-cha-d*
   1s-son 1s-finger 3sr-3si-bite-DYN
   My son bit my finger.

I propose to treat these verbs as assigning an inherent Case to the object. Crucial to my account is the proposal that inherent Case is mediated by an ergative agreement projection in the same way that structural Case is. The assignment of inherent "Case" from the lexical head is really the assignment of a feature which limits the DP to a particular type of agreement projection in which it may occur.

Section 6.1 presents background on inherent Case. Section 6.2 discusses lexically inverted verbs in Abaza, developing an analysis in which they are transitive verbs which assign an inherent (ergative) Case to their direct object. Section 6.3 returns to the question of expletives, demonstrating how the assignment of inherent Case figures in the analysis of expletives. Section 6.4 discusses the impossibility of reflexives with inverted verbs. Section 6.5 discusses the behavior of lexically inverted verbs in the potential construction. In this construction, the order of agreement prefixes with respect to the potential prefix differs from the order in the potential of normal transitive verbs. This is shown to be predicted by my analysis. Section 6.6 discusses the behavior of lexically inverted verbs in the causative construction. This, too, follows from my analysis without the need for additional machinery.

6.1 Inherent Case

Numerous languages have specific verbs which assign to an argument a special Case (or case) different from the Case normally assigned to that position. For example, "dative" verbs in German or Russian require an object in the dative case, rather than in the accusative case normal for direct objects.

(369) ich helfe dir / *dich
 I help you (dative) / you (accusative)
 I help you. (German)

(370) ja vʲerʲu tʲebʲe / *tʲebʲa
 I believe you (dative) / you (accusative)
 I believe you. (Russian)

These verbs are often treated as assigning an INHERENT Case to their object. That is, the verbs themselves are lexically specified to assign a particular, exceptional Case. Inherent Case is assigned because of the Case recipient's relation to a particular (lexical) head. This differs from structural Case, which is assigned in a particular structural configuration.

6.2 Inverted verbs and inherent Case

In the normal pattern of agreement for transitive verbs in Abaza, the subject is registered in the ergative series and the direct object is registered in the absolutive series. A small class of two-argument verbs in Abaza utilizes a different agreement pattern. For these verbs the subject is registered in the absolutive series, and the object is registered in an ergative series, as in (368).

6.2 Inverted verbs and inherent Case

The verbs which constitute this class form a heterogeneous set semantically. Catford (1976) claims that the Northwest Caucasian languages historically allowed a productive contrast between the ergative-absolutive pattern and the nominative-accusative pattern, depending on the degree of affectedness of the object. Each transitive verb was thus able to occur freely in either pattern, with a slightly different semantic interpretation. The current synchronic split is presumably due to the fact that when the language generalized to the ergative-absolutive pattern, a few verbs were frozen in the nominative-accusative pattern, perhaps because they were used most commonly with that pattern before the generalization. A partial list of this type of verb is given in (371).

(371) cha   bite
      xʲəs   touch
      as   strike, hit[168]
      gʷəkʷs   attack
      zərʕʷa   forgive[169]
      cqraʕ   help
      ayxs   shoot at[170]

The order of syntactic arguments for these verbs is the same as that of a normal transitive verb, with subject followed by object. Compare the word order in (372), having an inverted verb, with that in (373), having a normal transitive verb. In both cases, the object is aʃʷ 'the door', and in both cases this object follows the overt subject. The two cases differ in that the subject is registered in the absolutive Case in (372), and in the ergative Case in (373).

(372) a-čʲkʷən   a-ʃʷ   ʒʷəhʷa-la   d-ʕ-a-sə-y-d
      DEF-boy   DEF-door   hammer-INST   3sr-DIR-3si-hit-PRS-DYN
      The boy pounds on the door with a hammer.

---

[168]The verb as 'hit' is used in numerous idioms, particularly in describing the playing of musical instruments and games.

[169]The verb zərʕʷa 'forgive' is possibly derived either from some transitive root plus a potential prefix, z-, or from some intransitive root plus an incorporated benefactive, also z (see chapter 7). Neither analysis is available synchronically, as there is no related form without z. A similar historical derivation is possible for cqraʕ 'help' in which the incorporated comitative prefix c- merged with the root, leaving agreement with its object in the ergative. Again, no such synchronic account is available.

[170]Compare this with the simple transitive root xas 'shoot'. The two forms are clearly related, though the prefix ay- is not normally used compositionally in this way.

(373) sara   a-ʃʷ   ʃa-s-t'ə-y-d
     I   DEF-door   DIR-1s-open-PRS-DYN
     I open the door.

This order is valid for other inverted verbs, such as cha (368), xʲəs (374), and gʷəkʷš (375). It is also valid for all other tense and mood combinations, such as those in (376) and (377).

(374) sara   a-wasa-kʷa   sə-r-xʲəs-d
     I   DEF-sheep-PL   1s-3p-touch-DYN
     I touched the sheep.

(375) hara   a-ya   hə-y-gʷəkʷš-t'
     we   DEF-enemy   1p-3sm-attack-DYN
     We attacked the enemy.

(376) a-čʲkʷʷən a-q'ama-la   a-haqʷ   d-a-sə-n   y-pčʲə-d
     DEF-boy   DEF-sword-INST   DEF-stone   3sr-3si-hit-DEP   3si-break-DYN
     The boy broke the sword on the stone. (lit., The boy hit the stone with the sword and it [the sword] broke.)

(377) a-čʲkʷʷən a-qʷʷabəz   d-a-s-wa-mc'ara   yəbza-pʃdza
     DEF-boy   DEF-accordion   3sr-3si-hit-PRS-HAB   music-pretty

     ʃa-tə-y-ʃtə-y-d
     DIR-PV-3sm-pull-PRS-DYN
     The boy (habitually) plays good music on the accordion.

I propose that inverted verbs in Abaza are parallel to the dative verbs of Russian or German in that they have the lexical property of assigning a special (inherent) Case to their objects. In the framework I have developed, Case is assigned through the specifier-head relationship within an agreement projection. Inherent Case, then, is not directly assigned by V°, but is a feature assigned by V° which requires the specially marked DP to occur in a particular type of specifier for Case purposes.[171] I give evidence for this position in §6.5. This analysis requires that ergative and absolutive agreement projections be of a categorially different type, and not of a single type distinguished simply by relative position with respect

---

[171] This is identical to the treatment of the inherent ergative Case assigned to the subjects of transitive and ditransitive verbs in accordance with the Transitive Subject Condition in §2.2.3. The TSC must be a default, since it does not apply to inverted verbs. Perhaps, a verb only has the ability to assign a single inherent Case.

6.2 Inverted verbs and inherent Case

to T° and V°. The underlying structure of a sentence containing an inverted verb is thus identical to that of a transitive verb, as in (378), with the exception that the DP complement of V° is assigned a feature, [+ERG], requiring it to occur in the specifier of an ergative projection.

(378)

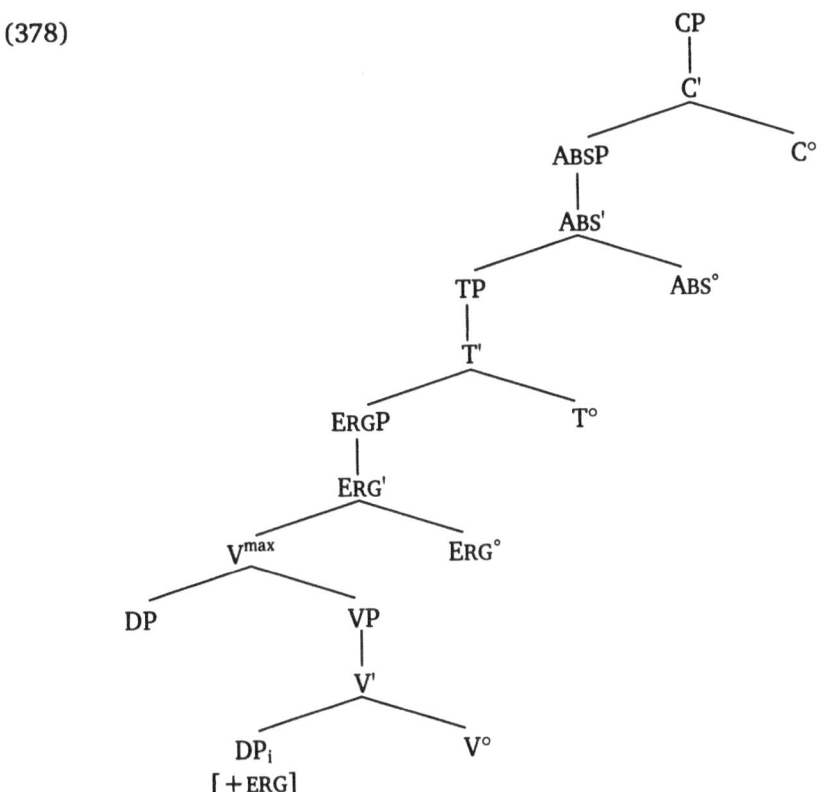

In this structure, V° assigns an inherent Case (feature) to its sister, DP_i in (378). The direct object, DP_i, can only move to the specifier of ERGP because of the feature [+ERG] which it bears. The subject can and must move to the absolutive specifier, since the absolutive specifier is available and must be filled, in accordance with the EPP. The structure in (378) leads to that in (379) after movement.

(379)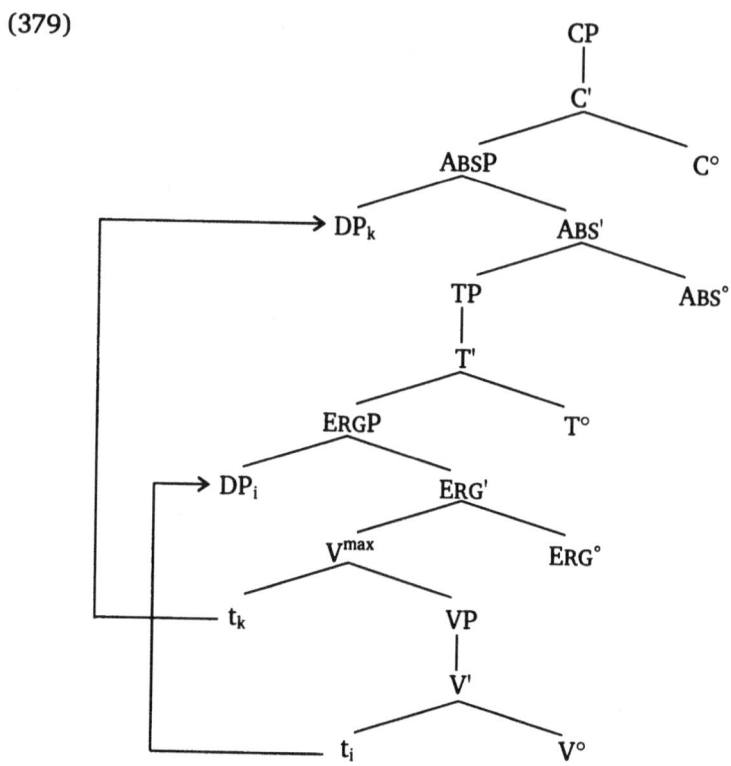

Such movement involves a violation of the Nesting Condition. One possible way of understanding this is that the Nesting Condition is a principle governing the free movement of arguments to agreement specifiers. Movement of an inherently Case-marked DP is not free, however, since its target site is limited by the lexical specification it bears. This suggests the Elsewhere Condition (Kiparsky 1973), which states that specific lexical requirements take precedence over general principles. As a lexical specification, inherent Case would take precedence over the more general Nesting Condition, a default principle for movement.

In summary, I claim that a lexically inverted verb differs from a normal transitive verb solely in that the inverted verb assigns an inherent Case to its object (in the form of a feature requiring it to occur in a particular kind of agreement projection), while a normal transitive verb has no such inherent Case to assign. This accounts for the contrast in agreement patterns between normal transitive verbs and lexically inverted verbs.

Before moving on to more complex constructions involving lexically inverted verbs in §§6.5 and 6.6, I discuss two related side issues. Section 6.3

returns to a discussion of expletives in Abaza. The analysis of lexically assigned Case developed thus far sheds light on what prevents an argument from moving into the specifier of ABSP, forcing the appearance of an expletive. Section 6.4 returns to the issue of the reflexive construction, as it interacts with both lexically inverted verbs and derived inversion. Reflexives are relevant at this point because inverted verbs, in spite of having two arguments, cannot be reflexivized morphologically.

6.3 Expletives

We return now to the question of expletives from §2.4.2.2. I repeat the relevant examples of absolutive expletives here in (380)–(382).

(380) *y-lə-rxaw-t'*
3si-3sf-get.underway-DYN
She got underway (to there). GAL, 113

(381) *y-sə-z-č'ə-r-t-t'*
3si-1s-BEN-PV-3p-call-DYN
They invited me. (lit., They called [it] for me.) GAL, 113

(382) *zurab   a-kolxoz   a-x-brigada-k'*
Zurab DEF-collective.farm DEF-3-brigade-INDEF

  r-partorganizacia-kʷa   r-sekretar-kʷa
  3p-party.organization-PL 3p-secretary-PL

  y-ʕa-rə-z-č'-i-t-t'
  3si-DIR-3p-BEN-PV-3sm-call-DYN
Zurab invited the secretaries of the party organizations of the three collective farm brigades. GAL, 113

In each of these cases, there is a (default) third-person singular irrational absolutive prefix, which does not register agreement with any argument. I argued in chapter 2 that this agreement occurs because of the Extended Projection Principle (EPP), which requires the specifier of ABSP to be filled. A null expletive is inserted in this position, and this expletive is registered through default agreement. Furthermore, I argued that the absolutive specifier was empty in these constructions because something prevented the thematic arguments of these verbs from moving to this position. We now have the machinery necessary to explain what prevents this movement.

Lexically inverted verbs are transitive verbs which assign an inherent ergative Case to their complements (objects). This suggests the possibility that there are intransitive verbs which assign inherent ergative Case to their single argument. This argument would thus be forced into the specifier of an ergative projection, leaving no argument available to move into the specifier of AbsP. The only possible way to satisfy the EPP, which requires that the specifier of AbsP be filled, is to insert an expletive.[172] A verb like that in (380) exhibits exactly this pattern.

The class of unaccusative verbs, in which the subject of a certain class of intransitive verbs originates in a position within VP, and not in the canonical (agentive) subject position, has been widely discussed in the literature (e.g., Perlmutter 1978, Burzio 1986, Belletti 1988). The position for unaccusative subjects within VP, i.e., complement of the verb, is exactly the position to which lexically inverted verbs assign an inherent Case feature. I propose, then, that the verb *rxaw* 'get underway' is an unaccusative verb which has the lexical property of assigning an inherent ergative feature to its sole argument.[173] The structure of (380) is given in (383).

---

[172]Recall from chapter 2 that TP necessarily extends to AbsP forcing the presence of AbsP in structures having tense.

[173]In Abaza, an unaccusative lacking the lexical specification [+ERG] will be indistinguishable from an unergative verb (in which the subject is adjoined to VP), since both subjects move to the specifier of AbsP.

6.3 Expletives

(383)

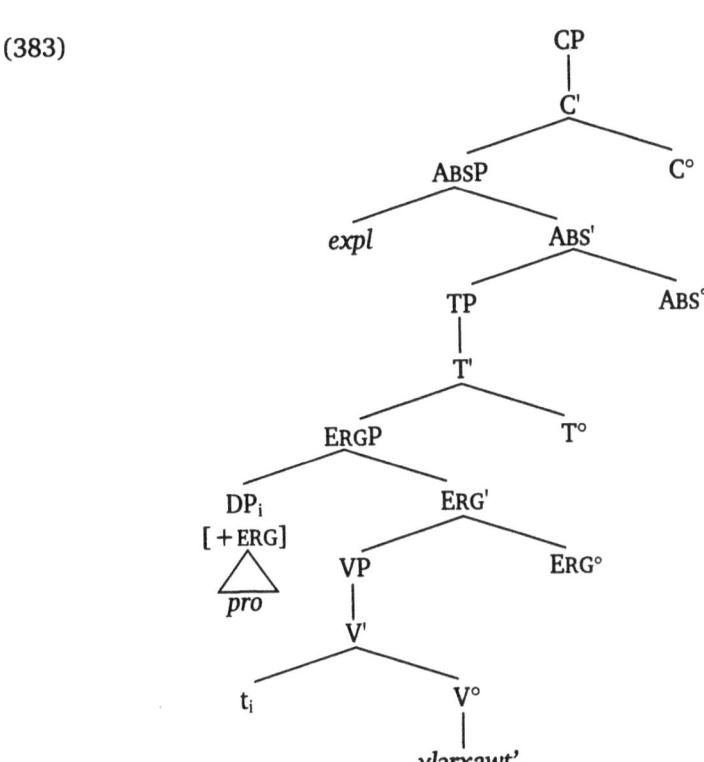

An analysis as an unaccusative is less plausible for a verb like zč'ət 'invite', since the subject is clearly agentive. Note, however, that this verb has two arguments. As a transitive verb, zč'ət inherently assigns ergative to its subject in accordance with the Transitive Subject Condition. The exceptional aspect of this verb is that it selects a benefactive PP complement, and the thematic argument of the verb occurs as the syntactic complement of this postposition. Since the object must be assigned Case within the PP, and the subject must occur in the specifier of an ergative agreement projection, neither argument is able to move to the specifier of AbsP, so an expletive is inserted there to satisfy the EPP.

Expletives occur in Abaza in those cases where no argument can move to the specifier of AbsP in order to satisfy the EPP. Verbs may lexically assign a feature, [+ERG], to an argument which requires the argument to occur in the specifier of an ergative projection. This feature is assigned either to a (di)transitive subject, in accordance with the TSC, or to the verb's complement when lexically specified. A configuration requiring an expletive results when an inherently Case-assigned complement is the only argument, as in an unaccusative, or when the nonsubject argument of a transitive verb is assigned Case independently, such as within a PP. The framework I have developed thus accounts directly for the expletive data.

6.4 Reflexives

Lexically inverted verbs are incompatible with the reflexive marker. The absolutive prefix cannot be replaced by the reflexive prefix, as in (384), which would be expected if the reflexive prefix were simply dependent on the absolutive prefix position. Nor can the ergative prefix be replaced by the reflexive morpheme, as in (385), which might be expected if the reflexive prefix were directly tied to the direct object position.[174]

(384) *č-s-as-d
REFL-1s-strike-DYN
(I struck myself)

(385) *sʕčʕasʕd
1s-REFL-strike-DYN
(I struck myself)

The underlying structure for both forms in (384) and (385) would be as in (386). The null anaphor, indicated with the feature [+REFL], must be in the object position, for if it were in the subject position, there would be a violation of Binding Condition A.

---

[174]The traditional Russian interpretation of lexically inverted verbs is that they are intransitive verbs with an indirect object. Sergei Pazov (pers. comm.) claims that the fact that the inverted verbs do not reflexivize is at least partial evidence for this position, since only truly transitive verbs may reflexivize.

6.4 Reflexives

(386)
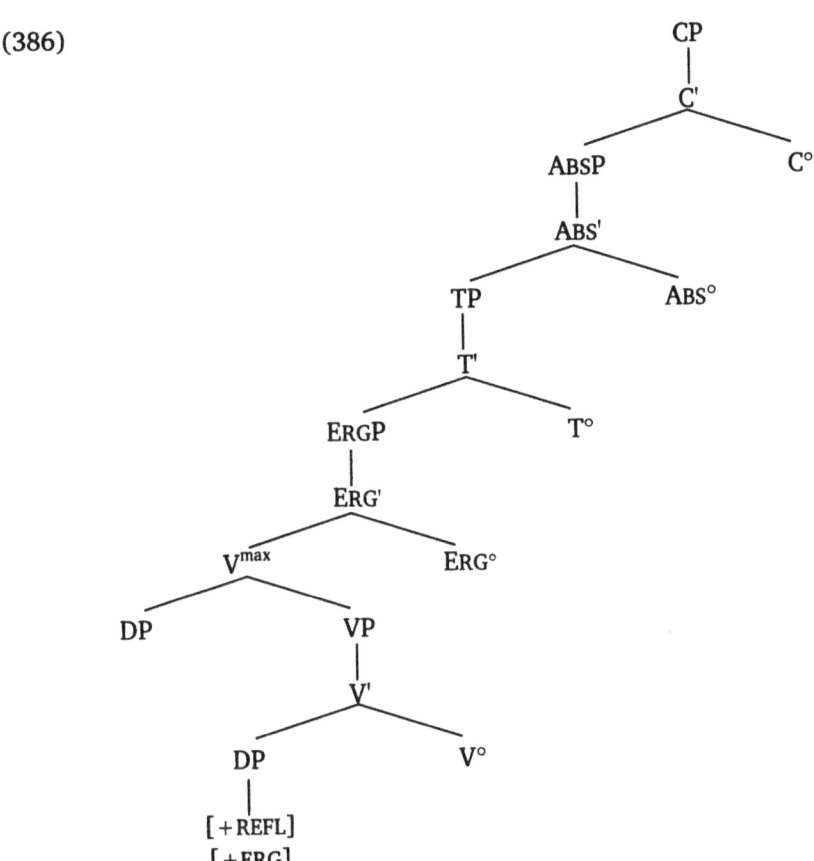

For inverted verbs, the direct object receives inherent Case, i.e., it is marked [+ERG] lexically by V°. For reflexives, the direct object is the reflexive anaphor with the feature [+REFL]. I argued above in §4.2.1 that there is a morphological gap such that there is no reflexive ergative form. The features [+ERG] and [+REFL] are thus incompatible. There is no configuration in which both can be successfully checked. If the anaphor moves to the specifier of ABSP, the feature [+REFL] can be checked, but the feature [+ERG] cannot. If the anaphor moves to the specifier of an ERGP, the feature [+ERG] can be checked, but the feature [+REFL] cannot because of the morphological gap.

A morphological gap such that there is no [+REFL] ergative prefix is a plausible language-specific solution for Abaza. A language-specific solution is desirable in that there are languages in which objects with inherent

Case can be reflexive anaphors, such as German, (387) and (388), and Russian, (389).[175]

(387) *Ich helfe mir / *mich*
 I help me (dative) / me (accusative)
 I help myself. (German)

(388) *Er hilft sich*
 he helps self (dative/accusative)
 He helps himself. (German)

(389) *ja vʲerʲu seʲbʲe / *s'eb'a*
 I believe self (dative) / self (accusative)
 I believe myself. (Russian)

Independently motivated factors in my analysis, i.e., the fact that there is no ergative reflexive form and the fact that inverted verbs lexically specify their objects as needing ergative Case, thus combine to correctly predict the impossibility of reflexive inverted forms.

6.5 The potential of inverted verbs

Lexically inverted verbs interact with derived inversion in an interesting way which supports my analysis. Agreement with the inherently Case-marked object is registered in an ergative series to the *right* of the potential prefix, as in (390). This contrasts with the agreement pattern seen with the potential of normal transitive verbs, (391), in which the ergative agreement series occurs to the left of the potential prefix.

(390) *s-z-y-əsə-y-d*
 1s-POT-3sm-hit-PRS-DYN
 I can hit him. SSAVC, 155

---

[175]Analyses in which the reflexive prefix is the head of a DP anaphor adjoined to the verb complex, as in §4.2.1, incorrectly predict that reflexives should be possible with lexically inverted verbs. It would be possible to rule out these ungrammatical forms with a constraint, similar to the one in the text, such that the anaphor DP could not be assigned the feature [+ERG]. Such a constraint is suspect, however, in that this would be the only DP in the language whose distribution was limited by a restriction on which Case it could receive. This is clearly more stipulative than the morphological gap which I propose. I take this as further evidence against these analyses.

6.5 The potential of inverted verbs

(391) d-s-zə-ƒʼə-y-d
   3sr-1s-POT-kill-PRS-DYN
   I can kill him/her.   SSAVC, 155

My analyses of derived inversion and of lexically inverted verbs predict this distinct pattern. In the potential of a normal transitive or ditransitive verb, as in (391), the subject must pass through the specifier of the auxiliary headed by the potential prefix before moving to an ergative specifier. The ergative projection must be higher than AUXP so that the transitive subject, which is specified [+ERG] by the TSC, can move into it. Thus, the ergative prefix occurs to the left of the potential prefix.

In a simple lexically inverted verb, on the other hand, the object instead of the subject is lexically specified [+ERG]. Since the subject, not the object, is required to pass through the specifier of AUXP, the ERGP whose specifier the object occupies is able to occur lower than AUXP; in fact, it must occur lower than AUXP because of the Closer Agreement Principle (CAP), which requires ergative agreement projections to occur as low as possible. Because this ERGP is lower than AUXP, the ergative agreement prefix in the verb complex occurs to the right of the potential prefix.

The subject is required to pass through the specifier of AUXP. Because it is not lexically specified [+ERG], the subject is free to move into the specifier of ABSP, which satisfies the EPP. The postmovement structure of (390) can be seen in (392).

(392)

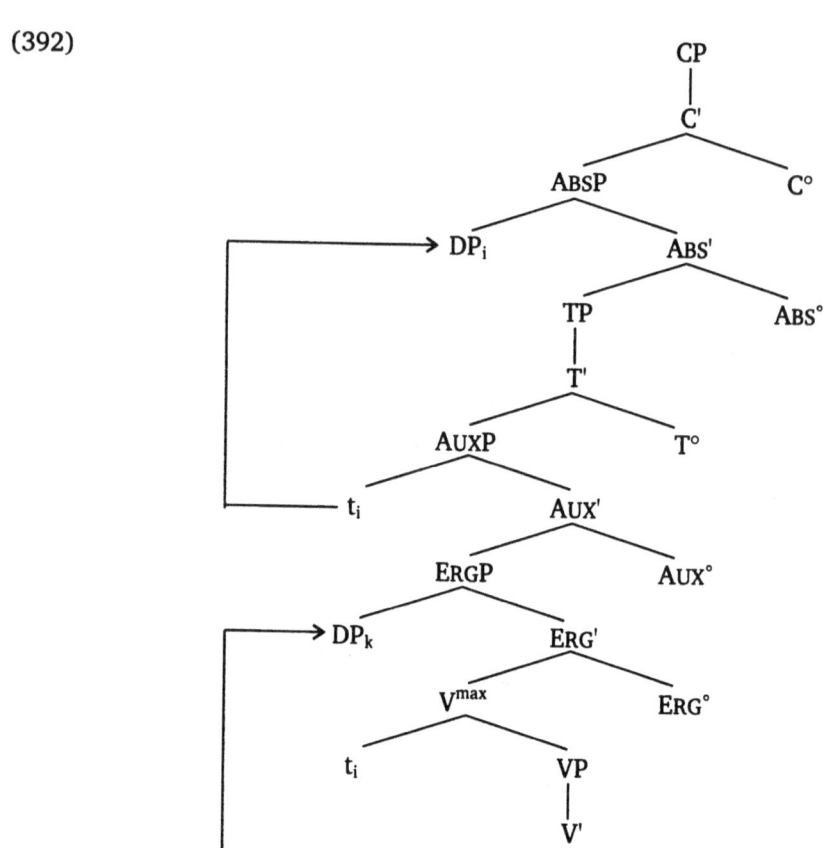

Interestingly, this structure obeys the Nesting Condition, albeit vacuously, unlike its nonpotential counterpart. The movement of the subject to the specifier of AuxP is A-movement. As A-movement, it does not interact with the A-bar movement of the object to the specifier of ErgP. The movements of the two arguments to their respective agreement specifiers do not interact, either crossing or nesting.

6.6 Lexically inverted verbs and the causative

This structure accounts for the potential construction with lexically inverted verbs entirely within the framework I have established.[176] Furthermore, it provides support for the treatment of the object in the lexically inverted verbs as receiving an inherent Case, since the behavior of the object is exceptional.

6.6 Lexically inverted verbs and the causative

We conclude our discussion of lexically inverted verbs by examining their interaction with the causative construction. This interaction lends support to the treatment of inherent Case as mediated through agreement projections.

When a lexically inverted verb is causativized, the causative prefix rʕ occurs to the immediate left of the verb root, as usual. The causative subject is registered in an ergative series to the left of the causative prefix, as expected. The object of the base verb is registered in an ergative series to the left of that, and the subject of the base verb is registered in the absolutive series. This can be seen in (393).

(393) d-a-s-r-əs-t'
    3sr-3si-1s-CAUS-hit-DYN
    I caused him/her to hit it.

Given the assumption that the order of morphemes reflects syntactic structure, and the analysis of causatives in chapter 4, the d-structure for a form like (393) is (394).

---

[176] I am not aware of any analysis in the Russian literature on Abaza dealing with this construction. It seems to me, however, that it would be problematic for the traditional account for the following reasons: (1) the ergative series to the immediate left of the verb root is generally taken to be the "subject" series, while the more distant ergative series is generally taken to be the "indirect object" series, and (2) the nonsubject argument in lexically inverted verbs is generally taken to be the indirect object of an intransitive verb. In the potential of lexically inverted verbs, what is taken to be the indirect object is registered in what is taken to be the subject series. This suggests the rearrangement of argument structure in the potential construction of lexically inverted verbs such that the indirect object becomes the subject.

(394)

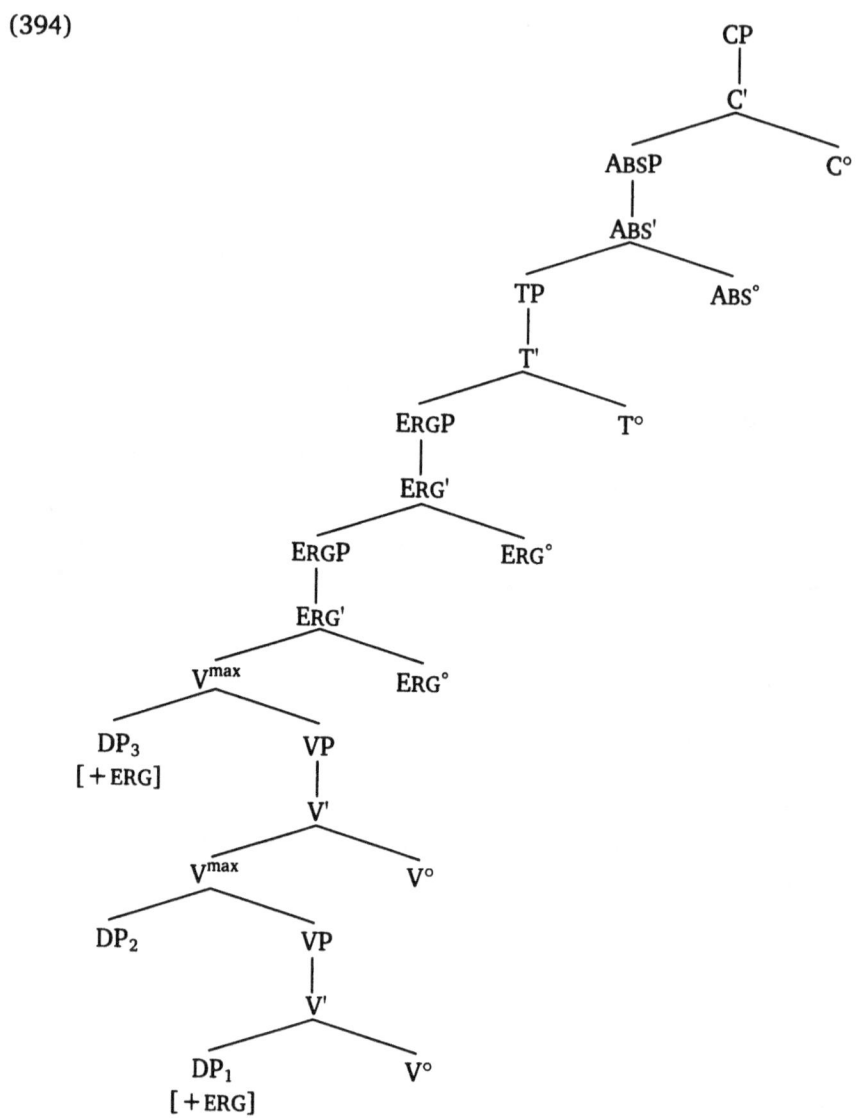

This is the d-structure predicted by my framework. The causative verb selects a lexical X^{max}, which may be headed by an inverted verb. There are two ergative agreement projections dominating the causative verb phrase, which is allowed by the free generation of ERGP and the Unused Agreement Filter (UAF) because both will be filled. These ergative

6.6 Lexically inverted verbs and the causative

projections occur as low as possible, i.e., directly dominating the causative V^{max}, in accordance with the Closer Agreement Principle (CAP).

In the structure (394), DP_1 is lexically marked [+ERG] by the inverted verb. The subject of the inverted verb, DP_2, is unmarked for Case. Because the causative verb is transitive, i.e., its complement position is filled, its subject, DP_3, is also lexically marked [+ERG].[177] In this structure, only the base subject, DP_2, can move to the specifier of AbsP. It must do so in order to satisfy the EPP. In order for the two arguments marked [+ERG] to satisfy the Nesting Condition, the causative subject, DP_3, must move to the lower ergative specifier, and the base object, DP_1, must move to the higher ergative specifier.[178] After movement, the resulting structure is (395).

---

[177]The same movement is predicted if the causative subject is not marked [+ERG] by the Transitive Subject Condition. Two arguments, the base subject and the causative subject, would then be unmarked for Case, and the lower one, the base subject, would have to move to the specifier of AbsP in order to satisfy both the Nesting Condition and the EPP.

[178]The only nonnesting interaction is that between the base subject and direct object. This is exactly the same result in simple lexically inverted verbs, and the same principle can be used to account for it, namely the Elsewhere Condition. See §6.2.

(395)

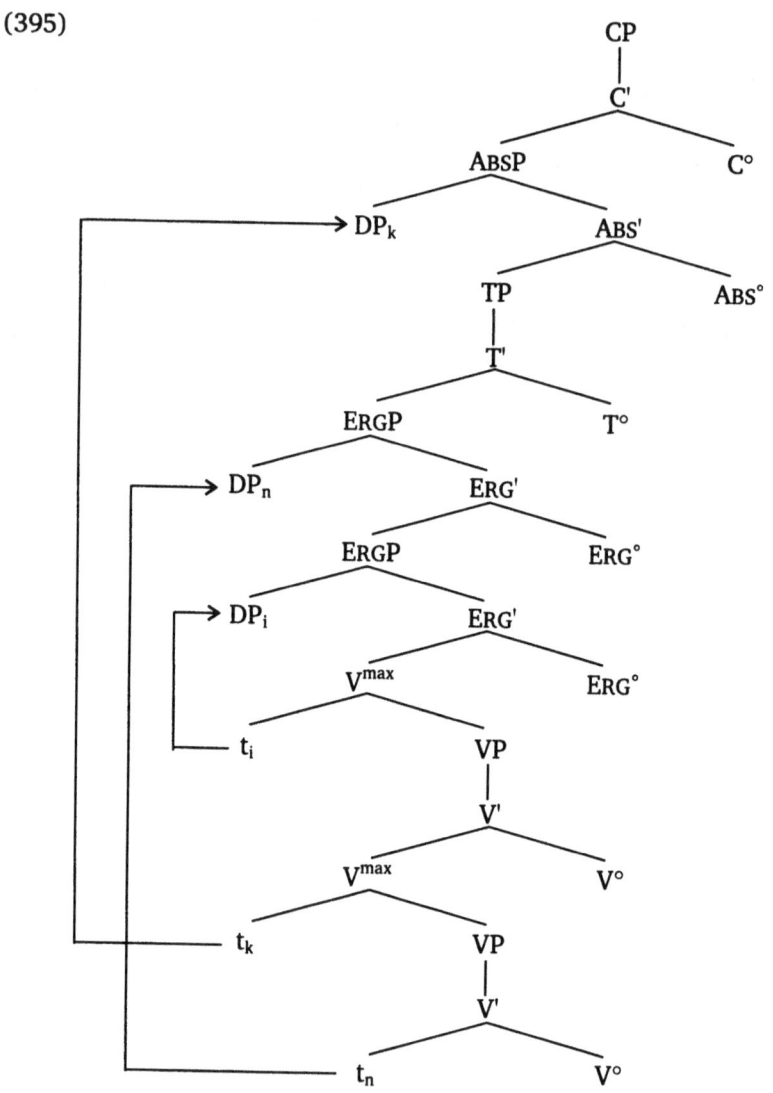

The framework I have developed forces the d-structure in (394) for the causative of a lexically inverted verb. Furthermore, this framework predicts the arguments in (394) will move to the agreement specifier positions as in (395). This results in a structure producing exactly the observed agreement pattern in (393). My framework thus correctly accounts for constructions involving the causative of lexically inverted verbs without any additional machinery.

6.6 Lexically inverted verbs and the causative

Such forms as the causatives of lexically inverted verbs support the analysis that inherent Case is mediated by an agreement projection. I assume that the order of prefixes reflects the order of syntactic checking, which is dependent on the syntactic structure. If inherent Case is assigned directly by $V°$ to its complement, then the morphological realization of this Case assignment, i.e., the agreement registered with the object, should occur in a position internal to the morphological realization of features which are checked higher in the syntactic structure. Because the verb-complement configuration occurs structurally below all the functional projections which mediate other feature-checking relationships, we would expect, therefore, that agreement with the object should appear adjacent to the verb when $V°$ assigns Case directly to its complement.

This prediction is not borne out, however. Agreement with the object of a lexically inverted verb complement to the causative verb is registered in an agreement series external to the causative verb and the ergative series which registers agreement with the causative subject. As already demonstrated, this is the expected position if inherent Case is mediated through agreement projections. The assignment of inherent Case through an agreement projection allows for the relevant agreement series to be nonadjacent to the head which assigns it (because it is assigning a feature and not the Case itself). It is difficult to account for the nonadjacency of the verb head and the morphological realization of this relation, i.e., agreement, if the verb head itself assigns inherent Case.

Lexically inverted verbs in Abaza exhibit an exceptional agreement pattern. I argue that this is the result of an inherent Case assigned by the inverted verb to its object. This inherent Case assignment is actually the specification of a feature [+ERG] on the DP which receives inherent Case. The interaction of lexically inverted verbs with the potential and causative constructions creates some complex alternations in the agreement patterns. The analysis I propose in chapter 2 in conjunction with my analysis of lexically inverted verbs as inherent Case-assigners correctly accounts for these patterns in a direct way and supports the claim that my analysis is comprehensive.

7

Postposition Incorporation

Certain oblique arguments in Abaza can be optionally expressed within the verb complex. These include benefactive and adversative (aka, malefactive), instrumental, comitative, and locative arguments. Associated with the morphology expressing these oblique relationships, there is obligatory agreement with the argument in that oblique role. I analyze this as the incorporation of a postposition (and its associated agreement head) into the complex of verbal heads.

Section 7.1 presents the basic data for this construction. Section 7.2 presents motivation for an analysis in which these are postpositions incorporated into the verb. This analysis is compared and contrasted with Baker's (1988) analysis of similar phenomena in other languages.[179] Section 7.3 discusses differences between Baker's data and the Abaza data. I propose that these differences result from the fact that in Abaza the postpositional head incorporates in conjunction with the ergative agreement head which dominates it. Section 7.4 deals with the issue of where these phrases occur within the structure. I propose a position adjoined higher than Baker assumes, external to VP. Section 7.5 discusses the problem of how the movement is licensed from the position proposed in §7.4.

7.1 Oblique arguments in the verb complex

There are four classes of verbal prefixes in Abaza which express various oblique relationships. Following Baker (1988), I will refer to these

---

[179]Throughout this chapter, any unspecified references to Baker refer to Baker (1988).

collectively as APPLICATIVES. These prefixes are associated with additional agreement morphology beyond that required by the basic thematic relations of the verb. In each case, the relevant applicative prefix occurs between the absolutive and ergative agreement series positions, and in each case the applicative prefix requires an additional agreement series to its immediate left, which has the phonological form of the ergative series.

These applicative prefixes may be used regardless of the transitivity of the verb, and the transitivity of the verb is not affected. The agreement pattern of the verb with its basic arguments is unaffected by the introduction of these prefixes. There are few or no verbs which require the presence of any of them, i.e., verbs are not subcategorized in terms of these prefixes.[180]

7.1.1 Benefactives and adversatives

The benefactive prefix is *z*-. It indicates who the action of the verb benefits or is supposed to benefit. The actual manner in which the benefactee is benefited is not rigid. Examples (396)–(398) demonstrate benefactive prefixes and their associated agreement prefixes to the left.

(396) *y-s-z-a-č'pa-d*
3si-1s-BEN-3si-do-DYN
It did it for me.   SSAVC, 163

(397) *y-l-zə-s-ʒʷ-d*
3si-**3sf**-BEN-1s-drink-DYN
I accepted her offer of a drink. (lit., I drank it for her.)   SSAVC, 148

(398) *ahʷa*   *r-zə-s-č'pa-b*
sword   3p-BEN-1s-make-FUT2
I will make them a sword.   SSAVC, 152

The adversative or malefactive prefix, *čʷ*-, has a similar (but opposite) meaning to that of the benefactive, indicating an argument which is adversely affected by the verb event. Examples (399) and (400) illustrate

---

[180]One exception is the verb *zč'ət* 'invite', discussed in §§2.4.2.2 and 5.2.1.2 with respect to (absolutive) expletives. A second possible exception to this is the verb *zərʕʷa* 'forgive', which I treat as an inverted verb. Tabulova (1976) provides a form of this as an example of a benefactive prefix. There is, however, no related verb lacking the benefactive prefix. (*rʕʷa* exists, with the meaning 'cause to dry', the causative from the root *ʕʷa* 'dry'.) It is possible that this developed historically from a benefactive, thus accounting for the inverted agreement pattern.

7.1 Oblique arguments in the verb complex

adversatives with intransitive and transitive verbs, respectively. The adversative can also express the source of something negative, such as in (401) with the intransitive verb ʃʷa 'fear', which utilizes the adversative to indicate the thing feared.

(399) *d-s-čʷ-ǰʷəkʷ-l-d*
    3sr-1s-ADV-out.go-DYN
    S/he escaped from me.   SSAVC, 163

(400) *y-s-čʷə-y-yəčʲ-d*
    3si-1s-ADV-3sm-steal-DYN
    He stole it from me.   SSAVC, 164

(401) *hara*   *a-la*   *h-a-čʷ-ʃʷa-y-d*
    we   DEF-dog   1p-3si-ADV-fear-PRS-DYN
    We are afraid of the dog.

7.1.2 Comitatives

The comitative prefix, *c-*, indicates an argument which is somehow a coparticipant in the action of the verb. Examples can be seen in (403)–(405). Examples (402) and (403) differ minimally in the presence or absence of a comitative verbal prefix. Examples (403) and (404) demonstrate the comitative with intransitive verbs, while (405) shows the comitative with a transitive verb.

(402) *də-mʃərqʷʼə-y-tʼ*
    3sr-joke-PRS-DYN
    S/he is joking.   GAL, 189

(403) *d-rə-cə-mʃərqʷʼə-y-tʼ*
    3sr-3p-COM-joke-PRS-DYN
    S/he is joking with them.   GAL, 189

(404) *qʼapʲan-y*   *asyat-y*   *mʕʷa*   *y-hə-c-ʕakʷəl-tʼ*
    Kaplan-and   Asiat-and   way   3p-1p-COM-set.out-DYN
    Kaplan and Asiat set out on the way with us.   GAL, 189

(405) awə́y   ana-m-wə   sosrəq'ʷa   yə-wnaʃʷa-la   aynəʒʷ
     that   when-NEG-agree   Sosruko   3sm-command-INST   giant

     y-ləmha-k'   ʕa-pə-r-q'ə-n   y-rə-c-ʕa-r-g-d
     3sm-ear-one   DIR-PV-3p-cut-PST   3si-3p-COM-DIR-3p-carry-DYN
     When that didn't work, they cut off one of the giant's ears and took
     it with them, as Sosruko commanded.   NART, 67-8

7.1.3 Locatives

The class of locative prefixes in the verb include at least the following, taken from Genko (1955).

(406) a. q- (qə-)   in the direction to (from)
      b. dzqa-   beside
      c. la- (lə-)   into, from within[181]
      d. n- (nə-)   into, from within
      e. čʷ- (čʷə-)   from (superficially)[182]
      f. q'ʷə-   from (behind)
      g. d- (də-)   about, in a row
      h. c'a- (c'ə-)   under (from under)
      i. kʷ- (kʷə-)   on top
      j. ʃ'ta-   (right) behind
      k. mc'a-   in front of
      l. qa- (qə-)   on the surface of

The following examples do not cover every prefix in (406), but they are representative of the way locative prefixes behave. Example (409) demonstrates that the oblique object may be overt and nonpronominal, in contrast to (408) with a null pronominal oblique object.

(407) s-č'ʷa-t'
      1s-sit-DYN
      I sat (down).

(408) s-a-kʷ-č'ʷa-t'
      1s-**3si-on**-sit-DYN
      I sat on it.

---

[181] This contrasts with the instrumental prefix *la-* in its position with respect to the directional prefixes.

[182] This may be better treated as the adversative prefix.

(409) a-ʔarama-kʷa   bqʷʼəl-kʼ   y-ta-l-cʼa-n   a-qarpa-gʲəy
      DEF-bunch-PL   barrel-INDEF   3si-in-3sf-put-PST   DEF-lid-INT

      abrahaqʷ   a-kʷ-l-cʼa-x-d
      boulder   3si-on-3sf-put-again-DYN
      She put the bunches in a barrel and on the lid she also replaced the
      boulder.   AT, 171-172

(410) y-a-mcʼa-gəla-pʼ
      3si-3si-before-stand-STP
      It stands before it.   GAL, 179

7.1.4 Instrumentals

The instrumental prefix *la-* indicates an object or thing with which an action is performed. Examples (411) and (412) of the instrumental prefix in the verb complex demonstrate that the applicative prefixes can have wh-agreement.[183] Note that example (412) utilizes the instrumental prefix without a concrete object, and seems to allow a manner interpretation.

(411) ahə   wʒʷə   wə-z-la-kʃa-x-wa-ya
      so   now   2sm-EWH-INST-strike-ASP-PRS-WHQ
      So, what will you strike (me) with now?   NART, 65

(412) wʒʷəbərg   w-qənhə-ta   wə-z-la-ʕayə-z-la
      right.now   2sm-turn-FTC   2sm-EWH-INST-come-PST-INST

      w-ca-x   y-hʷa-d   sosrəqʷa
      2sm-go-again   3sm-say-DYN   Sosruko
      "Turn around, right away, and go the same way you came here,"
      said Sosruko.   NART, 66

7.2 Motivation for a postposition incorporation analysis

I propose that applicative prefixes are postpositions incorporated into the verbal complex, similar to the analysis proposed by Baker (1988). In keeping with my assumption that the verb complex is formed in the lexicon and the features associated with each morpheme are checked in the syntax, I assume that the postpositions which incorporate are

---

[183]See chapter 8 for further discussion of wh-agreement.

phonologically null, but featurally contentful. This section provides motivation for the treatment as incorporated postpositions. One factor suggesting an analysis of applicative structures as postposition incorporation is that applicative constructions contrast with constructions having independent PPs and lacking any overt marking associated with the oblique argument in the verbal complex itself. By Baker's (1988) Uniformity of Theta Assignment Hypothesis (UTAH), these should both derive from the same underlying structure.

7.2.1 The UTAH

Baker (1988) analyzes applicative constructions in Bantu and other languages as involving the incorporation of a preposition into the verb. In motivating his analysis, he begins with the Uniformity of Theta Assignment Hypothesis (UTAH), as in (413).

(413) The Uniformity of Theta Assignment Hypothesis:
    Identical thematic relationships between items are represented by identical structural relationships between those items at the level of D-structure.   Baker (1988:46)

Baker then shows that there are languages in which the applicative construction coexists with constructions having independent PPs indicating the same thematic roles as the applicatives. Since the thematic relationships are the same in both constructions, the UTAH requires that the two types of constructions have the same d-structures. This means that both applicative constructions and constructions involving corresponding independent PPs have an underlying structure utilizing a PP, as in (414), 'I hand my exam to the teacher.'

(414)
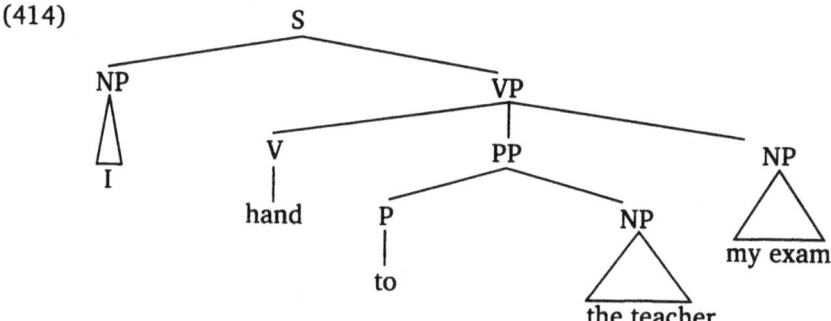

7.2 Motivation for a postposition incorporation analysis

This then requires an account of how the applicatives are derived from an underlying structure having independent PPs. Baker argues that the difference between an applicative construction and a construction involving an independent PP is that in the applicative construction the prepositional head, P°, incorporates into the verb, V°, while there is no such movement in the other case. The postincorporation structure is seen in (415) (from Baker 1988:234).

(415)
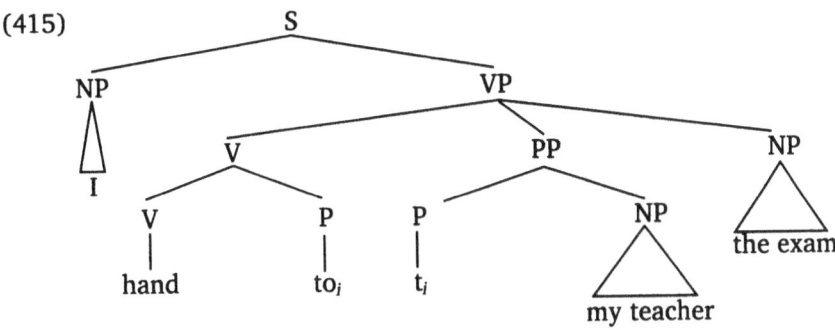

7.2.2 Independent postpositions in Abaza

This same argument based on the UTAH can be applied to Abaza. With the exception of the adversative prefix and perhaps a few of the locative prefixes, constructions with each of the applicative prefixes discussed in §7.1 have corresponding constructions with independent postpositional phrases, the object of which is the oblique argument in question.

It is possible to express the notion benefactive with an overt, independent postposition, *qaz*.[184] Recall that postpositions in Abaza agree with their objects.

(416) sara   qʷmarga-k'   s-pa   yə-qaz-la   y-s-əma-b
      I   toy-INDEF   1s-son   3sm-for-INST   3si-1s-have-STP
      I have a toy for my son.

(417) sara   bilet   **wara**   **wə-qaz**   y-ʕa-s-aw-d
      I   ticket   you   2sm-for   3si-PV-1s-find-DYN
      I found the ticket for you.

---

[184] I have found no discussion in the literature of this independent benefactive, but it occurs in my own field notes, as well as in texts. The phonological similarity between the independent postposition, *qaz*, and the verbal prefix, *z*- (*az*- in some cases), is certainly not coincidental. (The word *qa* 'head' is commonly used in the formation of idiomatic constructions.)

(418) awat   r-akʷ-b   a-dəwnay   də-z-z-əkʷə-w   **y-qa**
      they   3p-be-STP   DEF-world   3sr-EWH-BEN-be.in-PTC   3sm-head

   a-qaẑ-la   a-dəwnay   d-gʲə-kʷə-m
   3si-for-INST   DEF-world   3sr-INT-be.in-NEG
   He is living in the world for them, not for himself.   NART, 73

Example (418) actually contains two clauses, one with an independent postposition as benefactive, *aqaẑla*, and one with a benefactive as a verbal prefix, in *dəzzəkʷəw*. The use of the independent postposition appears to be required or motivated by the fact that the benefactive object is reflexive in this case.

I have discovered no independent postposition with an adversative usage either in the literature or in my own notes.

The literature I have seen does not refer to an independent comitative postposition, but my own notes indicate that there is one, which has a nearly identical form to the verbal prefix *c-* (*ca-*).

(419) ahmet bey   wačʷə   hara   **h-acə-ta**   sinema   h-ca-ta
      Ahmet Bey   tomorrow   we   1p-with-FAC   movies   1p-go-FAC

   ha-m-ca-wʃ-ta   gʲama   yə-w-dər-əw-ma
   1p-NEG-go-FUT-FAC   TAG   3si-2sm-know-PRS-YNQ
   You don't know whether Ahmet Bey will go to the movies with us tomorrow, do you?

Many of the locative verbal prefixes have counterparts as independent postpositions. In a few cases, such as *dzqa* 'beside' and *akʷ* 'on', the postpositions are identical or nearly identical to the corresponding verbal prefix (with only minor vowel variations if there are any differences at all). In other cases, for example *c'axʲ* 'under', the independent postpositions consist of what looks like the corresponding verbal prefix plus the (perhaps derivational) suffix, *-xʲ*. There are additionally some independent postpositions which have this shape (ending in *xʲ*), but which do not have a corresponding verbal locative prefix, e.g., *paxʲ* 'in front of, before' and *amʃt'axʲ* 'after'. Finally, there are postpositions which do not at all resemble their corresponding verbal prefixes, e.g., *wac'a* 'in' versus *la-* and *n-*.

(420) a-ẑʲəra   a-dzqa   (cf. *dzqa-* 'beside')
      DEF-smithy   3si-beside
      beside the smithy   SGSAL, 622

7.2 Motivation for a postposition incorporation analysis

(421) awəy   s-adzqa   d-č'ʷa-b
      s/he   1s-beside   3sr-sit-STP
      S/he is sitting next to me.

(422) a-haʒʷ   a-kʷ   (cf. akʷ- 'on')
      DEF-sheaf 3si-on
      on the sheaf   SGSAL, 622

(423) a-ʒʷʕʷand   a-kʷ-la   y-ala-y-jə-y-d-ta ...
      DEF-sky   3si-on-AV 3si-PV-3sm-throw-PRS-DYN-FAC
      He throws it into the sky...   NART, 73

(424) a-rəmdza   a-c'axʲ   (cf. c'a- 'under')
      DEF-chair 3si-under
      under the chair   SGSAL, 622

(425) a-čʲkʷʷən   a-c'la   a-c'axʲ   d-qʷmarə-y-d
      DEF-boy   DEF-tree 3si-under 3sr-play-PRS-DYN
      The boy is playing under the tree.

(426) a-čʲkʷʷən   a-c'la   a-paxʲ   d-ʕay-y-d
      DEF-boy   DEF-tree 3si-in.front.of 3sr-come-PRS-DYN
      The boy comes in front of the tree.

(427) sara   mčʲəbʒʲə-k'   a-mʃtaxʲ   s-nay-b
      I   week-INDEF   3si-after 1s-come-FUT2
      I will come next week (lit., after a week).

(428) a-bawra   a-wac'a
      DEF-barn 3si-in
      in the barn   SGSAL, 621

(429) hara   a-ʕʷaga   a-wac'a   čə-ha-ba-y-d
      we   DEF-mirror 3si-in   REFL-1p-see-PRS-DYN
      We see ourselves in the mirror.

The instrumental can also be expressed through the use of an independent postposition, which has the identical phonological form to the verbal instrumental prefix, la-. Examples (430) and (431) show a minimal pair with an independent postposition expressing the instrument in the former and a verbal prefix expressing the instrument in the latter.

(430) a-čʲkʷʰən kʲəm-la   d-qʷmarə-y-d[185]
      DEF-boy   top-INST   3sr-play-PRS-DYN
      The boy is playing with a top.

(431) a-čʲkʷʰən kʲəm   d-a-la-qʷmarə-y-d
      DEF-boy   top   3sr-3si-INST-play-PRS-DYN
      The boy is playing with the top.

The postpositional suffix (or clitic) *la* is used in a variety of constructions besides what is commonly referred to as instrumental, as seen in examples (416) and (418). This instrumental "postposition" differs from other postpositions in a number of crucial respects.[186] First, it never registers any agreement with its complement. Second, it is part of the phonological phrase of its complement, and not an independent word. In this way it acts like a clitic. Finally, the range of the possible categories of its complements is wider than any of the other postpositions, allowing DP, PP, and CP (with CPs of various moods allowed). Other postpositions allow DP and, in a few cases, CP (limited to indicative mood).

As in the cases Baker discusses, then, Abaza exhibits a complementarity between applicative affixes in the verb complex (with associated agreement) and independent postpositional phrases. Both constructions can be used to express benefactive, comitative, locative, and instrumental notions. By the UTAH, these must derive from identical underlying structures. This motivates an incorporation analysis following Baker.

Baker makes the additional observation that it is not necessary that the phonological form of the incorporated P° and that of the independent P° be identical, but he claims that it is additional support for the incorporation analysis when they are. Quite a few of the Abaza independent postpositions have the same phonological form as their counterparts which show up in the verb complex. I take this as further support for the incorporation analysis.[187]

---

[185]The verb *qʷmar* 'play' is only intransitive in Abaza. Without incorporation of *la*, only a single argument may be licensed (in the absolutive Case). The instrument *kʲəmla* in (430) is completely optional, and not subcategorized for.

[186]The only other element with a similar behavior and distribution to *la* is the factitive marker *ta*, which indicates a state or condition into which something changes. See §1.1.2.4 and Serdyuchenko (1956) for further discussion.

[187]In my analysis of Abaza, though, incorporated postpositions themselves are phonologically null. The phonological similarity discussed here is thus between the overt postpositions and the verbal prefixes which introduce the features checked by these null postpositions.

7.2.3 The use of applicatives versus independent PPs

The question arises as to what determines the use of incorporated versus unincorporated postpositions. A full analysis is beyond the scope of this study; I offer a few initial observations in this section.

One factor affecting the distribution of applicatives and independent PPs in Abaza is that the object of the postposition seems to need to be definite with applicatives. For example, in (432), the applicative construction is used for the instrument, and the instrument itself (the object of the postposition), amhač̣ʷa 'spoon', is definite. This contrasts with (433), which is identical except that the instrument is indefinite, and this leads to ungrammaticality. The equivalent of (433) can be expressed grammatically if an independent PP is used, as in (434).[188] A second definite versus indefinite pair following this pattern can be seen in (435) and (436).

(432) a-čʲkʷʰən   a-mhač̣ʷa   y-axʃa   d-a-la-yə-c-č̣ʲa-t'
     DEF-boy   DEF-spoon   3sm-sister   3sr-3si-INST-3sm-COM-eat-DYN
     His$_i$ sister ate with the boy$_i$ with the spoon.

(433) *a-čʲkʷʰən   mhač̣ʷa   y-axʃa   d-a-la-yə-c-č̣ʲa-t'
     DEF-boy   spoon   3sm-sister   3sr-3si-INST-3sm-COM-eat-DYN
     (His sister ate with the boy with spoons/the spoon/a spoon.)

(434) a-čʲkʷʰən   mhač̣ʷa-la   y-axʃa   d-yə-c-č̣ʲa-t'
     DEF-boy   spoon-INST   3sm-sister   3sr-3sm-COM-eat-DYN
     His$_i$ sister ate with the boy$_i$ with spoons/the spoon.

(435) arq'an-la   y-w-č̣ʷə-s-yəč-t'
     rope-INST   3si-2sm-ADV-1s-steal-DYN
     I stole it from you with a rope.

(436) arq'an   yə-w-č̣ʷ-a-la-ʕa-s-yəč-t'
     rope[189]   3si-2sm-ADV-3si-INST-DIR-1s-steal-DYN
     I stole it from you with the rope.

---

[188] This pattern is quite clear for the instrumental. Perhaps this is related to the different status of the independent postposition (as a clitic, and lacking overt agreement). I do not have the data to confirm or deny this pattern for the other types of postpositions.

[189] The form arq'an is ambiguous between definite and indefinite because of a rule that reduces a sequence of two [a] vowels to one. Native speakers clearly distinguish definite and indefinite in this case and others like it.

There is a strong tendency for independent postpositions to have overt objects. In the data available to me, there are only a few examples of independent postpositions with null objects, all first or second person. This may be a factor in determining whether a postposition must incorporate.

Both incorporated and independent postpositions in Abaza can have overt pronominal objects, as in (437) and (438).

(437) a-čʲkʷʼən   awə-la   d-qʷmar-i-tʼ
     DEF-boy   that-INST   3sr-play-PRS-DYN
     The boy is playing with that.

(438) a-čʲkʷʼən   awəy   d-a-la-qʷmar-i-tʼ
     DEF-boy   it/that   3sr-3si-INST-play-PRS-DYN
     The boy is playing with it/that.

7.3 The incorporation of AGR°-P°

These Abaza verbs with oblique relationships morphologically marked through prefixes have striking similarities to the data Baker discusses. Nevertheless, there are some differences as discussed in §7.3.1. Section 7.3.2 shows how Baker accounts for his set of data, and §7.3.3 proposes that Abaza differs from the languages Baker discusses in that the agreement head plus the postposition head (AGR°-P°), instead of just P°, incorporates into the verb. This distinction directly accounts for the empirical differences between the two types of languages.

7.3.1 Empirical differences

There are three major differences between the data that Baker analyzes as postposition incorporation and the comparable Abaza data.[190] First, in Baker's data, only transitive verbs support P-incorporation, in general. In Abaza, the transitivity of the verb has no effect on P-incorporation, which can occur freely with either transitive or intransitive verbs. Second, in Baker's data, the incorporation of the adposition results in a rearrangement of the argument structure of the verb. The incorporation of the

---

[190]One minor difference between the two sets of data is that Abaza allows the incorporation of a postpositional head from a comitative PP, in addition to benefactive, locative, and instrumental. This is not a surprising extension of the possible categories which may incorporate, though, and does not require any modification of the analysis presented here. Craig and Hale (1988) discuss similar data in three languages of the Americas, and include comitative as a possible type of PP involved in this construction.

7.3 The incorporation of AGR°-P°

postposition has no such effect in Abaza. Finally, in Baker's data, only a single adposition may incorporate into a verb. In Abaza, as many as three postpositions may incorporate into a single verb.

In many of the Bantu languages Baker discusses, only transitive verbs can host the applicative construction, i.e., P-incorporation. For example, it is not possible to form applicative structures from intransitive verbs in Chichewa.

(439) chiphadzuwa   chi-a-fik-a
      beautiful.woman SP-PERF-arrive-ASP
      The beautiful woman has arrived.   Baker (1988:255)

(440) *chiphadzuwa   chi-a-fik-ir-a   mfumu
      beautiful.woman SP-PERF-arrive-for-ASP chief
      (The beautiful woman has arrived for the chief.) Baker (1988:255)

In Abaza, both transitive and intransitive verbs may freely host applicatives. This has already been demonstrated for the different types of oblique prefixes in §7.1, for example with the adversative prefix in (441) and (442).

(441) d-s-č^w-ǰ^{w}ək^{w}l-d
      3sr-1s-ADV-out.go-DYN
      S/he escaped from me.   SSAVC, 163

(442) y-s-č^{w}ə-y-ɣəč^j-d
      3si-1s-ADV-3sm-steal-DYN
      He stole it from me.   SSAVC, 164

In the languages Baker analyzes, the argument structure of a verb with applicative morphology differs from that of a simple transitive verb. Specifically, an applicative object behaves as the direct object, and the underlying direct object behaves as an oblique,[191] that is, it occurs as an oblique, if at all. Consider the examples from Chichewa.

(443) afisi   a-na-ph-a   nsomba
      hyenas   SP-PAST-kill-ASP fish
      The hyenas killed the fish.   Baker (1988:254)

---

[191] Baker's term, "applicative object", refers to the object of the preposition after the head P° incorporates into the verb. I use this term for the object of the postpositions in the Abaza constructions as well.

(444) *afisi   a-na-ph-er-a   anyani   nsomba*
      hyenas SP-PAST-kill-for-ASP baboons fish
      The hyenas killed fish for the baboons.   Baker (1988:254)

Evidence that the applicative object has replaced the underlying direct object as the surface direct object can be seen in that the applicative object can trigger object agreement on the verb (445), can pro-drop (446), and can become the subject of a passive verb (448). These are all tests in Chichewa for being a direct object. In the applicative construction, the underlying direct object loses all of these properties.

(445) *amayi   a-ku-mu-umb-ir-a   mtsuko   mwana*
      woman SP-PRES-OP-mold-for-ASP water.pot child
      The woman is molding the water pot for the child.
                                                        Baker (1988:266)

(446) *amayi   a-ku-mu-umb-ir-a   mtsuko*
      woman SP-PRES-OP-mold-for-ASP water.pot
      The woman is molding the water pot for him.   Baker (1988:266)

(447) *kalulu a-na-gul-ir-a   mbidzi nsapato*
      hare   SP-PAST-buy-for-ASP zebras   shoes
      The hare bought shoes for the zebras.   Baker (1988:266)

(448) *mbidzi zi-na-gul-ir-idw-a   nsapato (ndi kalulu)*
      zebras SP-PAST-buy-for-PASS-ASP shoes   by   hare
      The zebras were bought shoes by the hare.   Baker (1988:266)

In Abaza, applicative prefixes do not trigger a rearrangement of the argument structure in this way. The underlying verbal arguments retain their underlying argument positions, and it is the applicative object which is treated differently. In both transitive and intransitive verbs, the applicative object is registered in an exceptional ergative series not associated with any basic verbal argument. One consequence of this is that in Abaza an "extra" agreement prefix occurs in the verb complex (registering agreement with the applicative object). Another consequence is that the presence of the applicative prefixes does not affect the transitivity of the verb.

Intransitive verbs remain intransitive. The subject is registered in the absolutive series normally, and it continues to be registered in the absolutive series when applicative prefixes are present. Compare (449)

7.3 The incorporation of AGR°-P°

and (450). Furthermore, intransitive verbs with applicative prefixes cannot be reflexivized, as would be expected if these became transitive.

(449) *də-mʃərqʷ'ə-y-t'*
3sr-joke-PRS-DYN
S/he is joking.   GAL, 189

(450) *d-rə-cə-mʃərqʷ'ə-y-t'*
3sr-3p-COM-joke-PRS-DYN
S/he is joking with us.   GAL, 189

Transitive verbs likewise remain transitive, maintaining the same argument structure, that is, the subject is registered in the ergative series and the direct object is registered in the absolutive series in both simple transitive clauses and in transitive clauses with applicative prefixes and their associated agreement. Compare (451) and (452), in which ergative and absolutive agreement prefixes are in bold.

(451) *y-p-s-qə-t'*
3si-PV-1s-break-DYN
I broke it.

(452) *yə-l-čʷ'ə-p-s-qə-t'*
3si-3sf-ADV-PV-1s-break-DYN
I broke it to her disadvantage.

When reflexivized, transitive verbs having applicative prefixes allow only the reflexive reading in which the subject is the antecedent and the direct object is the reflexive anaphor. The applicative object cannot be the antecedent to a direct object anaphor, as in (453), nor can the applicative object be a reflexive anaphor. This is consistent with the fact that there is no ergative reflexive prefix.

(453) *čə-y-čʷ'ə-s-ga-t'*
REFL-3si-ADV-1s-bring-DYN
I bring myself to his disadvantage. (*I bring him(self)$_i$ to his$_i$ disadvantage.)

In applicatives in Bantu and other languages Baker discusses, a maximum of one preposition may incorporate into the verb. Consider Baker's Chichewa examples in (454)–(456).

(454) *mbidzi zi-na-perek-a   msampha kwa nkhandwe*
zebras SP-PAST-hand-ASP trap   to   fox
The zebras handed the trap to the fox.   Baker (1988:383)

(455) *mbidzi zi-na-perek-er-a   nkhandwe msampha*
zebras SP-PAST-hand-APPL-ASP fox   trap
The zebras handed the fox the trap.   Baker (1988:383)

(456) **mbidzi zi-na-perek-er-er-a   kalulu nkhandwe msampha*
zebras SP-PAST-hand-APPL-APPL-ASP hare   fox   trap
(The zebras handed the trap to the fox for the hare.)
                                              Baker (1988:383)

In Abaza, at least two postpositions can incorporate into the same verb, as seen in example (457), where there is both a benefactive, *z-*, and a locative, *dzqa-* 'by'.

(457) *y-**bə-z-ʕa-yə-dzqa**-d-sə-r-c'a-t'*
3si-**2sf-BEN-DIR-3sm-by**-3p-1s-CSE-put-DYN
I made them put that near him for you (f).   GAL, 113

Multiple applicatives can apparently occur with any combination of applicative roles, if a plausible pragmatic context can be found. A benefactive plus a locative is shown in (458), a benefactive plus an instrument in (459), and a benefactive plus a comitative in (460). An instrument plus a comitative is shown in (461).

(458) *s-pha   ayʔazaʕʷ   a-stol*
1s-daughter   doctor   DEF-table

   *də-y-**z-a-kʷ**-s-c'a-y-t'*
   3sr-3sm-**BEN-3si-on**-1s-place-PRS-DYN
   I put my daughter on the table for the doctor.

(459) *də-r-**z-a-la**-ca-t'*
3sr-3p-**BEN-3si-INST**-go-DYN
S/he went with it for them.

(460) *d-**lə-c-yə-z**-ca-t'*
3sr-**3sf-BEN-3sm-COM**-go-DYN
S/he went with her for him.

7.3 The incorporation of AGR°-P°

(461) d-a-la-yə-c-čʲa-t'
    3sr-3si-INST-3sm-COM-eat-DYN
    S/he ate with him with it.

The number of multiple applicatives is not limited to two. It is possible to have three applicative prefixes plus their corresponding agreement in a single verb complex, as in (462).

(462) y-lə-cə-r-z-a-la-h-čʲpa-t'
    3si-3sf-COM-3p-BEN-3si-INST-1p-do-DYN
    We did it with her for them with it.

Although perfectly grammatical, such forms are not common. One major factor in limiting the occurrence of these multiple applicatives is presumably pragmatic. In addition, the requirement that the object of the incorporated version of a postposition be definite (see §7.2.3) plays a role in reducing the number of contexts in which they are possible. Compare (463), in which *mafina* 'car' must be definite or specific in the incorporated version, and (464) where it can be indefinite when the postposition does not incorporate.

(463) a-čʲkʷʼən   a-mafina   yə-ʕʷza-čʷa   də-r-z-a-la-ca-t'
    DEF-boy   DEF-car   3sm-friend-PL   3sr-3p-BEN-3si-INST-go-DYN
    The boy went with the car to/for his friends.

(464) a-čʲkʷʼən   mafina-la   yə-ʕʷza-čʷa   d-rə-z-ca-t'
    DEF-boy   car-INST   3sm-friend-PL   3sr-3p-BEN-go-DYN
    The boy went by car to/for his friends.

In many of the cases in which it would be possible to use multiple applicatives, they are not used. It may be that unincorporated PPs are easier to process and parse, leading to their use even when multiple incorporations are possible. Compare the form in (458) with the following:

(465) s-pha   ayʔazaʕʷ   yə-qaz-la   a-stol
    1s-daughter   doctor   3sm-for-INST   DEF-table

    d-a-kʷ-s-cʼa-y-t'
    3sr-3si-on-1s-place-PRS-DYN
    I put my daughter on the table for the doctor.

7.3.2 Baker's applicative analysis

Baker analyzes the constructions in (414) and (415) as involving incorporated prepositions. This does not directly account for the Bantu facts he discusses. Baker gives a unified account of these properties, in which he argues that each of the observed patterns derives from Case principles.

In Baker's analysis, when a lexical head incorporates into a $V°$, the Case assigning property of the newly created $X°$-$V°$ complex does not increase. In applicatives, the object of the adposition, which is "stranded" when the adposition incorporates into the verb, is assigned the objective Case of the verb, and the underlying direct object must get Case by some other means. Two principles account for these facts. One is the Case Frame Preservation Principle (CFPP), as in (466). The other is the assumption that traces (of lexical heads) do not assign Case, so that the trace of $P°$ does not simply assign Case to the applicative object.

(466) The Case Frame Preservation Principle:
   A complex $X°$ of category A in a given language can have at most the maximal Case assigning properties allowed to a morphologically simple item of category A in that language.
   Baker (1988:122)

The "bumping" of the direct object is the result of the fact that a simple item of category V can have at most two Cases associated with it.[192] When $P°$ incorporates into the verb, the CFPP limits the $P°$-$V°$ complex to having at most two Cases to assign. One of these Cases is reserved for the subject. The $P°$-$V°$ complex assigns its remaining Case to the applicative object, and the direct object is left to get Case in some other way.

Baker's analysis makes the crucial assumption that a trace cannot assign Case (1988:99, 120–121). When a $P°$ incorporates into the $V°$ which governs it, the $V°$ does not increase its Case assigning ability beyond a certain limit. At the same time, the object of the adposition loses its Case assigner ($P°$), since the trace cannot assign Case. Therefore, the object of the adposition

---

[192]Treating a (transitive) verb as assigning two Cases counts the Case assigned by INFL among those assigned by the verb. It is irrelevant to the present argument whether the maximal number of Cases assigned by a simple V is one (its direct object) or two (direct object and subject). In either case, the subject will be treated consistently in both simple and complex categories.

must receive Case from the P°-V° complex in order to be licensed.[193] This removes from the direct object its normal source of Case, so it must get Case either through inherent Case or through whatever licenses the second object in double object constructions.[194] The Case-assigning relationships of the basic verb are changed precisely because the applicative object requires Case. No other NPs can be licensed because the verb has exhausted its Case assigning ability, and there is no other source of Case.

Baker's Case-based analysis explains the relative frequency of applicatives with transitive verbs versus their relative infrequency with intransitive verbs. Transitive verbs have a Case to assign, and it will be assigned to the applicative object, while intransitive verbs have no Case to assign. Thus, they cannot license an applicative object.

Furthermore, Baker's analysis accounts directly for the fact that only a single adposition may incorporate. A verb has only limited means for assigning Case. If there were two PPs whose heads incorporated as applicatives, the object of only one could be assigned Case by the verb. This would leave the other applicative object Caseless, in violation of the Case Filter.

7.3.3 Case assignment in Abaza

If a language could assign Case to the objects of incorporated adpositions in some way other than by the P°-V° complex, we would expect no distinction between transitive and intransitive verbs with regard to adposition incorporation, no rearrangement of the verb's argument structure, and the possibility of multiple adpositions incorporating. This is the line I pursue for Abaza. The analysis I propose below is precisely that the object of the incorporated postposition receives Case from a source other than the P°-V° complex. Empirical evidence from the language bears out these predictions.

Abaza differs from the languages Baker discusses in that there is agreement morphology associated with the applicative prefix beyond the normal agreement associated with the host verb. As we have seen (§2.2.2), Abaza postpositions normally register agreement with their objects. The difference between Abaza and the languages Baker analyzes can be shown

---

[193]Incorporation creates a complex configuration of heads, in which an incorporating head does not, in fact, govern its underlying complement, under some interpretations. Baker proposes the Government Transparency Corollary (GTC) to ensure that the P°-V° complex may govern the applied object, in order to meet the requirements he assumes need to be met to assign Case. See (496) in §7.5.2.

[194]If neither of these options is available in a language, that language cannot have applicatives, or cannot have applicatives with overt direct objects (which require licensing through Case).

to follow from the fact that there is an agreement phrase dominating PP in Abaza which mediates agreement and Case assignment, while there is no such projection in the other languages. If this agreement projection is present in both independent and incorporated PPs, then the presence of agreement within the verb complex is accounted for since the agreement head must incorporate along with the postpositional head.

I propose that Case assignment within a PP whose head incorporates into the verb is identical to Case assignment in independent PPs, and crucially that this process occurs before the incorporation of the postposition head into the verb complex. As with nonincorporating postpositions, P° raises to the ERG° immediately dominating it, where agreement with the postpositional object is mediated. The null P°-ERG° head then incorporates into the complex of verbal heads as a complex bundle of features, including both the content of P° and agreement features. Agreement with the applicative object appears within the verb complex precisely because checking with the DP has taken place prior to incorporation, and the P° which incorporates already bears the relevant features.

(467)

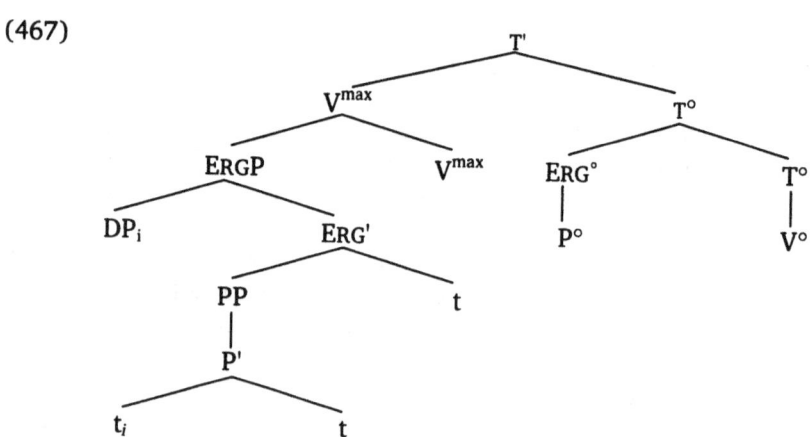

In this structure, the applicative object moves to the specifier of ERGP where it is assigned Case and its agreement features are checked. P° raises to ERG°, creating the configuration in which the relevant features of person and number are checked. The complex of heads, ERG°-P°, then incorporates into the head complex of the verbal extended projection, T°. (The structure in (467) represents an intransitive verb. For a transitive verb, V^{max} is replaced by ERGP.)

For the structures discussed thus far, in which the head of a selected complement, XP, incorporates into the head which selects XP, I have

7.3 The incorporation of AGR°-P°

assumed that the verbal complex is formed in the lexicon, inserted in the tree at V°, and this substitutes into successive head positions. The position of PPs involves adjunction to a maximal projection, but the substitution of a head from an adjoined maximal projection is ruled out since two overt heads cannot substitute into the same position, and the verbal complex raising through the extended projection already substitutes into this position. I, therefore, assume that the ERG°-P° head adjoins to T°, rather than substitutes into it. (See §7.4 for motivation that the head adjoins to T°.) The internal structure of this complex of heads is as follows:

(468)

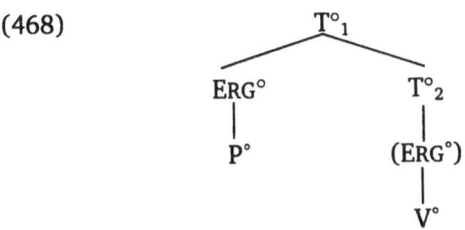

The mechanism of substitution is straightforward for the V°-(ERG°)-T°$_2$ and P°-ERG° substructures. A lower head substitutes into the head position directly above it, and the relevant (null) features are checked, e.g., when P° substitutes into ERG°, the ergative features are checked. The adjunction configuration, in which ERG° and T°$_2$ are sisters dominated by T°$_1$, requires a different means of checking. I continue to assume that the verb complex is formed entirely in the lexicon. This requires that P°-ERG° be phonologically null, but featurally contentful, like other heads in an extended projection. As in Chomsky (1992), checking may occur in either of two configurations: (1) when the fully formed word substitutes into a (phonologically) null head position or (2) in the adjunction configuration in (468). Once the features have been checked in this adjunction configuration, the complex of heads incorporates as a unit (again by substitution) into the next higher functional head, ABS°.

This analysis accounts for the fact that an agreement morpheme always occurs to the immediate left of an applicative prefix, since the agreement (head) and the postposition head form a constituent, associated with a complex of features which must be checked together by the overt head.

The difference between Abaza and Chichewa (or Bantu in general), then, is that there is no agreement projection dominating (or associated with) the prepositions in Chichewa which can independently mediate agreement and, crucially, assign Case.[195] This forces the applicative object to utilize the Case assigned by the verb, with the result that the applicative object behaves like the direct object of the verb. In Abaza, on the other hand, there are agreement projections dominating applicative PPs, and Case assignment to the object of the postposition can occur independently from the verb complex.

This analysis also accounts for the fact that Abaza applicatives register agreement with their corresponding applicative objects in a way not found in most other languages exhibiting applicative constructions. Furthermore, this analysis accounts in a direct way for the differences discussed in §7.3.1 between the Bantu (and Mayan, etc.) data discussed by Baker and the Abaza data.

Applicatives may not occur with intransitive verbs in many Bantu and other languages because an intransitive verb has no Case to assign, leaving the applicative object without Case, in violation of the Case Filter. Since, in Abaza, applicative objects receive Case independently from the verb, the Case-assigning properties of the verb are irrelevant in determining which verbs a postposition may incorporate into. This correctly predicts that applicatives should freely occur with both transitive and intransitive verbs in Abaza.

In Bantu and other languages, the applicative object requires Case from the verb, which forces a rearrangement of the argument structure such that the verb assigns Case to the applicative object. In Abaza, on the other hand, the applicative object independently satisfies the Case Filter without Case from the verb. The direct object is thus not forced from its Case position. This correctly accounts for the fact that the argument structure is not rearranged in Abaza.

Finally, in Bantu, only one applicative object can be assigned Case, since the verb has only one Case to assign. This follows from the CFPP, which states that no complex head may assign more Cases than a morphologically simple head of the same category. The Abaza data appear to be counterexamples to the CFPP, since verb complexes contain as many as five agreement prefixes while a morphologically simple verb can have at most three. In my analysis, however, even though agreement with applicative objects appears morphologically within the verb complex, applicative objects do not receive Case from the verb, but within the postpositional extended projection of which they are objects. The number of applicative objects in Abaza is thus not limited by the number of Cases a verb may assign. Applicative objects are licensed independently from

---

[195]This requires that Chichewa allow Case to be assigned other than in the specifier-head relation within an agreement projection.

the verb, so there can be multiple applicatives. This prediction follows directly from my analysis.

7.4 Adjunction positions

We return now to the issue of the adjunction site of applicative PPs.[196] I propose that they are adjoined to the maximal projection immediately below TP, a position higher in the structure than Baker assumes.[197] Three factors pointing to a position external to VP (V^{max}) are (1) the order of the prefixes within the verbal complex, (2) Li's Generalization, and (3) coreference possibilities between a subject and an applicative object. Also important are word order and the possible adjunction of locative PPs lower than nonlocative PPs, since locatives occur in the verb complex to the right of other applicatives.

7.4.1 Order of morphemes

One of the basic assumptions I make is that the order of the morphology represents the order of checking, and that agreement is checked "from the inside out". Applicative prefixes occur between the absolutive and the ergative prefixes. This indicates a structural position from which the ERG°-P° head can incorporate after the verb's ERG°, but before ABS°. I assume a verbal extended projection containing only CP, ABSP, TP, ERGP, and V^{max}. If PPs adjoin to TP, the incorporating head will adjoin to ABS°, as in the substructure (469). In this configuration, the features of the incorporated applicative will be checked after the absolutive features, leading to the wrong order of morphemes. The adjunction site must, therefore, be lower than TP.

---

[196]I refer to these as PPs for ease of presentation, recognizing that the highest category is actually ERGP. This avoids any possible confusion with an ERGP in the verbal extended projection.
[197]Baker analyzes the applicatives in Bantu (and Mayan, etc.) as originating within VP. The main reason is so that they can be assigned a θ-role by the verb.

(469)

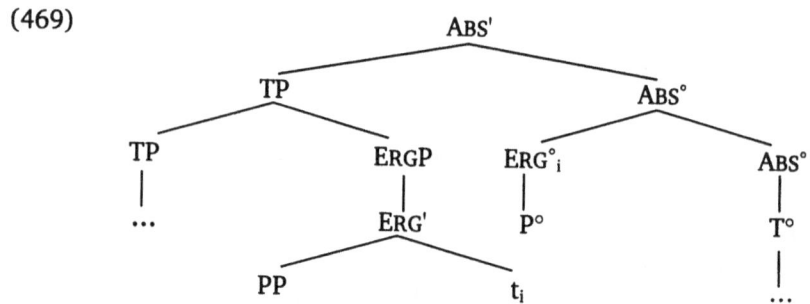

Specifying ERGP as a target adjunction site is problematic for those cases in which there is no such projection, i.e., with intransitive verbs. The adjunction of PP to V^{max} is problematic in that it predicts that the incorporated postposition should occur to the right of both the series which registers agreement with an indirect object and the potential prefix.[198] The generalization which best accounts for the position of PPs is that they (left or right) adjoin to the maximal phrase immediately below TP, whether ERGP or V^{max}, as in (470).[199] I adopt this position.

(470) a.   b.

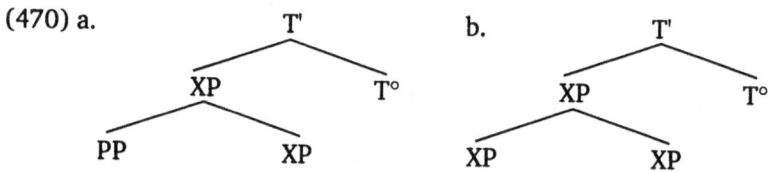

Multiple applicative PPs can be accounted for easily in an adjunction analysis by multiple adjunction to the same node. It is often possible in Abaza to have various orders of the applicative prefixes. (Compare, for example, (471) and (472).)[200] This is support for a syntactic account of applicatives in Abaza as opposed to a purely morphological or lexical account, because it directly accounts for the relative scope relations, since it provides a structural configuration in which the element with higher scope is also structurally higher. A

---

[198] I do not have any examples involving either ditransitive verbs or the potential with an applicative, but I predict that the applicative morphology should occur to the left of both, since the (nonlocative) applicatives generally occur to the left of directionals while the potential and the ergative series which registers agreement with an indirect object both occur to the right of directionals.

[199] One possible account of this is to require that TP govern these PPs. Perhaps, TP must assign some licensing feature under government.

[200] I believe that this leads to different scope relations, as well. Native speakers note a distinction between forms with the two orders of applicative prefixes, but I have been unable to determine the precise difference. I leave the matter for further research.

7.4 Adjunction positions

purely morphological or lexical account does not refer directly to the relative syntactic positions where scope is calculated.

(471) d-lə-z-yə-c-ca-t'
3sr-3sf-BEN-3sm-COM-go-DYN
S/he went for her with him.

(472) d-yə-c-lə-z-ca-t'
3sr-3sm-COM-3sf-BEN-go-DYN
S/he went with him for her.

7.4.2 Li's Generalization

I argued in chapters 4 and 5 that Li's Generalization holds in Abaza. That is, a functional head can only incorporate into another functional head. The incorporation of a functional head into a lexical head is prohibited. For PPs dominated by an agreement projection, as in Abaza, the head (complex) should only be able to incorporate into the verb complex within the functional range of heads, since the lexical P° must incorporate into the functional ERG° before incorporating into the verb complex. This requires PPs in Abaza to occur external to V^{max}, higher than the subject, which rules out a position for them within V^{max}. For adpositional phrases which are dominated at the highest level by a lexical projection (PP), as in the Bantu languages, the head should be able to incorporate at any point in the verbal extended projection.

7.4.3 Coreference possibilities

Further support for placing these phrases in a position outside of the VP comes from the coreference possibilities of subjects with an applicative object. It is possible for the comitative object, for example, to be coreferential with the subject of the verb, as seen in (473)–(475). Crucially, though, reflexive morphology may not be used in these cases. This contrasts with simple transitive cases, in which reflexive morphology is required for all persons and numbers when the subject and object are coreferent.[201]

(473) d-yə-c-yə-r-ca-t'
3sr-3sm-COM-3sm-CAUS-go-DYN
He$_i$ made him go with him$_i$.   GAL, 189

---

[201]Recall the discussion of reflexives in §4.2.

(474) b-hə-cə-ʕ-ga-p'
2fs-1p-COM-1p-carry-FUT2
We will take you with us.   GAL, 189

(475) k'amaʃ ...   a-č-č^wa   ʕ^waʒ^wa-gʲi   yə-c-y-c'a-n
      Kamash   DEF-horse-PL twenty-INT   3sm-COM-3sm-put-PST

      y-pa   y-fərg^wən   d-a-g^wək^ws-t'
      3sm-son   3si-van   3sr-3si-attack-DYN
      Kamash took with him twenty horsemen and fell on the khan's van(guard). [or the khan's son's vanguard]   GAL, 189

Coreference between the subject and the applicative object is not limited to comitatives. Example (476) illustrates coreference between a causative subject and a locative applicative object.[202]

(476) ...   hara   d-hə-la-hə-r-č'^wa-wa   ...
            we   3sr-1p-within-1p-CAUS-sit-PTC
"[He, so to speak, is not yet ready to walk,] **how can he be seated among us**?" [he said, and he objected] (lit., we, causing him to sit among us).   NART, 57

It is not surprising that reflexive agreement is not used in these examples, since reflexive agreement is limited in Abaza to the absolutive series, and agreement with applicative objects occurs only in the ergative series. It is surprising, however, that the argument registered in the ergative series, i.e., the applicative object, may be coreferential with the subject.

The fact that examples with coreferential subject and applicative object are grammatical without reflexive agreement indicates that the applicative object is not bound in its governing category.[203] If the PP were adjoined lower than the subject, i.e., within VP, its governing category would be V^{max}, in which case the coreferential subject would bind it in its

---

[202]I am not sure if it is possible to have coreference of this sort between subjects and benefactive or instrumental applicative objects. For instrumentals it is pragmatically difficult to create such a situation, since subjects using instruments are generally animate and instruments are generally inanimate.

[203]Likewise, the applicative object may not bind the subject. This will never happen, however, since the object of the PP cannot c-command anything outside of the postpositional extended projection. The ergative agreement projection above PP guarantees this.

7.4 Adjunction positions

governing category.[204] PPs in Abaza must, therefore, be adjoined higher than the subject (in contrast to a position within VP, where Baker posits them for the languages he discusses).[205]

Potentially problematic for this analysis is the fact that objects of unincorporated postpositions can be coreferent with the subject, and this relation may be expressed with the synthetic reflexive construction, as in (418), repeated here as (477). Optimally, these PPs should occur in the same position as the PPs from which the head incorporates, yet the binding facts seem different.

(477) awat   r-akʷ-b   a-dəwnay   də-z-z-əkʷə-w   y-qa
      they   3p-be-STP   DEF-world   3sr-EWH-BEN-be.in-PTC   3sm-head

      a-qaz-la   a-dəwnay   d-gʲə-kʷə-m
      3si-for-INST   DEF-world   3sr-INT-be.in-NEG
      He is living in the world for them. Not for himself.   NART, 73

7.4.4 Word order

Applicative objects may occur to the right of the subject, as in (478), but they may also occur to the left of the subject, as in (479). Applicative objects also generally occur to the right of the direct object, as in (480), although they may occur to the left of the direct object, as well, as in the second clause in (409).[206] PPs whose heads do not incorporate generally occur to the right of both subject and direct object as well, as in (481).

---

[204]Jim McCloskey (pers. comm.) has pointed out that it may be possible in some circumstances to restrict the governing category to the applicative PP by treating the "object" of the postposition as the subject of the PP, i.e., by locating it in the specifier position. If true, this could eliminate support for the claim that Abaza applicative phrases are adjoined high, based on the argument that the coreference possibilities in Abaza applicatives require that the applicatives not be c-commanded by the subject. It does not, however, provide evidence against the higher position for these phrases.

[205]This contrast is reminiscent of the possibility in English in a few cases to have either anaphors or non-anaphors in the same position:

He$_i$ wrapped the cloak around him$_i$.
He$_i$ wrapped the cloak around himself$_i$.

One possible solution for this dilemma is that the synthetic reflexive is not fully subject to the binding conditions. This is not implausible.

[206]I assume that in (409) the applicative object would also occur to the left of the subject if it were overt. I have no examples in which an overt applicative object occurs between an overt subject and an overt direct object. Examples with all of these occurring overtly are not common.

(478) hara   a-la   h-a-čʷ-ʃʷa-y-d
      we   DEF-dog   1p-3si-ADV-fear-PRS-DYN
      We are afraid of the dog.

(479) a-čʲkʲʷən   a-mhačʲʷa   y-axʃʼa   d-a-la-yə-c-čʲa-t'
      DEF-boy   DEF-spoon   3sm-sister   3sr-3si-INST-3sm-COM-eat-DYN
      His$_i$ sister ate with the boy$_i$ with the spoon.

(480) s-pha   ayʔazaʕʷ   yə-qaz-la   a-stol
      1s-daughter   doctor   3sm-for-INST   DEF-table

      d-a-kʷ-s-c'-i-t'
      3sr-3si-on-1s-place-PRS-DYN
      I put my daughter on the table for the doctor.

(481) sara   bilet   wara   wə-qaz   y-ʕa-s-aw-d
      I   ticket   you   2sm-for   3si-PV-1s-find-DYN
      I found the ticket for you.

There is a ready analysis of these facts if PPs are generally right-adjoined to V^{max}, but may optionally left-adjoin to V^{max}. The right-adjoined position places them to the right of all verbal arguments. When the verb head raises through its extended projection (in the syntax), it will move to the right of the PP, accounting for the fact that the PP (or just its object in cases where the ERG°-P° complex incorporates into the verbal complex) occurs to the left of the verb complex. If the PP left-adjoins to V^{max}, the PP and the applicative object occur to the left of the subject. The right-adjoined structure, including head movement of the verb, is given in (482) with single-bar level nodes left out.

7.4 Adjunction positions

(482)

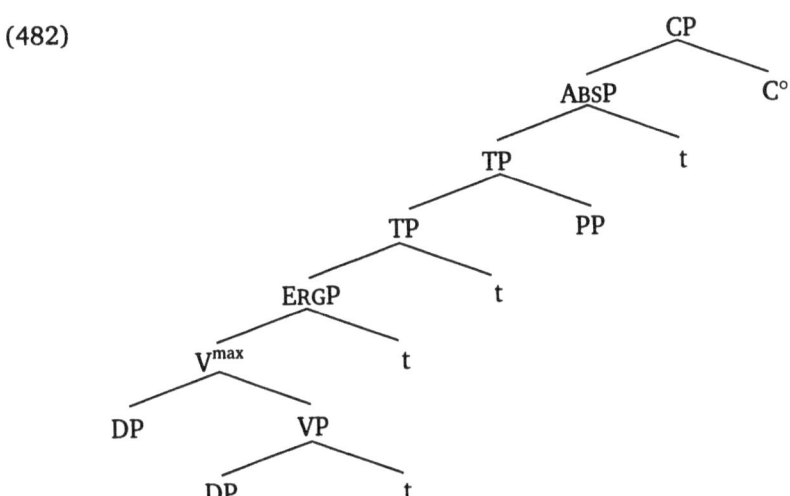

This analysis predicts that for multiple applicatives, the order of overt applicative objects should be reversed depending on whether the PPs are right or left adjoined. If the PP is right-adjoined, the lower applicative object, corresponding to the inner applicative verbal morphology, should occur to the left of the higher applicative object. Such an example can be seen in (483). With left-adjunction, the lower applicative object is predicted to occur to the right of the higher applicative object.[207]

(483) a-čʲkʼʷən   a-maʃina   yə-ʕʷza-čʷa   də-r-z-a-la-ca-tʼ
DEF-boy   DEF-car   3sm-friend-PL   3sr-3p-BEN-3si-INST-go-DYN
The boy went with the car to/for his friends.

7.4.5 The position of locative PPs

We address one final question concerning the position of PPs before turning to the question of licensing the incorporation of ERG°-P° into the verb complex. The position of incorporated locative postpositions within the verb complex differs from the position of the other incorporated postpositions with respect to the directional prefix ʕa-. Locative applicatives always occur to the right of an overt directional prefix, while the other applicatives always occur to its left. The benefactive, malefactive, comitatitive, and instrumental prefixes—each with its associated

---

[207]Examples (458) and (479) are apparent counterexamples. I have no explanation for the order in these examples. In both cases, the overt applicative object on the left is animate while the one on the right is inanimate. Perhaps the animacy hierarchy plays a role in this.

agreement—are shown in (484), (485), (486), and (487), respectively. Note that they occur to the left of the directionals.

(484) ɬapʃʷ   ʃalamat   ʃalamat   wə-z-ʃa-z-g-d   l-hʷa-d
      Tlapsh   miracle   miracle   2sm-BEN-DIR-1s-carry-DYN   3sf-say-DYN
      "Tlapsh, a miracle, a miracle I brought for you," she said.   NART, 53

(485) wara   saq'-ta   w-pʃc'az   amalʲ   a-ma-ztən
      you   vigilant-FAC   2sm-be.there   possibility   3si-have-COND

      a-mca   y-čʷ-ʃa-ʃ-g-b
      DEF-fire   3sm-ADV-DIR-1p-carry-FUT
      And you watch carefully, and if we are lucky enough, we'll carry away the fire (from him).   NART, 71

(486) awəy   ana-m-wə   sosrəqʷa   yə-wnaʃʷa-la   aynəʒʷ
      that   when-NEG-agree   Sosruko   3sm-command-INST   giant

      y-ləmha-k'   ʃa-pə-r-q'ə-n   y-rə-c-ʃa-r-g-d
      3sm-ear-one   DIR-PV-3p-cut-PST   3si-3p-COM-DIR-3p-carry-DYN
      When that didn't work, they cut off one of the giant's ears and took it with them as Sosruko commanded.   NART, 67–8

(487) arəy   ayxa   z-la-ʃa-ʃt'ə-r-x-wa   a-rəčʷa-gʲə-y
      that   iron   EWH-INST-DIR-PV-3p-lift-PTC   DEF-tongs-INT-and

      satanaya   l-akʷ-b   yə-z-z-rə-čʲpa-z
      Satanaya   3sf-be-ST   3sm-POT-EWH-CSE-make-PSP
      So those tongs which can be used to take hot iron were made (by him) with Satanaya's advice. (lit., It was Satanaya who caused him to be able to make the tongs...)   NART, 55

Examples of locative prefixes following directionals are given in (488) and (489).

(488) d-ʃa-hə-dzqa-yə-r-gəl-t'
      3sr-DIR-1p-beside-3sm-CSE-stand-DYN
      He caused him/her to stand next to us.   GAL, 179

7.4 Adjunction positions

(489) y-ʕa-sə-kʷ-d-wə-r-c'a-t'
3si-DIR-1s-on-3p-2ms-CAUS-place-DYN
You made them place it on me. GAL, 180

This suggests the analytical possibility that this difference in prefix position reflects different positions for locative and nonlocative PPs. This would be the case if, for example, locative PPs were adjoined to V^{max}, while nonlocative PPs were adjoined to ERGP. I argue, however, that this analysis is not adequate to account for the Abaza data.

Both locative and nonlocative applicative prefixes in the verbal complex occur in the same position with respect to the morphology associated with other functional heads, i.e., absolutive and ergative agreement. The arguments for the position of PPs given in §§7.4.1–7.4.4 are valid for both locative and nonlocative PPs. Without the adoption of another functional head between TP and ERGP, there are not enough fixed positions to provide distinct adjunction sites for locative and nonlocative PPs.

It would be possible to treat the directional prefix as heading a functional projection between ERGP and TP. I have no independent evidence for such a functional projection, however, and I am hesitant to propose a further proliferation of functional categories in the verbal extended projection based on such limited evidence. I, therefore, reject this analysis, noting that if independent evidence for such a functional projection arises, it would provide a distinct position for the adjunction of locative PPs.

I assume that the verb complex is built in the lexicon, and the features of this word are checked in the syntax. The semantic content of directionals does not need to be checked in the syntax because it is not relevant to the syntax, either featurally or structurally. The relative position of the locative and nonlocative applicatives with respect to the directionals, then, is determined solely by the morphological template or word-formation rules. Syntactically, this means that the locative applicatives must always adjoin lower than other applicatives in order for checking to proceed correctly. This is a morphological constraint on what can happen in the syntax.

I conclude that locative and nonlocative PPs are both adjoined to the maximal projection immediately below TP.

7.5 Legal movement

My proposal for applicatives in Abaza involves the movement of the ERG°-P° complex from within an adjoined PP (ERGP) into the verbal complex of heads. Like all movement, this movement leaves a trace, which must meet certain licensing conditions, i.e., it must be properly governed. Baker discusses how the traces of incorporated prepositions are properly governed. Crucially for Baker, incorporated prepositions move from PPs which are internal to VP, allowing the verb to assign a θ-role, which means that the PP node is not itself a barrier and hence will not block head-movement. This is not possible in my analysis, since the PPs are not within VP. The trace of the applicative head is properly governed when the PP is external to VP.

7.5.1 Proper government within VP

In Baker's analysis, the applicative construction involves a prepositional head, P°, incorporating into a verbal head, V°. This movement leaves a trace, and this trace must be licensed. In order to be licensed, the trace must satisfy the Empty Category Principle (ECP). The ECP requires that traces be governed by an appropriate element.

(490) The Empty Category Principle:
    Traces must be properly governed.   Chomsky (1986a:17)

Baker assumes that proper government involves (1) government and (2) either theta-coindexing or a chain relationship. His definition of proper government is given in (491) (Baker 1988:367).[208]

(491) Proper Government:
    A properly governs B iff:
        (i) A governs B, and
        (ii) A is theta-coindexed with B or A is a chain-antecedent of B.

Recall the definition of government repeated in (492). Government is based on the structural relationship (c-command) between the governor

---

[208]This is not significantly different from Chomsky's (1986a:17) definition:

    α properly governs β iff:
        (i) α antecedent-governs β, or
        (ii) α theta-governs β.

7.5 Legal movement

and the element it governs. Government is also subject to two locality constraints. A certain type of element, i.e., a barrier, cannot intervene between the governor and the element it governs, and the actual governor must be the closest possible governor.

(492) α governs β iff
  α c-commands β,
  every barrier for β dominates α, and
  minimality is respected.[209]

The government relation can be blocked by the presence of a barrier between the governor and the trace. Baker (1988:56) defines a BARRIER as in (493).[210]

(493) γ is a barrier between α and β iff
  (i) γ is a maximal projection that contains β and excludes α, and
  (ii) γ is not selected.

Baker (1988:57) defines SELECTION as in (494).[211]

(494) α selects β iff
  (i) α assigns a θ-role to β, or
  (ii) α is of category C and β is its IP, or
  (iii) α is of category I and β is its VP.

The theta-coindexation relation of (491) involves the assignment of a theta-role. The chain-antecedent relation requires (1) that the two

---

[209]Baker's definition of government does not mention minimality. It is clear, however, that minimality, which he treats as a type of barrier, is required for him. See Baker (1988:55–56).

[210]Compare Chomsky's 1986a definition of BARRIER:

  (i) γ is a barrier for β iff (a) or (b):
    a. γ immediately dominates δ, δ a blocking category for β;
    b. γ is a blocking category for β, γ ≠ IP.

  (ii) γ is a blocking category for β iff γ is not L-marked and γ dominates β.

  (iii) α L-marks β iff α is a lexical category that theta-governs β.

  (iv) α θ-governs β iff α is a zero-level category that θ-marks β, and α and β are sisters.

[211]Parts (ii) and (iii) of (494) can be generalized to include the relationship between any functional head and its sister.

elements be coindexed and (2) that relativized minimality (formalized later by Rizzi 1990) be respected.

The potential difficulty for the trace of an incorporated P°, under the definitions in (491)–(494), is that the trace of P° cannot be governed because PP is a barrier. Baker shows that PP is not a barrier to government.

In Baker's analysis, the PP whose head incorporates into V° is located within VP.[212] Crucially, this allows V° to assign a θ-role to PP. Since V° assigns a θ-role to PP, V° selects PP, by the definition in (494). Since PP is selected, it is not a barrier, under the definition in (493).

An incorporated P° thus governs its trace, under the definition in (492). P° c-commands the trace.[213] No barrier intervenes between P° and the trace. There is no closer head which could potentially govern the trace. The trace of P° is also properly governed, since P° governs the trace, and P° is a chain-antecedent of the trace. The ECP, (490), is thus satisfied. The relevant substructure is as in (495).

(495)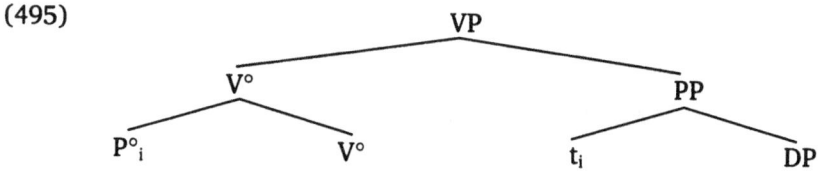

7.5.2 Proper government outside VP

The trace of P° satisfies the ECP in the cases Baker discusses precisely because PP is within VP, where V° assigns a θ-role to PP, with the consequence that PP is not a barrier for the trace of P°. In my analysis of postposition incorporation in Abaza, I argue that PP (ERGP) must be external to VP for a variety of reasons. This raises the question of how the trace of the incorporating P°-ERG° complex satisfies the ECP, since the barrierhood of ERGP cannot be voided by the verb assigning it a θ-role.

Craig and Hale (1988) analyze similar constructions in Rama (Chibchan, Nicaragua), Winnebago (Siouan, USA), and Nadëb (Maku, Brazil) as cases of postposition incorporation. They note the typological tendency for SOV languages "in which the syntactic projection of the

---

[212]Baker is not concerned with the precise position of these PPs. Two possibilities are (1) in the specifier of VP (which requires m-command for government, as opposed to c-command) and (2) as sister to the direct object and verb head (which requires non-binary branching). Adjunction to V' is also possible.

[213]The c-command relation holds for the structures Baker uses which lack single bar level categories. Under a more articulated structure of VP, m-command may be required for government, as in Chomsky's (1986a) definition. See footnote 207.

7.5 Legal movement

category V is not separate from that of the functional category INFL" (p. 335) to develop relational preverbs (i.e., incorporated postpositions) of this type. Their diagnostic for this nonseparation of V and INFL is whether verbal inflection is thoroughly integrated into the verb word. Abaza clearly fits their typology. It is SOV, it has postpositions, verbal inflection is indicated entirely within the verb word (complex) and, not surprisingly, it has "relational preverbs" or incorporated postpositions. In fact, Abaza provides perhaps even stronger evidence for incorporation, as opposed to just syntactic reordering of constituents, than the Rama, Nadëb, and Winnebago data in that the relational preverbs (incorporated postpositions) in Abaza occur within the morphological word, internal to the outermost prefixes.

I propose to interpret this phenomenon as a result of the interaction of the verb's head movement through its extended projection and the Government Transparency Corollary (GTC) in (496). In languages in which verbal inflection occurs entirely within the verb word, it is reasonable to analyze the morphological association of $V°$ and $I°$ as resulting from the movement of $V°$ to $I°$ (where $I°$ stands for the relevant collection of inflectional functional heads) in the overt syntax, as I argue for Abaza. The GTC extends the domain of government for a head which incorporates, such that the head into which it incorporates governs everything it originally governed.

(496) Government Transparency Corollary
    A lexical category which has an item incorporated into it governs everything which the incorporated item governed in its original structural position.   Baker (1988:64)

Thus, for Abaza specifically, and for the SOV languages discussed by Craig and Hale in general, the following extension of the government domain of the verb occurs. $V°$ incorporates into $ERG°$ ($AGR_O°$), and $ERG°$ governs what it normally governs plus everything $V°$ governed in its original position. $ERG°$ then incorporates into $T°$, and by the GTC, $T°$ governs everything that $ERG°$ governed, which includes everything $V°$ governed in its original position. In Abaza, the $P°$-$ERG°$ complex then incorporates into $T°$, which by the GTC thus governs everything governed by $P°$ and $ERG°$.

I propose that the inverse of the GTC is true, as well. That is, a lexical head, $X°$, which has incorporated into another head, $Y°$, governs everything that $Y°$ governs. In order to void the barrierhood of the ERGP which is adjoined to TP, however, it is crucial not only that the complex of heads including V° govern ERGP, but it is also necessary that ERGP somehow be selected in the sense of (494). Since these PPs (ERGPs) clearly are not part of the extended verbal projection, selection requires θ-assignment. The typological pattern discussed by Craig and Hale suggests that this is not just a language-specific Abaza property, and that the conflation of the verb and inflectional material results in expanded government relations, allowing an expanded domain in which θ-roles may be assigned. Since Baker has shown that the verbal head assigns a θ-role to PP when PP is within VP, it is not unreasonable to assume that V° may assign a θ-role to PP (ERGP) when PP is external to VP and the government domain of V° has been extended beyond VP by virtue of its incorporation into inflectional heads.

If V°, or the complex of verbal heads, is able to assign a θ-role to an adjoined ERGP, then ERGP will not be a barrier for the trace of ERG°. The reason is that ERGP will be selected, in the sense of (494), because it is assigned a θ-role, and hence not a barrier. With no intervening barrier, the trace of P° will be governed by P° and, because of the chain-antecedent relation, properly governed. The ECP will thus be satisfied.

8
Wh-Agreement

Chomsky (1981) suggests the possibility that the feature [+wh] is a φ-feature. This chapter supports and develops this idea, utilizing evidence from overt wh-agreement in Abaza.[214]

Wh-agreement is used in three constructions in Abaza: (1) content (wh-) questions, (2) relative clauses, and (3) shared through coindexing. In addition, wh-agreement is used to indicate agreement with a [+wh] reason question. The last case is a kind of agreement which differs from other agreement in certain crucial ways.

The feature [+wh] in Abaza exhibits some unusual behavior in a number of respects. First, it patterns with regular agreement. Second, a wh-phrase may *pro*-drop. Finally, a maximal projection which is coindexed with a [+wh] maximal projection must, under certain circumstances, be registered through wh-agreement on its own licensing head. These facts are used to argue that [+wh] is a φ-feature in Abaza.

In §8.1, the basic patterns of wh-agreement are shown within a discussion of wh-questions and relative clauses. Section 8.2 discusses the [+wh] reason question. Section 8.3 demonstrates that a wh-pronoun may *pro*-drop. This involves an interesting alternation with respect to mood morphology. Section 8.4 shows the circumstances under which the feature [+wh] is shared between two coindexed DPs.

---

[214]This chapter is a revision of O'Herin (1993).

8.1 Wh-agreement data

Abaza lexical categories morphologically register agreement with each of their syntactic arguments. When an argument is [+wh], the agreement with that argument is realized as wh-agreement. This places wh-agreement squarely within the normal agreement paradigm.

Wh-agreement patterns with other agreement as part of the basic paradigm (§8.1.1). The structure of wh-questions is compared with the structure of relative clauses. Movement facts show that wh-agreement is not (solely) a case of agreement with a wh-trace, since there is wh-agreement even if the wh-phrase remains *in situ*. Since [wh] patterns with other agreement, it shares the property of being a φ-feature with them (§8.1.2).

8.1.1 Wh-agreement patterns with other agreement

The agreement paradigms in Abaza are fully differentiated for person and number and partially differentiated for gender and rationality. In addition, each of the agreement series paradigms (ergative, absolutive) contains a separate marker indicating the feature [+wh]. For the ergative series, this is *z-*; for the absolutive series, it is *yə-*. The full ergative paradigm can be seen in (497), as agreement with the possessor of the noun *čə* 'horse'.

(497) a. *s-čə*   my horse
     b. *b-čə*   your (f) horse
     c. *w-čə*   your (m) horse
     d. *l-čə*   her horse
     e. *y-čə*   his horse
     f. *a-čə*   its horse
     g. *h-čə*   our horse
     h. *ʃʷ-čə*   your (PL) horse
     i. *r-čə*   their horse
     j. *z-čə*   whose horse

The full absolutive paradigm can be seen in (498) as subject agreement on the intransitive verb *qəčʲčʲa* 'laugh'.

8.1 Wh-agreement data

(498) a. s-qəč́ʲč́ʲa-d   I laughed
b. b-qəč́ʲč́ʲa-d   you (f) laughed
c. w-qəč́ʲč́ʲa-d   you (m) laughed
d. d-qəč́ʲč́ʲa-d   s/he laughed
e. y-qəč́ʲč́ʲa-d   it laughed
f. h-qəč́ʲč́ʲa-d   we laughed
g. ʃʷ-qəč́ʲč́ʲa-d   you (PL) laughed
h. y-qəč́ʲč́ʲa-d   they laughed
i. yə-qəč́ʲč́ʲa   who/what laughed?[215]

Wh-agreement is utilized for content (wh-) questions and for relative clauses. This is not simply agreement with a wh-trace.

8.1.1.1 Content questions. Three factors are involved in the formation of content questions in Abaza. The licenser of the wh-questioned argument necessarily registers wh-agreement with the questioned element. A different set of mood markers from those used for indicative statements is used, indicating a content question. There is optionally the movement of the question word to a designated position.

Any argument registered through agreement on the verb may be wh-questioned, regardless of which series registers its agreement. There may, however, be no more than one wh-agreement marker on a single licenser. As seen with nouns in (497), the wh-agreement marker in the ergative series is z-. As seen in (498), the absolutive agreement marker is y(ə)-. The [+wh] element in the paradigm differs from the other members of each paradigm both in form and in the specific features shared with the DP it agrees with, i.e., either person and number, or [+wh], which overrides person and number. For example, the argument of a verb corresponding to the absolutive series must be indexed on the verb with the relevant prefix based on person and number unless the feature [+wh] overrides it, in which case it is marked only as "[+wh] absolutive".

---

[215] The absolutive wh-prefix is identical to the absolutive third-person singular irrational and third-person plural prefixes, both of which are also y-. This is potentially ambiguous only if the agreeing XP could be third-person singular irrational (nonhuman) or third-person plural, and even then the wh-marker can often be distinguished by the stress pattern, as in (498) (the epenthetic vowel in the prefix in (498i) is due to stress factors). O'Herin (1992b, 1994) shows how this distinction can be derived from differing foot structure in the lexical entries of these prefixes.

The words *dəzda* and *dzačʷəya* are used to question 'who'.[216] They may question any argument position, i.e., any position licensed by a lexical head and registered by agreement on that head. Examples (499)–(502) show *dəzda* questioning a transitive subject. Note that the subject occurs after the object (*skʲtab*) in (499), and after the object (*afačʲəʕʷ*) and location modifier (*afincan apnə*) in (501). Example (502) contains a lexically inverted verb. As will be shown below, movement is to a position right-adjoined to ABSP.

(499) s-kʲtap   dəzda   y-na-z-axʷ
      1s-book   who   3si-PV-EWH-take
      Who took my book?

(500) dəzda   s-axčʲa   zə-yəčʲ
      who   1s-money   EWH-steal
      Who stole my money?

(501) a-fačʲəʕʷ   a-finỹan   a-pnə   dəzda   y-na-z-axʷ
      DEF-sugar   DEF-cup   3si-at   who   3si-PV-EWH-take
      Who took the sugar out of the cup?

(502) a-sabəy-kʷa   dəzda   yə-r-pʃə
      DEF-child-PL   who   AWH-3p-look
      Who is taking care of the children?

Example (503) shows *dzačʷəya* in an object position.

(503) izmir   dzačʷəya   yə-r-ba-kʷa-z
      Izmir   who   AWH-3p-see-PL-PST
      Who did they see in Izmir?

Example (504) shows an applicative object being questioned.

(504) dəzda   də-z-c-ca
      who   3sr-EWH-with-go
      Who did she go with?

---

[216]Apparently, both *dəzda* and *dzačʷəya* are historically derived from verbs of being. Thus, there are possible parsings into *də-z-da* 3sr-EWH-WHQ, with the verb root itself having been lost, and *d-z-ačʷə-ya* 3sr-EWH-be-YNQ. It may be that such examples have a sort of clefted construction, as in 'who is it who...?'. The form *dzačʷəya* is in free variation with *začʷəya* (Sergei Pazov, pers. comm.).

8.1 Wh-agreement data

The word *yač'ʷəya* is used to question 'what?'.²¹⁷ Example (505) shows *yač'ʷəya* as a subject, while examples (506) and (507) show it as an object.

(505) a-č'ʷal   yač'ʷəya   yə-ta-wa
     DEF-sack   what   AWH-in-PRS
     What is in the sack?

(506) a-c'la   a-pnə   yač'ʷəya   yə-w-ba-z
     DEF-tree   3si-at   what   AWH-2sm-see-PST
     What did you see in the tree?

(507) ahmet   w-ǰʲəp   yač'ʷəya   y-ta-y-c'a
     Ahmet   3sm-pocket what   AWH-in-3sm-put
     What did Ahmet put in his pocket?

We turn now to a discussion of the location of the landing site of wh-question words, which I take to be a focus position. This is reasonable, considering the close connection between focus and wh-interrogatives.²¹⁸ Hungarian, likewise, has a position which can be analyzed as a focus position immediately before the verb for wh-question words (see Horvath 1981).²¹⁹ There are three possible ways to account for something in this position: movement to an open structural position in the tree, movement of nonfocused elements away from this position, and adjunction. These will each be discussed in turn.

If the focus position is a nonadjoined position, the only possibility is the specifier of T, which must then actually be to the right of the head. This requires that V° raise through the series of functional heads to C°, which is already well established for Abaza. There are various reasons to reject this

---

[217] Like *dəzda* and *dzač'ʷəya*, *yač'ʷəya* can be viewed, historically at least, as a sort of cleft construction: 'what is it that...'. It breaks down into the absolutive wh-marker, y-, the root, *ač'ʷə* 'be' and the wh-question mood suffix (=complementizer), -ya. The related form *ač'ʷəya* is identificational:

    a-phas   lə-xʲəz   ač'ʷəya
    DEF-woman   3sf-name   what
    What is the woman's name?

[218] Both focus and wh-interrogatives involve an open formula. For wh-interrogatives, the variable represents new information. For focus, the variable represents new or contrastive information.

[219] Further support for treating this as a focus position is that the agreement prefixes in Abkhaz and Kabardian (both Northwest Caucasian languages related to Abaza) which correspond to these wh-agreement prefixes in Abaza actually register focus agreement (Konstantin Kazenin, pers. comm.).

option, however. One is the strong preference for heads to be final in Abaza. Except for a few adjoined structures, all heads are final with respect to both complements and specifiers. This is consistent with the claim made by Kayne (1992) that specifiers are universally on the left.[220]

A possible alternative account of this word order is that the focused (wh-) word actually remains *in situ*, and the remaining XPs within the VP scramble out to the left of it. Since the subject may also occur in this focused position, the landing site of this scrambling would have to be outside of the VP (V^{max}), either adjoined to a maximal projection, or else in various specifier positions of functional heads.

Abaza has relatively free word order in some respects, but I would argue that free scrambling of arguments is not a productively available option.[221] In (508), for example, *ansəmʃgʲəy* 'every day' and *labala* 'with a stick' are adjuncts. The word order possibilities allow the temporal modifier of VP, *ansəmʃgʲəy*, to occur before the subject, *ačʲkʷʼən*, as in (509a), or after the object, *ala*, as in (509b). The instrument, *labala*, may occur between the subject, *ačʲkʷʼən*, and the object, *ala*, as in (509c).[222] The relative ordering between the adjuncts is free within these limitations. The relative order of subject and object is fixed. The object may generally not precede the subject. Additionally, the verb complex must occur last. These possibilities can be accounted for by allowing the adjuncts to adjoin freely to VP, either to the left or to the right. Left-adjunction to VP places adjuncts between subject and object. Left-adjunction to V^{max} or any functional XP places adjuncts to the left of the subject. Right-adjunction to VP or any functional XP except CP places adjuncts between the object and the verb complex.

(508) a-čʲkʷʼən   ansəmʃgʲəy   a-la   laba-la   d-a-sə-y-d
      DEF-boy   daily   DEF-dog   stick-INST   3sr-3si-hit-PRS-DYN
      The boy hits the dog every day with a stick.

---

[220]Kayne (1992) also claimed that there is no rightward head movement, a claim which is falsified if the structure proposed here (V° to I° to C°) is correct.

[221]The relative freedom of word order varies greatly from speaker to speaker, ranging from quite free (so that arguments and adjuncts can occur in virtually any order) to almost completely rigid (so that there is only one possible ordering for each clause, plus the focus and antitopic positions). The question of word order is muddied somewhat by prolific *pro*-drop, so that text examples with more than one or two overt arguments are difficult to find, especially in unmarked orders. In addition, the presence of overt pronouns interacts with word order possibilities in ways I do not yet completely understand.

[222]This is the only example I am aware of in which a PP of the type discussed in chapter 7 may occur between subject and object. I have no account of the position here, since I argued in chapter 7 that these PPs adjoin higher than the subject. I note, however, that the individual who provided the sentences in examples (508), (509), and (510) generally allows freer word order than other speakers I know.

8.1 Wh-agreement data

(509) a. ansəmʃgʲəy ačʲkʷʼən ala labala dasəyd
b. ačʲkʷʼən ala ansəmʃgʲəy labala dasəyd
c. ačʲkʷʼən labala ansəmʃgʲəy ala dasəyd

In sentences in which the subject is wh-questioned, the permissible orderings are slightly different. Either the subject dəzda 'who' occurs first in the sentence, as in (510a), or it occurs to the immediate left of the verb, as in (510b). Again the relative ordering among the other elements is free. This freedom of order can be accounted for by the same means that allows various word orders in nonquestion sentences, namely by allowing adjuncts to freely adjoin at different places within the verbal extended projection.

(510) a. dəzda ansəmʃgʲəy ala labala yaswa
b. ala ansəmʃgʲəy labala dəzda yaswa

A problem with a scrambling account is that when there are layers of verbs, the focus position is (or at least may be) to the immediate left of the rightmost (highest) verb, as in (511).

(511) y-ca-nəs   dəzda   yə-z-taqə-z
AWH-go-INF   who   3si-EWH-want-PST
Who wanted to go?

Except for the possible case of the extraposition of relative clauses (always to the right), any scrambling in Abaza appears to affect only DPs, PPs, and adverbials, but not verb complexes. Therefore, dəzda 'who', the focused element in (511), must have moved to its surface location, since the verb complex ycanəs 'who to go' cannot have moved to the left of it.[223] As a subject of yəztaqəz, dəzda must have started to the left of ycanəs, since the specifier position of this verb is to the left of the complement position. Therefore, we are forced to an analysis of focus in which the focused element moves.

Among the possibilities for the landing site of moved wh-words, are a number of adjoined positions. These include right-adjunction to the

---

[223]The form y-ca-nəs is clearly verbal. The suffix -nəs is (one of) the infinitival suffix(es), and its verbal character can be seen in that it allows the full range of verbal agreement, specifically including absolutive agreement.

abaza-bəzʃʷa   y-sə-rdər-nəs   s-taqə-b
Abaza-language   3si-1s-learn-INF 1s-want-STP
I want to learn Abaza.

rightmost overt argument of V°, right or left-adjunction to V°, or any of the verbal functional heads up to ABS°, left-adjunction to C°, or right-adjunction to VP, V', or the maximal or single-bar projections of the functional categories in the verbal extended projection (except CP and C'). These possibilities are marked with * in (512).

(512)

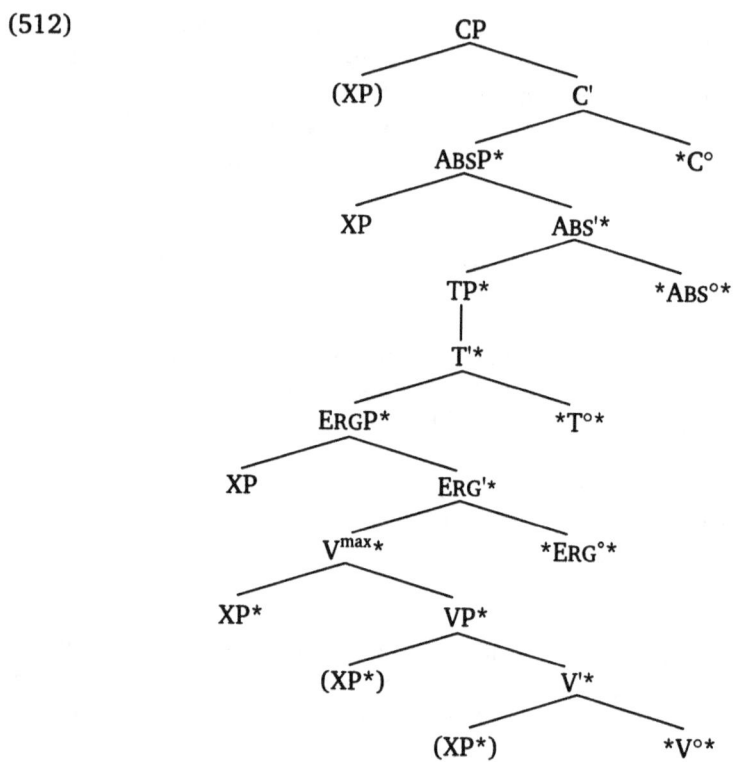

Of these possible landing sites, adjunction to an argument inside V^{max} can be rejected for a variety of reasons. There is not always a complement to the verb, in which case there would not always be an acceptable adjunction site. If adjunction were allowed to be to any XP within the VP, there is no elegant way to rule out adjunction to the subject (specifier) when there is an object (complement). Additionally, I have found no evidence that would indicate a treatment of the focused DP as a constituent with the relevant XP. Besides these language specific reasons for rejecting adjunction to an argument inside a VP, McCloskey (1992) argues for the Adjunction Prohibition, which disallows adjunction to argument categories. Furthermore, downward movement is less preferable than upward

8.1 Wh-agreement data

movement in general, since the trace cannot then be antecedent governed.

Adjunction to any of the heads, V°, ERG°, T°, ABS°, or C°, is likewise a less than desirable option due to Chomsky's (1986b; following Emonds 1976) claim that adjunction of maximal projections may only be to other maximal projections, and that only heads (X°) may adjoin to heads. Adjunction to V' or the single-bar projection of any of the functional categories has similar drawbacks.

This leaves adjunction to V^{max} and adjunction to one of the functional phrases as the best possibilities for the landing site. Two possible adjunction structures for Abaza focus are as in (513), with (513a) showing adjunction to V^{max} and (513b) showing adjunction to AbsP. It is not crucial whether it is the subject or object which is focused, though I use an intransitive structure for space reasons.

(513)

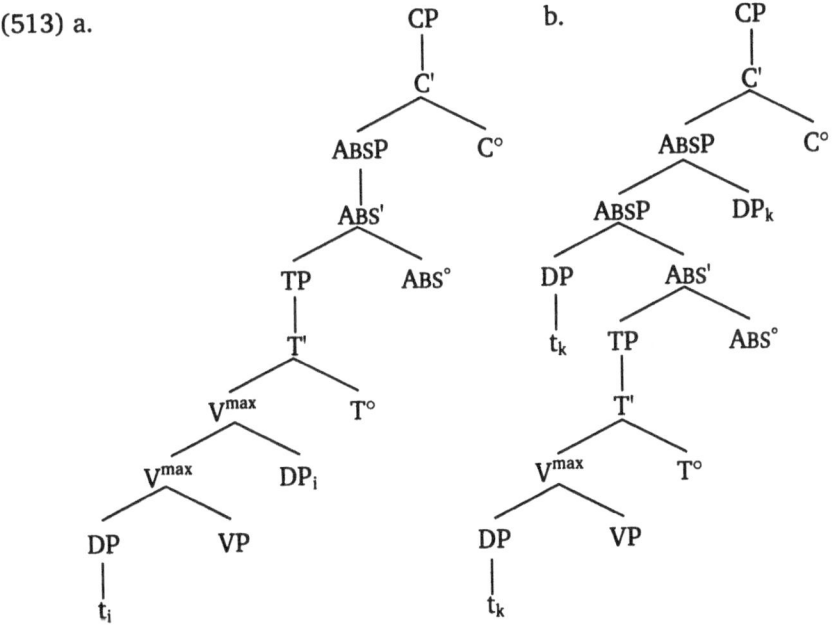

In (513a), the focused element moves first to the focus position, and from there it must move to the specifier of an agreement projection in order to be licensed. In (513b), the focused element moves first to the specifier of an agreement projection, and then into the focus position. Both of these movements are allowed in terms of the A/A-bar distinction. Like the specifier of an agreement projection, I assume that the focus position is an

A-bar position. Movement is therefore possible both from the specifier of an agreement projection to the focus position and from the focus position to the specifier of an agreement projection, since movement from one A-bar position to another is allowed.

The focused element in the focus position is an operator which needs to bind a variable, and should not itself be bound. This requires the operator to occur in the highest position in a chain. The focus position must, therefore, be higher than the highest agreement phrase.[224] Note that this requires the focused element to pass through the agreement specifier on its way to the focus position. Nothing prohibits the agreement specifiers from being filled earlier than LF, but in the absence of independent factors, such as focus movement, they are not forced to be filled until LF.

One possible difficulty for this position for focus phrases is that under some theoretical interpretations the adjunction to AbsP could be a barrier for the movement of Abs° to C°. This will not be the case under the definition of barrier I adopted in (493) in §7.5, however. This definition allows the verbal complex of heads to cross over the adjunction site on its way to C°.

The possible positions for wh-phrases in Abaza, then, are (1) *in situ* and (2) adjoined to AbsP.[225] There is interesting cross-linguistic confirmation of this combination of positions found in Tuller (1992), where focus constructions (which include wh-phrases) in Chadic languages are analyzed as occurring *in situ*, in the specifier of C, and adjoined to VP. Her motivation for adjunction to VP is that a feature [FOCUS] is assigned by I°, and adjunction to VP provides a position where I° can assign this feature through government. It may be that the locus of this feature is in C° in Abaza, instead of in INFL.[226] This would account for its position adjoined to the phrase which is sister to C°.

---

[224]In general, the argument registered in the absolutive series is immediately adjacent to the verb without being focused. This makes it difficult to demonstrate that absolutive arguments may move to the focus position, since both the underlying and focus positions occur to the immediate left of the verb at some level. It is therefore possible to claim that absolutive arguments are never focused, and the focus position is adjoined lower than to AbsP. I do not make this claim.

[225]It is theoretically possible that a questioned argument could move to the specifier of C position. An observation in support of this possibility is the fact that adverbial elements may not occur to the left of a questioned subject as freely as to the left of a nonquestioned subject. I take this to be either a gap in my data or a stylistic preference, since it is clear that no object may move to the sentence-initial position. It is likely that wh-phrases move for independent reasons to the specifier of C at LF. See Huang (1982).

[226]Under a more articulated structure of INFL, Tuller's feature [FOCUS] would presumably reside in T°. This places the focused element in a position adjoined to ErgP or VP (V^{max}). This is possible for Abaza, as well, if absolutive arguments may not, in fact, be focused.

8.1 Wh-agreement data

With the focus position established as adjunction to ABSP, the structure for a transitive clause having a focused DP, such as (514), is as in (515). The direct object moves to the absolutive specifier at LF.

(514) s-k'tap   dəzda   y-na-z-ax^w
     1s-book   who   3si-PV-EWH-take
     Who took my book?

(515)

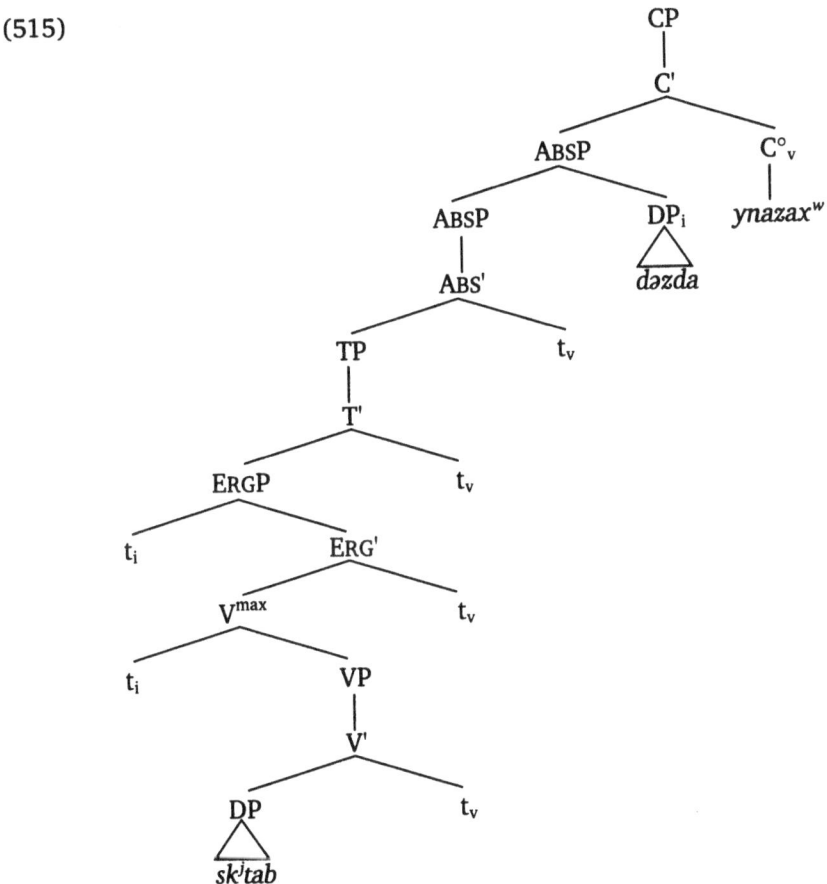

8.1.1.2 Relative clauses. The verb of the relative clause bears one of several tense/aspect combinations which are distinct in some ways from nonrelative clauses, although one set of patterns is the same as for participles. Mood is not marked overtly on the verb complex in relative clauses. I take this as evidence that the verb in relative clauses raises only to ABS°, and not from there to C°. This mirrors the pattern found in languages such as German, in which I° to C° movement is impossible in relative clauses.[227] Further evidence will be seen below that supports the view that verb movement in relative clauses targets a position lower than C°.

The verb in a relative clause obligatorily agrees with all its arguments. This includes the relativized argument, which bears the feature [+wh]. The agreement patterns here are identical to those found in wh-questions, as seen in (516)–(519).

(516) y-awə-y-ʃtə-z   a-haqʷ-dəw
      AWH-PV-3sm-throw-PST   DEF-stone-big
      the big rock that he threw

(517) z-tdzə   yə-w-xʷaʕ-z   a-qac'a   d-aba-ta-w
      EWH-house   3si-2sm-buy-PST   DEF-man   3sr-where-be.in-PRS
      Where does the man whose house you bought live?

(518) z-aba   ankara   y-ca-waʃ   a-čʲkʷən   d-čʲəmazʕʷa-xa-d
      EWH-father   Ankara   AWH-go-FUT   DEF-child   3sr-sick-become-DYN
      The child whose father is going to Ankara became sick.

(519) z-phʷəs   y-pa   yə-z-zak-wa   a-qac'a   awəy
      EWH-wife   3sm-son   3sm-EWH-hit-PTC   DEF-man   s/he

      d-l-əzdzərʕʷə-y-d
      3sr-3sf-hear-PRS-DYN
      The man whose wife his son hits hears her.

---

[227]If German verb second phenomena (in independent indicative clauses) can be accounted for by movement of I° to C°, then the inability of the verb to occur in second position in relative clauses (and other dependent clauses) is an indication that there is no I° to C° movement:

     (i)   Ich habe dem Mädchen das Buch gegeben.
           I gave the book to the girl.
     (ii)   Das Mädchen, dem ich das Buch gegeben habe,...
           The girl to whom I gave the book...
     (iii)   *Das Mädchen, dem habe ich das Buch gegeben,...
     (iv)   *Das Mädchen, dem ich habe das Buch gegeben,...

Thanks to Jim McCloskey (pers. comm.) for pointing out these facts to me.

8.1 Wh-agreement data

There are two major differences between relative clauses and wh-questions. One is that the relativized argument[228] can never appear overtly. I take this to indicate the presence of a null relative operator originating in the argument position to be relativized.

The second difference between relative clauses and wh-questions is that this null relative operator moves to the specifier of C position in the relative clause. Evidence for this movement can be seen in examples like (519), where the relative operator takes with it the head N, $zph^wəs$, of which it is possessor, from object position past the subject, *ypa*, to the specifier of C at the left of the clause. This presumably also happens in (517) and (518), but vacuously. Example (520) shows a pied-piped postposition. Huang (1982) suggests the possibility that the relativization process in Chinese likewise involves the movement of an abstract operator.

(520) zə-wac'a   xʃə   yə-z-ta-s-čʷa-z   finÿan dəzda
      EWH-in   milk   3si-EWH-in-1s-pour-PST   cup   who

yə-pə-z-čʲə
3si-PV-EWH-break
Who broke the cup into which I had put the milk?

The structure of the relative clause from (518) is as in (521). Note that the DP *ankara* does not require Case through an agreement projection by virtue of its role as a location. (See §3.1.2.)

---

[228]Only arguments can be relativized. Nonarguments must be incorporated in order to be relativized.

(521)

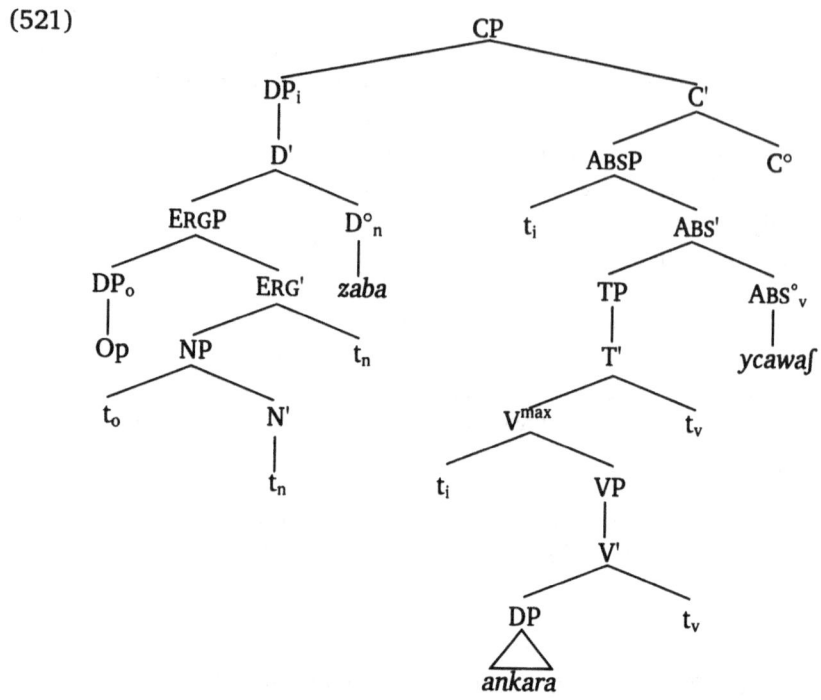

Here the relative operator is coindexed with the head noun $ač^jk^{\prime w}ən$ 'boy'—not shown in (521). It originates as the possessor of the subject, hence in the specifier of the subject DP. As a relative operator, it must move to the specifier of C position of the relative clause. Because its head noun cannot be stranded,[229] it is pied-piped along with the operator to the specifier of C position. The verb of the relative clause registers agreement with its subject. As a simple intransitive, *ca* 'go' takes the absolutive case for its subject. The agreement here is wh-agreement. This makes it appear that the feature [+wh] has percolated up from the specifier of the subject NP to give the whole DP the feature. Such a "percolation" happens regularly with [+wh] possessors, but only with possessors, i.e., not with postpositions or verbs. This supports the structure in which postpositional objects occur in the complement, not specifier, position of the PP. The difference between the behavior of nouns and postpositions can thus be accounted for in purely structural terms.

One difference between the structure of DPs and PPs, as discussed above, is that the possessor is in a specifier position while the object of a

---

[229]Neither may postpositions be stranded in Abaza. This may be due to the Left Branch Condition of Ross (1967).

8.1 Wh-agreement data

postposition is in a complement position. This structural difference between DP and PP can account for the agreement pattern difference seen here. If [+wh] is a feature which is shared via specifier-head agreement, a [+wh] possessor will both trigger wh-agreement on the licensing head (noun or noun-determiner complex) and pass the feature to that head. The object of a postposition, which is in complement position, will not share the feature [+wh] with the postposition, although wh-agreement will appear on the postposition as a result of its licensing a [+wh] argument.[230] This percolation is independent of movement to the specifiers of agreement projections.

8.1.1.3 Agreement with a wh-trace. Chung and Georgopoulos (1988) discuss a phenomenon in Palauan and Chamorro which they call wh-agreement. This is a process of agreement with a wh-trace, rather than with a wh-word itself. The wh-agreement pattern found in Abaza is fundamentally different from the wh-agreement in Palauan and Chamorro. First, wh-agreement in Abaza is part of the pervasive regular agreement paradigm, behaving according to the same pattern as other agreement.

Second, wh-agreement in Abaza occurs whether or not there is movement. As shown above, wh-words in Abaza may optionally move to a (focus) position to the left of the verb, or remain *in situ*. In both cases wh-agreement is obligatory. Example (522) shows a case where the subject *dəzda*, is questioned, but it is still to the left of the object, *kʲtab*, and thus *in situ*. Examples (523) and (524) show the optionality of focusing the questioned subject *dəzda* 'who'. In both cases the wh-agreement pattern is identical.

(522) dəzda   kʲtab   z-əma-m
      who   book   EWH-have-NEG
      Who doesn't have a book?

(523) y-ca-nəs   dəzda   yə-z-taqə-z
      AWH-go-INF   who   3si-EWH-want-PST
      Who wanted to go?

---

[230]The feature [+wh] is apparently *not* shared between a verb and its subject. The subject, adjoined to VP, is in a different position from a possessor in the specifier of NP. Nevertheless, [+wh] is not shared between a verb and its indirect object in the specifier of VP. The fact that φ-features are generally nominal may account for the incompatibility of the feature [+wh] with the category [+V].

(524) dəzda   y-ca-nəs   z-taqə-zʃʷa   yə-z-ba-w-z
     who   AWH-go-INF   EWH-want-NFF   3si-EWH-see-PRS-PST
     Who seemed to want to go?

Even though wh-agreement with a wh-trace can occur in Abaza, this differs from that in Palauan and Chamorro in that it is not a special agreement used only to indicate the presence of a wh-trace. The feature [+wh] agrees with the licensing head in the same way that other features agree with their licensing heads, even when moved, for example by raising, as in (525). Any trace left in an argument position must provide access to the features of the moved XP to the licensing head, regardless of whether the feature [+wh] is present or not.

(525) a-qac'a   də-čʷaʒʷa-rnəs   y-taqə-zʃʷa   y-ba-w-n
     DEF-man   3sr-speak-INF   3sm-want-NFF   3sm-see-PRS-PST[231]
     The man seemed to want to speak.

8.1.2 [wh] as a φ-feature

The feature [wh] has been shown to pattern with other agreement features in Abaza. These other features comprise a set including at least person, number, gender, and rationality. These are the types of features generally assumed to be φ-features. Chomsky (1981:330) listed several of the φ-features, and included the possibility that [wh] is among them: "The set φ includes person, number, gender, Case, and perhaps other features (e.g., perhaps [wh-])."

I propose that the feature [wh] is, in fact, treated as a φ-feature in Abaza.[232] Besides patterning with other agreement, two facts about its behavior support this analysis. First, wh-agreement may license *pro*-drop of a corresponding wh-phrase. This is a natural result of the feature's membership in the set of φ-features, since these are what allow *pro*-drop. Second, a wh-phrase shares the feature [+wh] with a coreferent DP under the right structural configuration. These behaviors of the feature [+wh] are discussed in §§8.3 and 8.4.

---

[231]Note that all the features of the raised DP must be recorded in the trace. This can be seen in that the ergative series, which is used on *taqə* 'want' and *ba* 'seem', is concerned with the gender (masculine, feminine, inanimate) of third-person singular arguments, while the absolutive series, used on *čʷaʒʷa* 'speak', is concerned with the rationality of third-person singular arguments. The features of *aqac'a* 'man' are [+masculine] and [+rational], and all are correctly realized in their respective agreement series.

[232]Thanks to Jim McCloskey (pers. comm.) for suggesting this possibility.

A precise definition of φ-features is lacking in the literature.[233] The introduction of the idea of agreement heads and phrases suggests the possibility that φ-features are those features which may head agreement phrases. This allows for some variation from language to language, as with, for example, different tense possibilities, yet maintains one general set of possibilities for languages to draw from. It also accounts for the related fact that φ-features form a closed class. Crucially for the discussion here, it also accounts for the result that [wh] (and [REFL]) are φ-features in Abaza.

8.2 The manner adverbial yač̣ʷəya

Before moving on to the behavior of the feature [+wh], we look at a case of what appears to be wh-agreement as discussed in §8.1. This is involved in agreement with yač̣ʷəya 'why'. Abaza uses yač̣ʷəya to question both 'what' and 'why'. There are two factors which differentiate the two uses. The first is the order of yač̣ʷəya in the sentence. If it is questioning 'why', then it necessarily occurs sentence initially, as in (526)–(528). If it is questioning 'what', then it occurs either *in situ* or to the immediate left of the verb, as in (529)–(531).

(526) yač̣ʷəya   a-tdzə   ʃʷə-(z)-z-na-m-ʃəl
      why   DEF-house   2p-RWH-can-PV-NEG-enter
      Why weren't you able to enter the building?

(527) yač̣ʷəya   rəc'a-gʲa   ʃarda   ʃʷ-zə-nə-m-xa-wa
      why   more-even   hard   2p-RWH-PV-NEG-work-PRS
      Why don't you work (even) harder?

(528) yač̣ʷəya   sahat   aʕba   r-pnə   a-pqa-la   y-z-ʕay-z
      why   hour   eight   3p-at   3si-before-AV 3p-RWH-come-PST
      Why did they come before eight o'clock?

(529) a-č̣ʷwal   yač̣ʷəya   yə-ta-wa
      DEF-sack what   AWH-in-PRS
      What is in the sack?

---

[233]Although see Everett (1996).

(530) a-c'la   a-pnə   yač'ʷəya   yə-w-ba-z
DEF-tree   3si-at   what   AWH-2sm-see-PST
What did you see in the tree?

(531) ahmet   w-cəp   yač'ʷəya   (y)-y-ta-y-c'a
Ahmet   3sm-pocket   what   AWH-3si-in-3sm-put
What did Ahmet put in his pocket?

The second differentiating factor between the two uses of *yač'ʷəya* is the agreement. The 'what' interpretation always triggers wh-agreement in the prefix series corresponding to the argument which is questioned. This can be seen in the absolutive wh-agreement markers (AWH) in (529)–(531). Note that the intransitive verb in (529) uses the absolutive series to register agreement with the subject, where the transitive verbs in (530) and (531) use the absolutive series to register agreement with the object.

The 'why' interpretation of *yač'ʷəya* triggers a different sort of wh-agreement on the verb. This agreement (glossed RWH, for 'reason wh-agreement') is *in addition to* the prefixes for each argument, so there is essentially an "extra" agreement marker in these cases. Such an agreement marker is not a part of any regular agreement pattern, since it does not alternate with any other agreement markers, and is used only in this special case.

If this is to be treated as a form of wh-agreement, two issues need to be resolved: (1) what forces the [+wh] reason adverbial to occur at the left edge of the sentence? and (2) why does only wh-agreement occur in this position in the verb complex, and why may it occur there? I address (1) first.

Rizzi (1990:46–51) proposes to treat wh-reason adverbials as base-generated in the specifier of C position. This eliminates the problem of how the trace of these adverbs is properly head-governed, since there is no clause-internal trace. If it were base-generated lower than in the specifier of C, there is a question as to what would head-govern it. It would have to be outside the VP, since reason adverbials modify the VP. The V° could not then head-govern the trace. Rizzi also shows that there are difficulties with allowing any of the functional heads to govern the trace of a moved reason adverbial.

A second piece of evidence Rizzi uses to support this proposal is that *pourquoi*, the reason adverbial in French, does not behave like other wh-phrases (including adverbials modifying VP). Other adverbials may be left *in situ*, but *pourquoi* cannot, and *pourquoi* may not trigger stylistic inversion as the other adverbials may. He argues that base-generation of

8.2 The manner adverbial yač'ʷəya

pourquoi in the specifier of C adequately and correctly accounts for this behavior.

The analogous question word in Abaza, *yač'ʷəya*, 'why' likewise behaves differently from other question words in Abaza, with respect to both position in the sentence and agreement. It is not possible, however, to follow Rizzi's analysis of *pourquoi* and base-generate *yač'ʷəya* in the specifier of C. This would account for the requirement that it always occur at the left edge of the sentence, since there is no nonadjoined position to the left of the specifier of C. From this position, however, any agreement with this position should occur external to the absolutive prefix, since the syntactic position is structurally higher than the absolutive projection. Under my assumption that the order of morphemes mirrors the order of checking, and consequently syntactic structure, the locus of RWH agreement must occur lower than AbsP. It must also occur higher than the position of PPs, since RWH agreement occurs to the left of applicatives:

(532) y-zə-y-zə-č'ʷgʲa-z   arəy   a-kʷə-n
      3p-RWH-3sm-BEN-angry-PSP   this   3si-be-PST
      Why they were angry with him was this:....   NART, 56

This limits the possible positions for *yač'ʷəya* to adjunction to TP and the specifier of TP. The specifier position would guarantee the position at the left edge of the sentence, whereas the adjunction position falsely predicts the possibility of occurring to the immediate left of the verb complex. I, therefore, adopt the position that this manner phrase occurs in the specifier of TP.

I have analyzed all agreement as mediated through agreement projections. I extend this analysis to the manner phrases under discussion. This requires an (ergative) agreement phrase immediately dominating TP. This is allowed by the free generation of ERGP and the Closer Agreement Principle (CAP). The underlying structure of (526) is thus as in (533). This structure correctly places the "extra" agreement prefix in the verb complex between the applicatives and the absolutive.

(533)

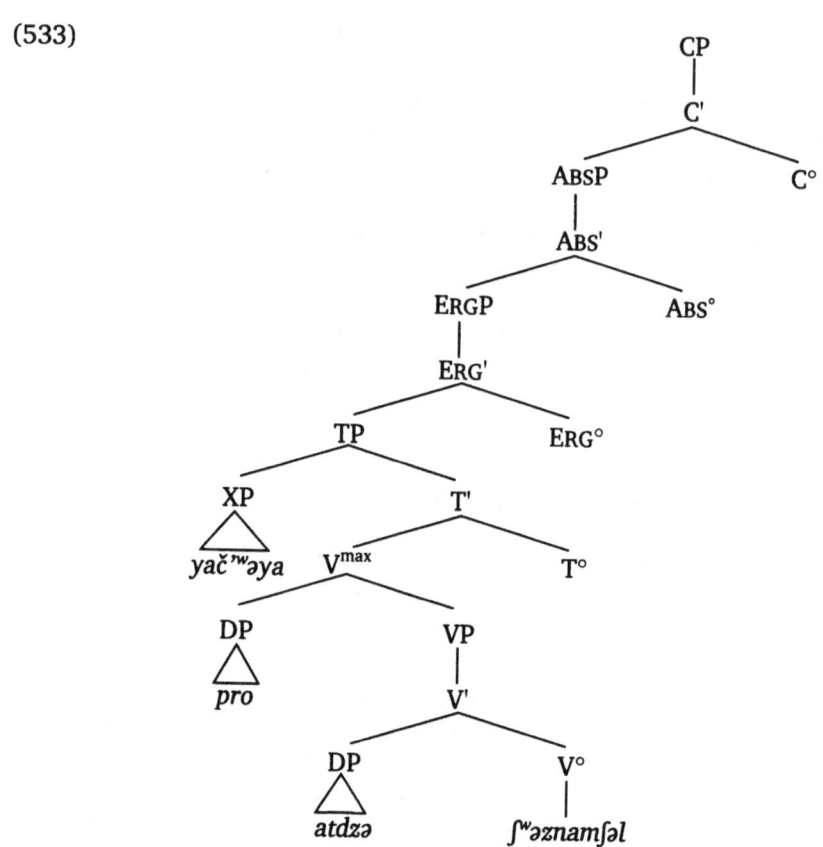

One final question to address is why there is never any non-wh agreement in the same position as the wh-prefix which registers agreement with *yač'ʷəya* 'why'. The answer is likely that there is no DP which ever occurs in that position needing Case. The question word *yač'ʷəya* 'why' is clearly a DP, as seen in its behavior in questioning nominal arguments. The non-wh reason adverbial is generally an independent PP, headed by *qaz* 'because'. As a PP, it does not require Case like its [+wh] reason counterpart. If only reason adverbials are permitted in the specifier of TP, and these are the only two reason adverbials, then only wh-agreement will be registered since only the wh-reason adverbial needs Case. Agreement is not registered independently from Case assignment.

8.3 Pro-drop

If the feature [+wh] is a φ-feature in Abaza, another phenomenon to be expected is that wh-phrases should behave the same as non-wh phrases with respect to *pro*-drop. Abaza allows *pro*-drop of a phrase if it shows agreement on a licensing head. This is true also of the [+wh] pronouns *dəzda* 'who' and *yač'ʷəya* 'what', 'why'.

The question word *dəzda* is itself subject to *pro*-drop, with the wh-agreement marker indicating the [+wh] nature of the *pro*. This can be seen in (534). Note that this requires the use of the WHQ mood marker, *da*, which only shows up when there is no overt question word.[234] Furthermore, when *dəzda* is present, there is no overt mood marker in the verbal complex.[235]

(534) *arəy k'tab yə-z-č'ʷə-w-da*
 this   book   3si-EWH-belong-PRS-WHQ
 To whom does this book belong? (or, Whose book is this?)

Since mood resides in C, this means that *-da* is a [+wh] (question) complementizer that agrees with the questioned word in rationality (i.e., 'who' as opposed to 'what'). A corresponding [+wh] question complementizer *-ya* agrees with a null irrational questioned word 'what'.[236] An important question is how C° has access to the relevant features of rationality from the questioned element. There are at least two possibilities.

The first possibility is that the [+wh] *pro*, which must be present in this construction, obligatorily moves to the specifier of C. The relevant features can then be shared via the specifier-head relationship. It is not clear, however, how it can be required only for a [+wh] <u>pro</u> to move to the

---

[234]If *dəzda* can be parsed as in fn. 216, then there is always exactly one occurrence of the suffix *-da*, either on the matrix verb or on *dəzda*. In the latter case, the "main" clause constitutes a headless relative: [who is the one [(who) owns the book?]].

[235]It is possible that the verbal complex consists of only heads including V° through ABS° when an overt question word is present, and has not raised all the way to C°. This could be involved in the lack of rationality agreement in the examples with an overt question pronoun. It is unclear how to motivate this, however.

[236]It seems likely that historically the *-d(a)/-y(a)* distinction in the suffixes corresponds to the distinction in the third-person singular within the absolutive series between rational (*d*), interpreted as 'who', and irrational (*y*), interpreted as 'what'. It is not clear that it is necessary to account for this synchronically.

specifier of C position without allowing (or requiring) wh-question words to move there in general.[237]

The second possibility does not involve the movement of a [+wh] *pro* to the specifier of C position. The feature [±rational] on the questioned element stands in a relationship with the verb such that the verb has access to the value of the feature. When V° raises through the agreement heads, the verb complex takes the information about the rationality of the wh-phrase with it. Again, when the complex of heads raises to C°, access to the feature is carried along. Thus, C° has access to information regarding the rationality of a wh-questioned element via the verb which has raised into it.[238] It is also possible that the information is passed to C° from V° via the chain which the verb heads, since the trace stands in the necessary relationship with the questioned element to access the feature value.

8.4 Wh-agreement under coreference

Bouchard (1984:17) makes the claim in (535) regarding φ-features (his F-features), namely that XPs with the same referential index share the same φ-features. If [+wh] is a φ-feature in Abaza, it should be expected that a DP coindexed with a [+wh] DP should also bear the feature [+wh]. This is true in a number of cases.

(535) *Agreement* (=Bouchard's (15)):
 α assigns (redundantly) its F-features to β if α and β have the same R-index, where F-features are person, number, and gender.

In (536), the question word *dəzda* 'who' has been *pro*-dropped, and the matrix verb is marked with the complementizer *-da*. The possessor of *pha*

---

[237] Jim McCloskey has suggested that the Doubly-Filled COMP Filter (DFCF) may be involved here. This is possible if the DFCF can apply at LF and if wh-phrases in Abaza obligatorily move to the specifier of C at LF. In that case, only one overt element is allowed. It cannot account for the distribution in Abaza if the DFCF can only apply at PF or s-structure. This is because the wh-phrase generally either remains *in situ* or moves to the focus position, where it would not be involved in the DFCF, but a wh-phrase in either of these positions still prohibits the occurrence of an overt [+wh] C°.

[238] An alternative way to account for the complementarity of *dəzda* and *-da* is to list two lexical entries meaning 'who'. The form *-da* would have the additional (morphological) requirement that it (right-)adjoin to the verb complex. It is unclear what sort of morphological subcategorization would guarantee that it got to the correct position, and there may be additional problems in getting it to antecedent govern its trace from the position it occupies.

8.4 Wh-agreement under coreference

'daughter' is coindexed with the questioned word, and the agreement triggered by this possessor is, in fact, wh-agreement.

(536) z-pha   k'anǰʲə-k'   l-zə-z-čʲpa-rnəs
      EWH-daughter doll-INDEF   3sf-BEN-EWH-make-INF

   d-zə-rgʷəya-da
   3sr-EWH-promise-WHQ
   Who promised her (own) daughter to make a doll?

Examples (537) and (538) contrast two interpretations of a single basic sentence, which differ only with respect to the type of agreement. In (537), the possessor of *pa* 'son' is necessarily coreferent with the head noun of the relative clause and with the relative operator. Wh-agreement is triggered by the possessor. Example (538) differs only in that the possessor of *pa* has necessarily disjoint reference from the relative operator. Agreement triggered by the possessor is not wh-agreement, but normal third-person singular masculine agreement. Note that *zpa/ypa* 'son' is the object of the postposition *pnə* 'by', which functions as an oblique subject in a sort of passive construction.

(537) [[z-pa   y-pnə-la]   y-zak-xa-z]   a-qac'a
      EWH-son   3sm-by-AV   AWH-hit-ASP-PST DEF-man

   də-s-dər-y-d
   3sr-1s-know-PRS-DYN
   I know the man who$_i$ was hit by his$_i$ son.

(538) [[y-pa   y-pnə-la]   y-zak-xa-z]   a-qac'a
      3sm-son   3sm-by-AV   AWH-hit-ASP-PST DEF-man

   də-s-dər-y-d
   3sr-1s-know-PRS-DYN
   I know the man who$_i$ was hit by his$_k$ son.

In (539) the "real" [+wh] DP is *dəzda* 'who', which is in focus position adjoined to ABSP. There are two cases of coindexation triggering wh-agreement in this example: the possessor of the matrix object, *qʷmarga* 'toy', and the possessor of *aba* 'father', the subject of a relative clause modifying the object of a postposition. The structure of (539) is as in (540), where the numerical indexing indicates movement chains, and

the bold DPs are coreferential with the wh-question pronoun subject of
the main clause, which thus shares its feature, [+wh], with the bold DPs.

(539) z-qʷmarga   z-aba   yə-č̓pa-wz   ayʃa   a-c'axʲ
      EWH-toy   EWH-father   AWH-build-PST   table   3si-under

          dəzda   yə-qa-z-č̓ʷax-əz
          who   3si-PV-EWH-hide-PST
      Who hid his/her toy under the table his/her father built?

8.4 Wh-agreement under coreference

(540)

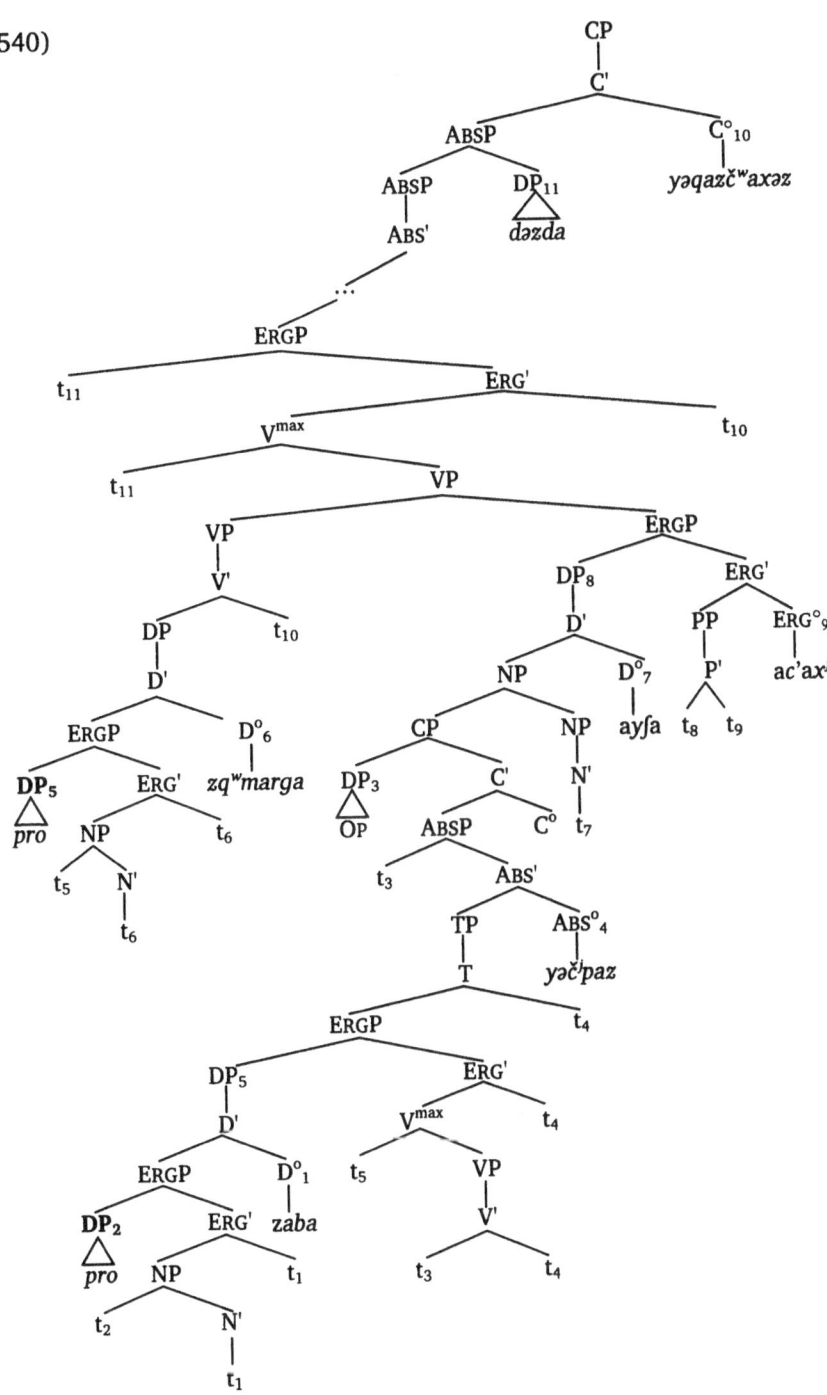

The feature [+wh] is not shared from a [+wh] DP to just any other coindexed DP in the sentence, however. Consider examples (541) and (542).

(541) z-pa   bzəy   də-z-ba-wa   a-qacʼa   y-phas (*z-phas)
      EWH-son   good   3sr-EWH-see-PRS   DEF-man   3sm-wife

    d-ʕa-y-də-d
    3sr-PV-3sm-get-DYN
    The man$_i$ who loves his$_i$ son picked up his$_i$ wife.

(542) z-phʷəs   y-pa (*z-pha)   yə-y-zak-wa   a-qacʼa   awəy
      EWH-wife   3sm-son   AWH-3sm-hit-PRS   DEF-man   s/he

    d-l-əzdzərʕʷə-y-d
    3sr-3sf-hear-PRS-DYN
    The man whose$_i$ wife his$_i$ son hits hears her.

In (541), the possessor of *phas* 'wife' cannot be [+wh], even though it is coreferent with the relative operator (possessor of *pa* 'son'). Likewise in (542), the possessor of *pa* 'son' cannot be registered by wh-agreement, even under coreference with the relative operator.

The data on wh-agreement under coreference can be accounted for by the generalization in (543).

(543) α shares the feature [+wh] with β iff:
    (1) α is [+wh]
    (2) α binds β, and
    (3) β does not bind α.

Binding is defined as in (544) (cf. Chomsky 1981:184–185).

(544) α binds β iff
    (i) α c-commands β, and
    (ii) α and β are coindexed.

This accounts for all the examples in (536)–(539), since the binding configurations are satisfied in each case. It also accounts for the ungrammaticality of wh-agreement in the indicated positions in (541) and (542). In (541) there is no way for the relative operator to c-command anything outside the relative clause. In (542) the relative operator cannot c-command anything outside of the DP of which it is the possessor.

The question arises as to why there should be such a rule in Abaza. If pronouns are referentially free, i.e., they have no independent reference of their own, then they have to get their reference from somewhere. Suppose that when a pronoun gets its reference from a coindexed DP that c-commands (=binds) it, it receives all the φ-features (referential information) of that DP. In the non-wh case, the features of person and number are shared. In the [+wh] case, these features are shared, as is the feature [+wh], but this latter feature overrides person and number as it always does in Abaza. In essence, a referentially free pronoun seeks a reference from a coindexed element "higher up" (i.e., c-commanding it).

In a sentence like (541), the possessor of 'wife' does not look down into the relative clause for its reference. The relative operator will share some of the φ-features of the possessor of wife, but as a relative operator it also bears the feature [+wh] independently. This feature overrides other features morphologically for the relative operator and for everything coindexed with the relative operator which it c-commands, but nothing above that.

In a sentence like (542), where neither of the DPs in question c-commands the other, neither will give the other its referential features. Therefore, the feature [+wh] is not passed from one to the other.

The proposal in (543) is thus a modification of Bouchard's proposal in (535), such that (1) [+wh] is taken to be a φ-feature, and (2) the sharing of φ-features moves in a downward direction. The proposal in (543) could be modified to say that all φ-features are shared in this way, with the understanding that [+wh] overrides other features of person and number morphologically.

8.5 Conclusion

The feature [+wh] in Abaza has the following unusual properties:

(545) a. it patterns with other agreement features,
    b. [+wh] pronouns have the ability to *pro*-drop, and
    c. DPs have the ability to agree in the feature [+wh] under coreference.

These facts all follow from a treatment of the feature [+wh] as a φ-feature for Abaza. As a φ-feature, it patterns quite naturally with the other φ-features (person, number, gender, rationality). Rich agreement systems tend to allow *pro*-drop, and it is reasonable to assume that the ability of wh-pronouns to *pro*-drop in Abaza is a result of the fact that the feature [+wh] patterns in the agreement system.

These phenomena are observed in content questions and relative clauses. Additionally, wh-agreement is used when a pronoun is coreferential with a [+wh] DP which asymmetrically c-commands it. This is not unexpected if a pronoun gets its referentiality (and φ-features) from the DP which binds it.

The wh-reason adverbial *yač'ʷəya* 'why' exhibits some unusual properties, namely that its position is fixed at the left edge of the sentence, and that wh-agreement registered with it occurs between the absolutive and applicative prefixes, where other agreement prefixes do not occur. Only the fact that *yač'ʷəya* is a DP and that it is base-generated in the specifier of TP are needed to account for these properties. Given these assumptions, everything else falls out from the system I have developed.

Appendix

Summary of Dynamic Verbs and Stative Predicates

Dynamic verbs

	Intransitive	Transitive
Simple	ABS-V | S	ABS-ERG-V | | DO S
Causative	ABS-ERG-CV-V | | S CS	ABS-ERG-ERG-CV-V | | | DO S CS
Potential	ABS-POT-V | S	ABS-ERG-POT-V | | DO S
Causative and Potential	ABS-ERG-POT-CV-V | | S CS	ABS-ERG-POT-ERG-CV-V | | | DO CS S
Incorporated Postposition	ABS-ERG-P-V | | S PO	ABS-ERG-P-ERG-V | | | DO PO S

	Ditransitive	**Inverted**
Simple	ABS-ERG-ERG-V | | | DO IO S	ABS-ERG-V | | S DO
Causative	ABS-ERG-ERG-ERG-CV-V | | | | DO IO S CS	ABS-ERG-ERG-CV-V | | | S DO CS
Potential	ABS-ERG-POT-ERG-V | | | DO S IO	ABS-POT-ERG-V | | S DO

Statives

	Simple	**Causative**
Intransitive Verb	ABS-V | S	ABS-ERG-CV-V | | S CS
Transitive Verb	ABS-ERG-V | | DO S	ABS-ERG-ERG-CV-V | | | DO S CS
Intransitive Postpositon	ABS-P | S	ABS-ERG-CV-P | | S CS
Transitive Postposition	ABS-ERG-P | | S PO	Does not occur
Unpossessed Noun/Adjective	ABS-N | S	ABS-ERG-CV-P | | S CS
Possessed Noun	ABS-ERG-N | | S PS	Does not occur

References

Abney, Steven Paul. 1987. The English noun phrase and its sentential aspect. Ph.D. dissertation. MIT.

Allen, W. Sidney. 1956. Structure and system in the Abaza verbal complex. Transactions of the Philological Society, 127–176.

Allen, W. Sidney. 1965. An Abaza text. Bedi Kartlisa, revue de kartvelologie, 19–20, 159–172.

Anderson, Stephen. 1976. On the notion of subject in ergative languages. In Charles Li (ed.), Subject and topic, 1–23. New York: Academic Press.

Aydemir, Izzet. 1973. Türkiye Çerkesleri. Kafkasya: Kültürel Dergi. YIL: 10. Sayi: 39–42, 215–237. (Turkish Circassians, in Caucasus: Cultural Magazine 10(39–42):215–237.)

Aydemir, Izzet. 1974. Türkiye Çerkesleri. In Kafkasya: Kültürel Dergi. YIL: 11. Sayi: 43, 34–36. (Turkish Circassians, in Caucasus: Cultural Magazine 11(43):34–36.)

Aydemir, Izzet. 1975. Türkiye Çerkesleri. In Kafkasya: Kültürel Dergi. YIL: 11. Sayi: 47, 39–48. (Turkish Circassians, in Caucasus: Cultural Magazine 11(47):39–48.)

Baker, Mark. 1985. The mirror principle and morphosyntactic explanation. Linguistic Inquiry 16:373–416.

Baker, Mark. 1988. Incorporation. Chicago: University of Chicago Press.

Belletti, Adriana. 1988. The case of unaccusatives. Linguistic Inquiry 19:1–34.

Bittner, Maria. 1992. Ergativity, binding, and scope. Rutgers University: ms.

Bittner, Maria, and Ken Hale. 1996a. Ergativity: Toward a theory of heterogeneous class. Linguistic Inquiry 27(4):531–604.

Bittner, Maria, and Ken Hale. 1996b. The structural determination of case and agreement. Linguistic Inquiry 27(1):1–68.

Black, Cheryl. 2000. Quiegolani Zapotec syntax: A Principles and Parameters account. SIL International and the University of Texas at Arlington Publications in Linguistics 136. Dallas.

Boboljik, Jonathan. 1993a. Nominally absolutive is not absolutely nominative. In Jonathan Mead (ed.), The Proceedings of the Eleventh West Coast Conference on Formal Linguistics, 44–60. Stanford: Center for the Study of Languages and Information.

Boboljik, Jonathan. 1993b. On ergativity and ergative unergatives. In Colin Phillips (ed.), Papers on Case and Agreement II, 45–88. MIT Working Papers in Linguistics 19.

Bok-Bennema, Reineke. 1991. Case and agreement in Inuit. New York: Foris.

Bouchard, Denis. 1984. On the content of empty categories. Dordrecht: Foris.

Bouda, Karl. 1940. Das Abasinische, eine unbekannte abchasische Mundart, in Zeitschrift der Deutschen Morgenlandischen Gesellschaft. Bd. 94. H. 2. (Abaza, an unknown Abkhaz dialect, in Journal of the German Oriental Society 94:2.)

Bowers, John. 1993. The syntax of predication. Linguistic Inquiry 24:591–656.

Burzio, Luigi. 1986. Italian syntax. Dordrecht: Reidel.

Campana, Mark. 1992. A movement theory of ergativity. Ph.D. dissertation. McGill University.

Catford, John C. 1976. Ergativity in Caucasian languages. Resources in Education, Jan.–June 1976. Arlington, Va.

Cheng, Lisa Lai-Shen. 1991. On the typology of Wh-Questions. Ph.D. dissertation. MIT.

Chkadua, L. P. 1970. Sistema Vremen i Osnovnyx Modal'nyx Obrazovaniy v Abxazsko-Abazinskix Dialektax. Tbilisi: Izdatel'stvo <Mecniereba>. (The system of tenses and basic modal formations in the Abkhaz-Abaza dialects, Tbilisi: Publisher "Mecniereba".)

Chomsky, Noam. 1981. Lectures on Government and Binding. Dordrecht: Foris.

Chomsky, Noam. 1986a. Barriers. Cambridge, Mass.: MIT Press.

Chomsky, Noam. 1986b. Knowledge of language. New York: Praeger.

Chomsky, Noam. 1991. Some notes on economy of derivation and representation. In R. Freidin (ed).), Principles and Parameters in comparative grammar, 417–454. Cambridge, Mass.: MIT Press.

Chomsky, Noam. 1992. A minimalist program for linguistic theory. MIT Occasional Papers in Linguistics 1. Cambridge, Mass: MITWPL.

Chung, Sandra, and Carol Georgopoulos. 1988. Agreement with gaps in Chamorro and Palauan. In Michael Barlow and Charles Ferguson (eds.), Agreement in natural language, 231–267. Stanford: Center for the Study of Languages and Information.

Chzykl'a, ShaxIymbi. 1991. Azh'ira abzh'i. Cherkessk: Stavropol' gIviragIatsIshtirta K'archa-Cherkes qvshara. (The Voice of the Smithy, Cherkessk: Stavropol Book Publisher, Karachaevo-Cherkessk Department.)

Colarusso, John. 1975. The Northwest Caucasian languages: A phonological survey. Ph.D. dissertation. Harvard. [Published 1988, New York: Garland.]

Colarusso, John. 1976. The languages of the Northwest Caucasus. Paper presented at the McMaster Conference on The Languages and Literatures of the Non-Russian Peoples of the Soviet Union, October 22–23, 1976. McMaster University: ms.

Colarusso, John. 1989. Proto-Northwest Caucasian (or how to crack a very hard nut). In Howard I. Aronson (ed.), The Non-Slavic Languages of the USSR: Linguistic Studies, 20–55. Chicago: The Chicago Linguistic Society.

Colarusso, John. 1992. Phyletic Links between proto-Indo-European and proto-Northwest Caucasian. In Howard I. Aronson (ed.), The Non-Slavic Languages of the USSR: Linguistic Studies, 19–54. Chicago: The Chicago Linguistic Society.

Craig, Colette, and Ken Hale. 1988. Relational preverbs in some languages of the Americas: Typological and historical perspectives. Language 64:312–344.

Déprez, Viviane, and Amy Pierce. 1993. Negation and functional projections in early grammar. Linguistic Inquiry 24:25–67.

Dixon, R. M. W. 1979. Ergativity. Language 55:59–138.

Doherty, Cathal. 1996. Clausal structure and the modern Irish copula. Natural Language and Linguistic Theory 14:1–46.

Dybo, Vladimir, Sergei Nikolaev, and S. Starostin. 1978. A tonological hypothesis on the origin of paradigmatic accent systems. Estonian Papers in Phonetics. Papers of the Symposium (Tallinn, November 1978). Studies on accent, quantity, stress, tone. Tallinn: Academy of Sciences of the Estonian S.S.R., Institute of Language and Literature.

Dzhandar, A. M. 1991. Uryshv-Abaza Aychvazhvaga. Cherkessk: Stavropol'skoe Knizhnoe Izdatel'stvo, Karachaevo-Cherkesskoe Otdelenie. ([Russko-Abazinskiy Razgovornik], Russian-Abaza Phrase Book, Cherkessk: Stavropol Book Publisher, Karachaevo-Cherkessk Department.)

Emonds, Joseph. 1976. A transformational approach to English syntax: Root, structure-preserving, and local transformations. New York: Academic Press.

Ernst, Thomas. 1992. The phrase structure of English negation. The Linguistics Review 9:109–144.

Everett, Daniel L. 1996. Why there are no clitics: An alternative perspective on pronominal allomorphy. Summer Institute of Linguistics and the University of Texas at Arlington Publications in Linguistics 123. Dallas.

Genko, A. N. 1955. Abazinskiy Yazyk. Moskva: Izdatel'stvo akademii nauk SSSR. (The Abaza language, Moscow: Publisher of the Academy of Sciences of the USSR.)

Grimshaw, Jane. 1991. Extended Projection. Brandeis University: ms.

Haegeman, Liliane. 1991. Introduction to Government and Binding theory. Oxford: Blackwell.

Harbert, Wayne, and Almeida Toribio. 1991. Nominative objects. Cornell Working Papers in Linguistics 9:127–192.

Hewitt, Brian George. 1989. Abkhaz. London: Routledge.

Horvath, Julia. 1981. Aspects of Hungarian syntax and the theory of grammar. Ph.D. dissertation. UCLA.

Huang, Cheng-Teh James. 1982. Logical relations in Chinese and the theory of grammar. Ph.D. dissertation. MIT.

Iatridou, Sabine. 1990. About Agr(P). Linguistic Inquiry 21:551–577.

Inkelas, Sharon. 1993. Nimboran position class morphology. Natural Language and Linguistics Theory 11:559–624.

Ionova, Sariyat Khasambievna. 1993. Abazinskaya Toponimia. Cherkessk: Karachaevo-Cherkesskiy Nauchno-issledovatel'skiy Institut Istorii, Filologii i Ekonomiki (Abaza Toponymy. Cherkessk: Karachaevo-Cherkessk Scientific Research Institute of History, Philology and Economics).

Johns, Alana. 1992. Deriving ergativity. Linguistic Inquiry 23:57–87.

Kathman, David. 1993. Expletive verb marking in Abkhaz. Berkeley Linguistic Society 19.

Kayne, Richard. 1992. Word order in universal grammar. Paper presented at the Workshop on Specifiers, University of California, Santa Cruz, March 1992.

Kiparsky, Paul. 1973. "Elsewhere" in phonology. In Stephen Anderson and Paul Kiparsky (eds.), A Festschrift for Morris Halle, 93–106. New York: Rinehart and Winston.

Kitagawa, Yoshihisa. 1986. Subjects in Japanese and English. Ph.D. dissertation. University of Massachusetts, Amherst.

K'lych, Rauf. 1988. Asuffiksoidkvi ashatakvi ynaraxvua ashchIypIa preverbkva. Cherkessk: Stavropol' gIviragIatsIshtirta K̆archa-Cherkes qvshara. (Academic dictionary of combinations of preverbs and roots, Cherkessk: Stavropol Book Publisher, Karachaevo-Cherkessk Department.)

Klychev, Rauf. 1991. Kratkiy Ocherk Abazinskogo Yazyka. In Dzhandar 1991. (A short sketch of the Abaza language.)

Klychev, Rauf. 1994. Lokal'no-Preverbnoe Obrazovanie Glagolov Abazinskogo Yazyka. Cherkessk: TOO <Adzh'pa>. (The spatio-preverbal formation of verbs of the Abaza language. Cherkessk: TOO "Adzhpa.")

Klychev, Rauf, and Nurya Tabulova-Malbakhova. 1967. Kratkiy Grammaticheskiy Ocherk Abazinskogo Yazyka. In Tugov. (A short grammatical sketch of the Abaza language.)

Koopman, Hilda, and Dominique Sportiche. 1988. Subjects. UCLA: unpublished ms.

Koopman, Hilda, and Dominique Sportiche. 1991. The position of subjects. Lingua 85:211–258.

Kratzer, Angelika. 1994. The event argument and the semantics of voice. Unpublished ms.

Kuipers, Aert. 1965. On one-vowel systems. Lingua 13:111–124.

Kuroda, S.-Y. 1988. Whether we agree or not. Lingvisticae Investigationes 12:1–47.

Laka, Itziar. 1990. Negation in syntax: On the nature of functional categories and projections. Ph.D. dissertation. MIT.

Larson, Richard. 1988. On the double object construction. Linguistic Inquiry 19:335–391.

Lasnik, Howard, and Juan Uriagereka. 1988. A course in GB syntax. Cambridge, Mass.: MIT Press.

Levin, Juliette. 1983. On the nature of ergativity. Ph.D. dissertation. MIT.

Levin, Juliette, and Diane Massam. 1984. Surface ergativity: Case/theta relations reexamined. Proceedings of the Fifteenth Annual Meeting, NELS, GLSA, University of Massachusetts, Amherst, 286–301.

Li, Yafei. 1990. X°-binding and verb incorporation. Linguistic Inquiry 21:399–426.

Lomtatidze, K. V. 1945. Kategoria Kauzativa v Abxazskom Yazyk. Soobshchenia A.N. Gruzinskoj SSR. t. VI, No. 1, Tbilisi. (The category of causative in the Abkhaz language. Communication of the Academy of Sciences of the Georgian SSR. Vol. 6, No. 1. Tbilisi.)

Longobardi, Giuseppe. 1994. Reference and proper names. Linguistic Inquiry 25:609–665.

Mahajan, Anoop. 1989. Agreement and agreement phrases. Itziar Laka and Anoop Mahajan, eds., MITWPL 10:217–252.

Mahajan, Anoop Kumar. 1990. The A/A-Bar distinction and movement theory. Ph.D. dissertation. MIT.

Marantz, Alec. 1984. On the nature of grammatical relations. Cambridge, Mass.: MIT Press.

Massam, Diane. 1985. Case theory and the projection principle. Ph.D. dissertation. MIT.

May, Robert. 1985. Logical form: Its structure and derivation. Cambridge, Mass.: MIT Press.

McCloskey, James. 1992. Adjunction, selection and embedded verb second. Santa Cruz: Linguistics Research Center. LRC-92-07.

Murasugi, Kumiko. 1992. Crossing and nested paths: NP movement in accusative and ergative languages. Ph.D. dissertation. MIT.

Nartiraa: Abaza uagIa repos. 1975. Cherkessk: Stavropol' glviragIatsIshtirta K'archa-Cherkes qvshara. (The Narts: The Abaza Folk Epic. Cherkessk: Stavropol Book Publisher, Karachaevo-Cherkessk Department.)

Nichols, Johanna. 1986. Head-marking and dependent-marking grammar. Language 62:56–119.

O'Herin, Brian. 1985. Abaza discourse features. University of Texas at Arlington: ms.

O'Herin, Brian. 1992a. Long-distance dependencies in morphology. Paper given at the Fifth International Morphology Meeting, Krems, Austria, July 7–9, 1992.

O'Herin, Brian. 1992b. Metrical structure in Abaza. University of California at Santa Cruz. ms.

O'Herin, Brian. 1993. Wh-agreement in Abaza. In Geoffrey K. Pullum and Eric Potsdam (eds.), Syntax at Santa Cruz 2:25–56.

O'Herin, Brian. 1994. Metrical stress in Abaza. The Nart epic and Caucasiology. Papers of the Sixth Colloquium of the Societas Caucasologica Europoea, ed. by Asker Gadagatl. Maykop: Adygea.

Ouhalla, Jamal. 1988. The syntax of head movement. Ph.D. dissertation. University College London.

Ouhalla, Jamal. 1990. Sentential negation, revised minimality, and the aspectual status of auxiliaries. The Linguistics Review 7:183–231.

Pazov, Sergei U. 1990. Frazeologia Abazinskogo Yazyka. Karachaevsk: Karachaevo-Cherkesskiy gosudarstvennyy pedagogicheskiy institut. (Phraseology of the Abaza Language, Karachaevsk: Karachaevo-Cherkessk National Pedagogical Institute.)

Perlmutter, David. 1978. Impersonal passive and the unaccusative hypothesis. Proceedings of the Berkeley Linguistics Society 4.

Pesetsky, David. 1982. Paths and categories. Ph.D. dissertation. MIT.

Pollock, Jean-Yves. 1989. Verb movement, universal grammar and the structure of IP. Linguistic Inquiry 20:365–424.

Postal, Paul, and Geoffrey Pullum. 1988. Expletive noun phrases in subcategorized positions. Linguistic Inquiry 19:635–670.

Rivero, María Luisa. 1994. Clause structure and V-movement in the languages of the Balkans. Natural Language and Linguistics Theory 12:63–120.

Rizzi, Luigi. 1986. Null objects in Italian and the theory of *pro*. Linguistic Inquiry 17:501–557.

Rizzi, Luigi. 1990. Relativized minimality. Cambridge, Mass.: MIT Press.

Rizzi, Luigi. 1991. Argument/adjunct (a)symmetries. Université de Genève: ms.

Rizzi, Luigi, and Ian Roberts. 1989. Complex inversion in French. Probus 1:1–30.

Ross, John Robert. 1967. Constraints on variables in syntax. Ph.D. dissertation. MIT.

Schafer, Robin. 1994. Nonfinite predicate initial constructions in Breton. Ph.D. dissertation. UCSC.

Sells, Peter. 1985. Lectures on contemporary syntactic theories. CSLI Lecture Notes, Number 3. Stanford: Center for the Study of Language and Information.

Serdyuchenko, G. P. 1955. Yazyk Abazin. Moskva: Izdatel'stvo akademii pedagogicheskix nauk RSFSR. (The language of the Abazas, Moscow: Publisher of the Academy of Pedagogical Sciences of the RSFSR.)

Serdyuchenko, G. P. 1956. Kratkij Grammaticheskij Ocherk Abazinskogo Yazyka. In Zhirov and Ekba, 591–646. (A short grammatical sketch of the Abaza language.)

Shlonsky, Ur. 1991. Quantifiers as functional heads: A study of quantifier float in Hebrew. Lingua 84:159–180.

Speas, Margaret. 1990. Phrase structure in natural language. Studies in Natural Language and Linguistic Theory 21. Dordrecht: Kluwer.

Spruit, Arie. 1986. Abkhaz studies. Ph.D. dissertation. Leiden.

Stowell, Tim. 1991. Determiners in NP and DP. In Katherine Leffel and Denis Bouchard (eds.), Views on phrase structure, 37–56. Dordrecht: Kluwer Academic Publishers.

Tabulova, Nur'ya Tatlustanovna. 1976. Grammatika Abazinskogo Yazyka. Cherkessk: Karachaevo-Cherkesskoe otdelenie Stavropol'skovo knizhnogo izdatel'stva. (Grammar of the Abaza language, Cherkessk: Stavropol Book Publishers, Karachaevo-Cherkessk Department.)

Tobyl', Nurya. 1992. Abaza Byzshva Aorfografiya Azhvar. Cherkessk: K˘archa-Cherkes Respublika GIvyragIacIshchtyrta. (Orthographic dictionary of the Abaza language. Cherkessk: Book Publishers of the Karachaevo-Cherkessk Republic.)

Travis, Lisa. 1984. Parameters and effects of word order variation. Ph.D. dissertation. MIT.

Tugov, Vladimir B., ed. 1967. Abazinsko-Russkiy Slovar'. Moskva: Izdatel'stvo <Sovetskaya Enciklopediya>. (Abaza-Russian dictionary. Moscow: Publisher "The Soviet Encyclopedia".)

Tuller, Laurice. 1992. The syntax of postverbal focus constructions in Chadic. Natural Language and Linguistic Theory 10:303–334.

Tygv, Vladimir. 1987. TsIarakIvyzhv SakIvpI. Cherkessk: Stavropol' GIvyragIatsIshchtyrta K'archa-cherkes X'vshara. (I am Tsarakwuzh, Cherkessk: Karachay-Cherkessk division of the Stavropol Book Publishers.)

Vallduví, Enric. 1990. The informational component. Ph.D. dissertation. University of Pennsylvania.

Williams, Edwin. 1980. Predication. Linguistic Inquiry 11:203–238.

Woolford, Ellen. 1993. Four-way case systems: Ergative, nominative, objective, and accusative. University of Massachusetts: ms.

Zamakhshirievna, Kunizheva L., ed. 1989. Abaziny: Istoriko-Etnograficheskiy Ocherk. Cherkessk: Karachaevo-Cherkesskoe Otdelenie Stavropol'skogo Knizhnogo Izdatel'stva. (The Abazas: Historical-ethnographic sketch. Cherkessk: Karachay-Cherkessk department of the Stavropol Book Publishers.)

Zhirov, Khamid D., and N. B. Ekba. 1956. Russko-Abazinskij Slovar'. Moskva: Gosudarstvennoe Izdatel'stvo Inostrannyx i Nacional'nyx Slovarej. (Russian-Abaza dictionary. Moscow: National Publishers of Foreign and National Dictionaries.)

www.ingramcontent.com/pod-product-compliance
Lightning Source LLC
Chambersburg PA
CBHW052152300426
44115CB00011B/1635